THE
SLICKROCK DESERT

ALSO BY STEPHEN W. HINCH

AUTHOR:

Outdoor Navigation with GPS

Hiking and Adventure Guide to the Sonoma Coast and Russian River

Guide to State Parks of the Sonoma Coast and Russian River

Handbook of Surface Mount Technology

CONTRIBUTING AUTHOR:

Fiber Optic Test and Measurement

Printed Circuits Handbook, 3rd Ed.

Encyclopedia of Electronics, 2nd Ed.

THE
SLICKROCK DESERT

Journeys of Discovery in an
Endangered American Wilderness

STEPHEN W. HINCH

ATENERA PRESS • SANTA ROSA, CALIFORNIA

ATENERA
PRESS

Atenera Press
Santa Rosa, California
publisher@atenera.com
www.atenera.com

First Edition

ISBN: 978-0-9661999-0-1 (paperback)
Library of Congress Control Number: 2022900557

Front Cover: Mesa Arch and The Washer Woman, Canyonlands National Park, Utah; Inset: Ancestral Pueblo Ruin, Cedar Mesa, Utah

Title Page: Fiftymile Point from Davis Gulch, Grand Staircase-Escalante National Monument, Utah

Back Cover: Pictographs, Grand Gulch, Utah; Rain over Grand Canyon, Arizona

Photographs by the author except where noted.

For my family: Nicki, Juliana, Greg, Katie, and Jasper

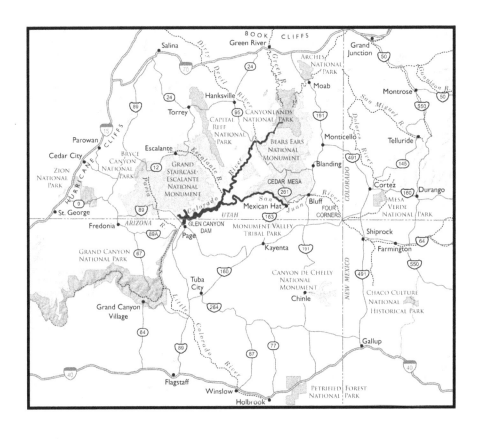

The Slickrock Desert

CONTENTS

Pothole Point and Junction Butte, Canyonlands National Park, Utah

1

SUNRISE

DAWN IS NOT YET a glimmer in the sky when I awake. Inside my down sleeping bag I am wreathed in warmth, but my face, exposed to the icy air, stings from the cold. The only sensible thing to do is roll over and go back to sleep. Sensible perhaps, but a nagging thought percolates through the cobwebs of my mind: "You came a thousand miles to photograph the dawn. You can't give up now. Get up. Get up!" Reluctantly, I listen.

I start by extending an arm just far enough to reach the thermometer hanging from my backpack. Twenty-nine degrees. No surprise. When I set up my tent yesterday it was snowing. If it is still snowing this morning, sunrise will be a non-event and I can blithely go back to sleep.

Wishful thinking. Snow never lasts long in the desert.

Still wrapped in down I wriggle over, unzip the tent door, and peer out. A layer of clouds covers the dark sky, but I can see a few stars, too. It is not snowing, and even last night's snow is mostly gone. Sunrise could be spectacular. My fate is sealed. Time to get up.

I have been to Canyonlands National Park before, but only as a tourist together with my family. On this trip I am solo, free to go where I want when I want—an essential privilege for a dedicated photographer. I arrived yesterday after a long drive from Salt Lake City through uncertain weather. Sleet turned to snow as I pulled into my campsite at the Needles District Campground. Being a frigid weekday afternoon in April, I had the entire place to myself.

The Needles is one of the four districts of Canyonlands. It isn't the most visited—that would be Island in the Sky, a 15-mile-long mesa rising over a thousand feet above the surrounding lands. Being the district closest to the town of Moab, with a first-rate visitor center and a well-paved road all the way to Grand View Point, Island in the Sky is the most heavily trafficked district. For that, it is a region I only rarely visit.

The Needles, a ninety-minute drive from Moab, is a land of fantastic rock formations. It has its own visitor center and a few paved roads, but to reach the best spots you need a true four-wheel-drive vehicle or a sturdy backpack and legs to match. The tortuous climb over Elephant Hill is not a drive for the faint of heart.

To the west lies The Maze, the most remote of the four regions—an all-day drive over rough four-wheel-drive trails into a land of fantastic spires, towers, domes, and canyons. This district also includes Horseshoe Canyon, a small, isolated unit that protects some of the finest rock art panels in the Southwest. From Moab, Horseshoe Canyon is a four-hour drive over washboard dirt roads followed by a seven-mile roundtrip hike to the best rock art panels. The six-hundred-foot descent at the beginning of the hike isn't the issue. It's the six-hundred-foot climb at the end that is the challenge.

The Green and Colorado Rivers form the fourth district. They offer world-class river rafting with prices to match.

WHEN I ARRIVED yesterday, I set up my tent and headed out to an intriguing site marked "Pothole Point" on the park map—a broad expanse of rough sandstone where dozens of shallow depressions have eroded into the rock surface. I saw the photographic possibilities, but the inclement weather made for a dull view. I promised myself I would come back to catch today's first rays of dawn light. An easy promise to make last evening, much harder to fulfill this morning.

I shed my down cocoon, dress warmly, and emerge from the tent into perfect blackness. Sunrise is more than an hour away. I listen for the sounds of nature but hear none. No singing birds, no chirping insects, nothing. The silence echoes through my ears. Apparently, the natives are smarter than I. They are still asleep. Or frozen. I don't envy them in this weather.

In the dark, my mind wanders. Why am I here on this frigid morning when I could have slept in a comfortable bed, eaten a savory breakfast, and driven to a secure, well-paid job? The answer is obvious. I am here to get away from that predictable life, to exercise components of my brain that would otherwise atrophy. I am not discouraged by that other life; I will not hesitate to return to it soon. But it is not my entire life. I need time in the wilderness, time to cleanse and re-energize my mind. That is why I am here.

Breakfast can wait; sunrise won't. I drive to Pothole Point, extract a backpack full of camera gear and head out, only to quickly discover a problem. The red dirt trail disappears onto the rough slickrock, and in the predawn darkness I can't tell how to get back to where I was yesterday. Thoughtlessly, I failed to pack a flashlight. I must tread carefully to avoid twisting my ankle in an unseen pothole or skewering my leg on the spines of a hidden cactus.

Relying on dim light from the nascent dawn, I finally find yesterday's view: a large, water-filled pothole surrounded by rocky terrain, with the acute walls of Junction Butte and Island in the Sky looming in the distance. In these pre-digital days, my camera of choice is a 4x5-inch view camera, the go-to camera for any serious landscape photographer of the time. It is slow, cumbersome, expensive, and looks exactly like the cameras Matthew Brady used during the Civil War. In skilled hands it produces postcard-size color transparencies with amazing detail far surpassing anything possible with a smaller camera. That level of skill doesn't include me, but I convince myself that with enough practice, it could.

I don't use the view camera exclusively; I sometimes resort to 35mm film. Eventually I will replace both cameras with a high-quality digital camera, but at the time of this trip such cameras don't exist and won't for more than a decade.

Working deliberately, I frame the scene as I envisioned it. When I am happy, I lock camera and tripod in place. Now there is nothing to do but wait for the dawn.

As I stand huddled against the cold, I study my surroundings. The eroded depressions around me go by a number of names—potholes, tinajas, tanks, gnammas, huecos, waterpockets. Researchers tend to use the bland term, "weathering pits." In canyon country they are most common on sandstones formed from what were once windblown dunes, known as aeolian sandstones. Compared to marine sediments, aeolian sandstones are less dense and more susceptible to erosion. Once a pit forms on the surface, it serves as a catchment for rainwater that further fractures the rock when it freezes, slowly enlarging the pit. The process is aided by certain species of bacteria that consume silica-based minerals from the rock. Over time, multiple pits can merge to become a single much larger pothole like the one in front of me now.

The water in the pothole froze overnight, giving it a mottled, crusty appearance. I idly wonder how the organisms within it are faring in the cold. Sand-filled potholes are entire ecosystems in miniature. Throughout the long dry months they lie dormant, betraying scant evidence of the denizens slumbering patiently within them. When the rains return and the pools fill with water, they erupt in activity. Fairy shrimp, tadpole shrimp, spadefoot toads, nematode worms, and a wide variety of bacteria and algae flourish in the tiny seas. Most live just long enough to reproduce and die, leaving only eggs to await the next rain—a tenuous legacy. But as the water evaporates, some enter a suspended state known as cryptobiosis. Certain species of shrimp can survive losing over ninety percent of their body water while in this state. When rain falls again months or years later, they absorb enough water in a matter of minutes to become fully rehydrated.

One microscopic eight-legged creature, the tardigrade or water bear, lives a fantastic life. It is unfazed by temperatures above 300 degrees and below minus 300 degrees Fahrenheit. Dehydrated tardigrades are known to have survived the frigid vacuum and intense radiation of outer space.

Their fate in potholes seems to be to serve as a food source for the larger inhabitants—the original freeze-dried dinner.

One day we may learn how well tardigrades survive on the moon. In 2019, a joint venture of two private Israeli companies launched a spacecraft carrying, among other things, thousands of dehydrated tardigrades to the Sea of Serenity. The idea was to leave them untouched for the indefinite future. Centuries from now, scientists could retrieve them and attempt to rehydrate them. An interesting premise, but there was one problem. The landing was meant to be soft, but it wasn't. The spacecraft crashed and may well have scattered tardigrades across the surface of the moon. Fortunately, the moon has almost no water, so they are unlikely to spontaneously reanimate. But there is always a chance in the distant future some of them could cling to the spacesuit of an astronaut exploring an ancient wreck. The tiny hitchhikers could unknowingly be brought to a more favorable environment not ready for them. As we will see in a later chapter, it wouldn't be the first time foreign life unwittingly transported by man has overrun native species.

Ever since this desert came into being after the last ice age, potholes have served as water sources for its inhabitants. That's fine for the wildlife, but I have no desire to drink from them myself. I recall the words the naturalist Ann Zwinger wrote in her book, *Wind in the Rock*, when, during a hot, tiring hike in Cedar Mesa, she examined her cup after filling it from a pothole: "Upon closer inspection the sediment does not sink because it is swimming, a whole school of daphnia—minute crustacea.... Without another thought I simply down it, daphnia and all, figuring it is going to be a lot harder on them than on me."

No thanks. Besides, there is barely enough water in this desert for the residents. Add people who see potholes as playthings, and you end up with not enough to go around. What little remains becomes contaminated with skin oils and chemicals deadly to the inhabitants. With the proliferation of hikers, mountain bikers, hunters, and backpackers throughout canyon country today, what was marginally acceptable fifty years ago is no longer so. Stay out of potholes and leave the water for the natives.

I turn again to the sky. Slowly, almost imperceptibly, the first light of dawn flows over the eastern horizon like water trickling over a dam.

Clouds blanket much of the sky, but shafts of light peek through sporadic openings. As sunrise nears, the clouds grow in color, transitioning from deep crimson through bright vermilion to light salmon. When the first tiny arc of the sun emerges, Junction Butte becomes bathed in a brilliant orange glow. Well before then I started my photography, exposing both 4x5-inch and 35mm transparencies.

A sunrise such as this can't be left only for film. Photography is just a pretext for my trip, a way to justify an outsider's compulsion to explore this wondrous land. I reserve time to enjoy the sunrise unencumbered, gazing in appreciative awe at unfolding waves of color. I take in the smell of juniper; I listen to the falling tremolo of a canyon wren who has emerged to welcome the day. This is why I rose before dawn. This is why I have come to immerse myself in the primitive beauties of the angular cliffs and the broad skies of the Slickrock Desert. It is the start of a beautiful day. It is the start of a beautiful trip.

Elephant Canyon, Canyonlands National Park, Utah

The Narrows, Grand Gulch, Utah

2

SLICKROCK COUNTRY

ASK A NATURALIST to describe the major North American deserts and you're likely to be told there are four: the Mojave Desert, the Sonoran Desert, the Chihuahuan Desert, and the Great Basin Desert. The first three stretch along the southwestern United States from Southern California to Southern Texas and into Mexico, while the last sprawls from the eastern edge of Central California across all of Nevada and on into Utah. You'll undoubtedly hear about numerous other deserts as well—the Escalante Desert, the Black Rock Desert, the Amargosa Desert, the Colorado Desert, the Forty Mile Desert, to name a few—but these are all subdivisions of the big four, like Manhattan and the Bronx are boroughs of New York City.

The canyons and mesas of southeastern Utah don't fit neatly into this definition of desert. Maps sometimes show it as an isolated extension of the Great Basin Desert, somewhat akin to how the Yucatan Peninsula juts far to the east of the rest of Mexico. But this is like confusing a farm tractor with a sports car because both have an engine and four wheels. There may be similarities, but even a newly arrived visitor from Alpha Centauri would hesitate to call them the same thing.

Anyone who has ever explored both the sagebrush ranges of Nevada and the pinyon-juniper canyons of southern Utah will quickly recognize these are not the same ecosystems. In Nevada, there's no place to hide. The low sagebrush scrub hardly comes up to a child's waist, and the nearest slope may be ten miles away. In southern Utah, it's impossible to walk a straight line for any appreciable distance. If the junipers or pinyon pines don't stop you, the mesas and canyons will. Even naturalists struggle with the issue. Some don't think southern Utah is a desert at all. Others choose to classify it as a fifth desert—Canyon Country, the Painted Desert, the Navajoan Desert, or the Colorado Plateau Province.

The author Edward Abbey, the Southwest's cantankerous favorite son, in his classic book, *Desert Solitaire*, called it the Slickrock Desert, not for its dominant plant community but for its most distinguishing feature, the naked rock that looms everywhere across the land. Covering roughly the southeastern quarter of the State of Utah, it extends east to Colorado's Mesa Verde region and south to the Grand Canyon. It is bounded by the Book Cliffs to the north and the Hurricane Cliffs to the west, with isolated segments stretching as far west as Valley of Fire, Nevada. All told, it encompasses a total area in excess of 100,000 square miles. It holds perhaps the largest collection of parklands on earth—Arches, Bryce Canyon, Canyonlands, Grand Canyon, Capitol Reef, Chaco Culture, Petrified Forest, Mesa Verde, and Zion National Parks, plus an assortment of national monuments, state parks, tribal parks, and broad expanses of Bureau of Land Management (the original BLM) public lands.

NOT LONG AGO I loaded my backpack—a gawky external frame affair left over from the 1980s—with three days of provisions and headed out into the Slickrock Desert, to a place called Cedar Mesa. No tent, for in this arid land a tent is a weighty luxury; just a down sleeping bag (another relic from the 1980s), a waterproof bivy sack (newly purchased from my local REI store), a backpacker's stove, a bevy of freeze-dried backpacker meals, and plenty of water. You don't need much to explore this land as long as you remember to bring water. Water is the currency of the desert. Don't count on finding any along the way.

I turned off the highway and drove many miles down a rough dirt road. At the head of Collins Canyon, I parked and surveyed the landscape. A faint trail disappeared down the canyon, eventually reaching an even larger canyon far below—a fifty-mile-long gash in the land known as Grand Gulch. Other than mine, there were no vehicles in sight. I had seen none along the way. The few tire tracks in the dirt were old and faded. I would be the only one on this trail today. Perhaps the first in a week. I shouldered my pack, scooped up two plastic water bottles, and started down.

The descent was long and arduous. The pack, more loaded with camera gear than supplies, weighed heavily on my back. The water bottles were equally heavy. I'm never in the best of shape for these kinds of sojourns, but I gamely pressed on. Overhead, clouds from the last remnants of a recent storm darkened the sky while a cold, biting wind blew fiercely across my face.

Collins Canyon is one of the easier entries into Grand Gulch, although "easier" doesn't mean "easy." It's a 300-foot descent over a two-mile-long trail built by cowboys over a century ago to move cattle. A gate and an old cowboy camp part way down remain from that time. In places, I could see evidence of the dynamiting that had been done to create the trail. If I had been better at noting the twists and turns along the way, I could have avoided two lengthy box-canyon detours on my return climb.

When I reached Grand Gulch, I extracted my camera gear, stashed my pack and water bottles behind a nondescript clump of bushes, and marked their location with my GPS receiver. Wouldn't want to misplace them in this arid, unforgiving land. Suddenly free of weight, my back rejoiced.

Grand Gulch is much like any other arroyo in slickrock country except for one thing. It is perhaps the best place anywhere to see relatively undisturbed relics of an ancient civilization. The Anasazi, or Ancestral Puebloans, flourished here intermittently for over a thousand years, from before the time of Christ to about the year 1300. Then, for reasons known only to them, they abandoned the region and seem to have moved southeast to form the pueblos of New Mexico. Remnants of their presence in

Grand Gulch remain even today in the form of intact ruins, rock art, and the detritus of daily living. All are protected by law, so if you go, leave everything as you find it.

I trekked up and down the Gulch for three days, photographing ruins, studying figures on the rock, and examining an occasional pottery sherd or desiccated corncob. I saw not a single soul the entire time.

I had deliberately not done much pre-trip planning. Although I knew there would be rock art on the canyon walls and ruins scattered about the cliffs, exactly what and where was a mystery. Like early archaeologists I wanted to make my own discoveries, not simply follow the guidance of others.

When I reached the canyon floor, I had a choice. I could turn left and go up canyon or turn right and go down canyon. Figuring downhill was easier than uphill, I turned right. A good choice. In a few hundred feet I reached a towering opening that had been cut through a canyon wall by millennia of flash floods—a feature called *The Narrows* on my topo map. The water here originally flowed around the wall in a great counterclockwise meander shaped like the letter C. Eventually the erosional power of repeated floods was enough to break through the thin neck of the wall to form a natural shortcut, leaving the former river channel abandoned. Numerous pools of water, remnants of the recent rains, served as warnings that flash floods were not mere historical phenomena, they could return at any time.

As afternoon turned to evening, I headed back to retrieve my cached supplies. Several times I was startled by flurries of frantic activity behind nearby shrubs. Flocks of what looked like oversize quail but without plumes atop their heads scampered quickly away by running rather than flying. Black stripes reminiscent of burglars' masks across their eyes and more stripes like prison garb on their bellies revealed them to be coveys of chukar, a species first introduced from the Middle East as a game bird in the late nineteenth century. Unlike most experiments with non-native species, the introduction of chukar to the Southwest seems not to have been detrimental to the region.

With clouds continuing to billow and winds continuing to gust, prudence dictated I find shelter for the night, preferably high enough to avoid being swamped should more rain fall. Alcoves along the walls could provide the necessary refuge, but they were all covered in prehistoric graffiti: figures of birds, sheep, Frankenstein monsters, goggle-eyed aliens. Camping is prohibited near rock art, so I pressed on.

&

THE ROCK ART of the American Southwest is an enigma. Some things we know, but there is much we don't. First the known. In canyon country there are two primary forms: *pictographs*, figures painted onto the rock, and *petroglyphs*, figures carved into it. In this part of Grand Gulch I saw many more pictographs than petroglyphs.

Prehistoric artists created pictographs using a variety of materials: ochre or crushed hematite for red, kaolin clay or gypsum for white, charcoal for black, turquoise or lapis for blue, and malachite or azurite for green, all held together by binders made from animal blood, fats, or plant oils.

Considering how susceptible pictographs are to the ravages of nature, it's a wonder any still exist. Only those sheltered from weather remain, and even those are disappearing. In some, the colors have faded unevenly, leaving behind eerie, skeleton-like shapes. In others, the underlying sandstone is spalling away, eroding entire strips of art at a time. I saw both modes of failure near Collins Canyon and realized that these few remnants of a lost civilization were only transitory. In another hundred years they may well have vanished forever. I promptly pulled out my camera to record as many as I could.

Pictographs, Grand Gulch, Utah

Petroglyphs, the other art form, range from simple scratchings in the rock to elaborate art created with stone chisels and hammerstones over an extended period. The few petroglyphs I saw here tended toward the simple side.

Petroglyphs are especially prevalent on rock walls covered with desert varnish—a thin, dark patina of oxidized iron and manganese minerals. Ancient artists created petroglyphs by pecking away the varnish to expose the lighter base rock.

Desert varnish can take thousands of years to form, a fact that can be used to give some idea of the age of the carving. The older the petroglyph the more desert varnish will have repatinated atop the chipped areas. A technique called chronographic dating compares the thickness of the varnish in the chipped areas to that of the background layer. Unfortunately, the technique is costly and not well developed. There is no way yet to confidently predict how quickly the varnish will grow back. It depends on such factors as the chemistry of the rock, the prevalence of the coating materials, and even the air temperature and extent of exposure to water and sunlight. Simpler methods can sometimes be used. A petroglyph of a horse and rider, for example, can be no older than the time of the first European entry into the region.

So much for the forensic analysis. What we don't know is what they mean. Do they tell a story or were they idle work simply to pass the time? Possibly some of each. With only a few exceptions, the pictographs near Collins Canyon tend toward the straightforward—ducks, sheep, anthropomorphs, and similar to the walls of today's public restrooms, the occa-

Pictographs, Grand Gulch, Utah

sional crude outlines of sexual organs. Many archaeologists say these may be associated with ceremonial fertility events. But perhaps that gives them too much credit. I could imagine them as the surreptitious work of giggling adolescents, with tribal elders lamenting them as evidence of the decline of civilization.

Elsewhere in canyon country, though, are haunting scenes of deeper meaning. Many were created by an even older people known as the Desert Archaic culture centuries before the first Ancestral Puebloans. At places like Sego Canyon, the San Rafael Swell, or Horseshoe Canyon, legions of ghostly figures lacking arms or legs float ethereally over the land. Helmeted aliens shoot laser death rays toward imagined antagonists. A grotesque, multi-armed Cyclops stares intently from its single eye. What inspired prehistoric artists to create scenes more from nightmares than from life? Were they the products of tormented minds—shamans on vision quests or artists high on psychedelic drugs? Archaeologists today generally see this as the most likely explanation. Canyon country certainly provides plenty of stimulants for those who know how to find them. For those who know how to keep from overdosing.

But perhaps we shouldn't discount the possibility these were indeed scenes extracted from life. Since at least the nineteenth century, reports have circulated throughout the West of strange, otherworldly objects seen hovering silently overhead before streaking away at enormous speeds, sometimes abducting hapless victims as they depart. Area 51, the secret Air Force base rumored to house the bodies of alien life forms, lies not far away. Perhaps such visits began long before the arrival of the first Europeans, and the fading art on canyon walls stands as mute testimony to ancient horrors.

Enough! Alien abductions and laser death rays are not topics to dwell on when you are about to spend three nights alone in the wilderness.

❧

I CONTINUED MY SEARCH for a campsite while passing rock walls covered with more graffiti than a railroad boxcar. One pictograph portrayed four shapes uncannily reminiscent of sombrero-topped Mexicans in mid-siesta. Another figure wielded what looked like a sword ready to cut off the head of a duck. Everywhere were handprints, butterflies, centipedes, fertility symbols, and strange shapes I couldn't decipher. The one figure I didn't see was Kokopelli, the well-endowed, humpbacked flute player found throughout the Southwest. His claim to fame seems to have been his ability to seduce impressionable young maidens.

Eventually I found a sheltered ledge on an east-facing wall far enough from rock art to be habitable and rolled out my sleeping bag. The air was already cold—the alcove had long been in shade, though I knew it would get early morning sunlight. As a crescent moon eased slowly westward, I drifted off to a nightmare-free sleep.

The dawn broke clear and mild, with not a cloud in the sky. After yesterday's tedious hike I had slept well. The wind had continued off and on most of the night, but rather than bothering me it tended to keep me cool.

My first destination was the one ruin I knew about: Bannister House, an inaccessible structure in an alcove halfway up a south-facing canyon wall. Two long wooden rails gave it the namesake appearance, although

Pictographs, Horseshoe Canyon, Utah

experts debate their significance. Were they simple barricades or did they have a religious significance—portholes to another world?

Walls of the living structure consisted of numerous upright wooden posts filled with brush and coated in adobe, a construction technique called *wattle-and-daub* or *jacal*, implying it was of Pueblo II age, around A.D. 900-1100. But outer walls of stone masonry showed the influence of Pueblo III techniques, suggesting it may have been used even into the 1200s. Like many ruins it was oriented to capture warmth from the low sun on winter days but recessed enough to be shaded when the sun was much higher in the summer. I pondered the difficulty of building a rock structure on the side of a cliff without any modern construction conveniences. I studied the rubble of a collapsed rock wall that had once served as the only way up to the ruin. When did it fall? Were people living there at the time?

One afternoon while studying an extended wall of pictographs, I was stopped in my tracks by the sight of two ancient handprints, one above the other. Handprints are ubiquitous in Grand Gulch, often in collections

Bannister House, Grand Gulch, Utah

of dozens at a time. No one knows what they mean. No one alive. Perhaps they marked a clan's territory. Perhaps they were just a way to say, "We were here." What was striking about these two prints was, one was that of a child. Its stiffly clenched fingers contrasted sharply with the casually spread palm of the adult's handprint above it. Here was a precious moment frozen in time from eons ago—a young child, anxious to emulate his (or her?) elders, making his first handprint. I could imagine the child waiting with anticipation as the father first coated his own hand with wet clay and pressed it against the wall. "Do it like this." And then it was the child's turn. Coated with clay, the father lifted the child's hand and pressed it against the wall. All the excitement and promise of a life yet to be lived were captured in this one imprint. I couldn't help but wonder how life had unfolded for that tiny child from long ago.

That's the thing about the Slickrock Desert. Away from the press of civilization, you have time to clear your mind and think. What you think about is up to you. The desert won't tell you. It is a muse, not a guru. It doesn't have answers, it only provides inspiration. It's the reason I never tire of returning to this barren, inhospitable, beautiful land.

Ancient Handprints, Grand Gulch, Utah

The Castle, Capitol Reef National Park, Utah

3

CANYONS AND MESAS

IT IS A LAND unlike any other on earth. A land where naked expanses of rock are sliced by rivers to depths of thousands of feet. A land where towering mesas stand as isolated remnants of rock layers long since eroded away. A land where hidden hoodoos, fins, and arches await discovery by the intrepid adventurer. A land where something monumental has clearly happened, but where even geologists can't agree on what it was.

For over a billion years, the Slickrock Desert was a broad expanse that sat at or below sea level. Over the eons, shallow seas alternated with sandy lowlands from the time of the earliest life to the age of dinosaurs, leaving behind polychromatic layers of limestone, sandstone, shale, and dolomite thousands of feet deep.

Around 140 million years ago, the Colorado Plateau slowly began rising. Mountain ranges came first, in two episodes called the Sevier and Laramide orogenies. Later, the entire plateau began rising like a loaf of leavened bread. Why? Possibly because of events occurring over 700 miles to the west. According to the Theory of Plate Tectonics, the surface of the earth is broken into a number of rigid rocky plates that ride on top of a molten, syrupy layer known as the mantle. Some of these plates consist of thin, dense layers under the ocean. Others, thicker but less dense, form the continents. As the plates drift along, they occasionally run into each other in what resembles an ultra-slow-motion car crash. Sometimes two plates grind past each other while at other times one plate slides under the other. On occasion, a plate breaks apart, with the various pieces moving away from each other. That's why the east coast of South America fits with the west coast of Africa like two pieces of a jigsaw puzzle. One hundred and fifty million years ago they were both part of the same supercontinent called Pangaea. Over the intervening eons Pangaea broke apart and South America drifted away from Africa, opening the Atlantic Ocean in its wake.

Until the mid-1960s, most geologists dismissed Plate Tectonics as the realm of crackpots; they couldn't imagine how masses the size of continents could move, so they rejected it. As a budding paleontologist in elementary school early that decade, I studied the geographies of South America and Africa and concluded it was obvious they had once been connected. Why couldn't professional geologists see this? Just because you can't explain why something happened doesn't mean it didn't happen. My youthful insight was vindicated a few years later when extensive seismic measurements of seafloor spreading in the mid-Atlantic provided the missing explanation.

The rise of the Colorado Plateau was an outcome of the breakup of Pangaea. As the supercontinent fractured, an oceanic plate—the Farallon Plate—began burrowing under a continental plate—the North American Plate—along what is now the coast of California. Over the next 100 million years, the Farallon Plate was completely consumed in the magma under the North American Plate. The enormous pressures created by these colliding plates compressed the lands to the east, giving rise to the Rocky Mountains, forming Nevada's basin-and-range topography, and uplifting the Colorado Plateau more than a mile into the sky.

Today, the Colorado River and its tributaries are the most obvious natural influences upon the land. Many geologists believe they are only recent influences—perhaps only over the last 6 million years. Earlier rivers meandered widely, and the most direct ancestor to the Colorado appears to have flowed in a direction opposite of today's river. No one is sure why, but the evidence is convincing. Gravel deposits eroded from mountains in the Mojave Desert of California can be found hundreds of miles away in Utah, carried eastward by the ancestral river.

Not every geologist agrees with the idea of a young Colorado River. Some claim it to be much older. They point to measurements of radioactive isotopes that suggest the river's most notable feature, the Grand Canyon, is at least 70 million years old. As for me, I will let the professionals fight it out. I gave up on paleontology as a career goal when I entered high school and took my first course in electronics.

Enough theory. The best way to understand this country is to get out and see it for yourself. It is time for me to do so again.

~

"THE TRICK TO DRIVING over quicksand," says the ranger, "is not to drive too slow and not to drive too fast. If you go too slow you'll get stuck, but if you go too fast, you'll throw wet sand up into your engine and be in even worse shape." Left unsaid is what constitutes driving "too slow" or "too fast." That will be an experiment for the driver to conduct in real time.

I am the driver in question. He is the ranger at the visitor center in Canyonlands National Park, administering advice while I fill out paperwork for a permit to drive the backcountry. I have come once again to the Needles District to explore. My plan is to drive Salt Creek Canyon and its surroundings, camping for several nights while photographing the landscape along the way. I have heard rumors that vehicles may soon be prohibited in this canyon, and I want to explore it while I still can. At my age and in my slovenly physical condition, hiking this route for many miles is out of the question.

The youthful ranger appears to be fresh out of school and has probably never driven my planned route. But after giving my Jeep Cherokee a quick look to confirm it is capable of the journey, he hands me the permit along with a park map and wishes me well.

The Jeep is a rental I picked up in Grand Junction after a turbulent flight from Denver. I suppose if I had read the contract carefully, I would have noticed it prohibits use off paved roads or on roads that are not regularly maintained. But what does it mean to be regularly maintained? And how much maintenance is required? Surely a road indelibly marked on a map duly issued by the United States Government should qualify. I've driven many city streets that probably should not. It's a question I only belatedly consider long after the trip is over.

If I were a romantic, I would follow John Steinbeck's lead and personify my Jeep by giving it an exotic name like Nellybelle or Rocinante. If I were a miscreant, I would follow Ernest Hemingway's lead and stock up on enough liquor to intoxicate an infantry platoon. But I am neither. I am an engineer, trained to analyze a situation dispassionately before acting. Although I long ago abandoned engineering life for the lure of management, I am told I maintain that dispassionate disposition. My wife often commiserates with other women about how unromantic it is to be married to an engineer. True to form, my jeep remains nameless.

As for liquor, when at home nothing beats a cool gin-and-tonic on a warm summer evening or a stout single-malt scotch on a cold winter night. And living in California's wine country, we always have an ample supply of the grape laid up. But when in slickrock country I don't want to dull my sense of the experience, so the alcohol stays home. Perhaps if I lived here full time, I'd soon see the need to drink.

My gear is limited to what I can carry onboard an aircraft or check in a single suitcase: down sleeping bag, hiking boots, flashlight, a few cooking utensils, a jacket, and one change of clothes. And of course, an ample supply of photographic equipment. When preparing for the trip my biggest concern was what to do for a stove. My regular backpacker's stove burns white gas, which would never be allowed on an aircraft. Nor would the associated gas bottle, even if empty. In the end, I pack a small butane-fueled stove attachment and purchase the butane canister in Grand Junction while stocking up on food.

I head out from the visitor center and down the highway to a side road on the left, initially paved but soon reduced to a dirt trail. Almost immediately I understand why the ranger offered his advice. What appears to be the trail stretches for several hundred yards nearly straight ahead. But it is completely covered in water for its full visible length. Only now do I realize this is called Salt Creek Canyon for a reason. After recent rains,

I will be driving through a river, not a road, with no idea of the quality of the roadbed. For a moment I have second thoughts, but I'm in a Jeep. According to television ads, this should be as easy as rolling rocks off a cliff. I shift into four-wheel-drive and venture in.

Any doubts are soon dispelled. I catch a glint to my right just as a car shoots across my bow from a side trail. It's a low-slung station wagon I recognize as being advertised for off-road adventures but only marginally qualified. It speeds along aggressively, kicking up a rooster-tail of water as it goes. Every seat is occupied, and people wave from open windows as they pass. It disappears around a distant corner and I do not see it again. But if they can do it, so can I.

I experiment with speeds and find one I like. As long as I keep moving there seems to be no danger of sinking into the mire. The worst of the water is soon past, and the road only occasionally enters the creek. The passageway is narrow, rough, full of dangerous rocks. At one point while traversing a particularly difficult stretch, I hear a loud bang from underneath the vehicle. Fearing the worst, I get out to check. The case

Salt Creek Canyon Trail, Canyonlands National Park, Utah

protecting the differential gear on the rear axle consists of two halves bolted together along a flange. The flange is visibly bent, victim of a boulder I couldn't avoid while cresting a rise. The case itself looks undamaged, so the situation doesn't appear serious. I continue on without problem, thankful I won't be the one who must take the differential apart when it eventually needs service.

The road spirals like a party streamer over the rough terrain, following the general flow of the creek. White and red walls of Permian-age Cedar Mesa sandstone rise two hundred, three hundred feet on either side. If I remember my geology, the white layers are the remains of beach sands and the reddish layers those of iron-rich sediments that washed in from nearby mountains during primeval floods. The entire assemblage was cemented together by calcium carbonate that leached into the rock when it was subsequently covered by ancient seas. Now, as rainwater dissolves this natural cement unevenly along fracture lines, portions of

Paul Bunyan's Potty, Canyonlands National Park, Utah

the rock collapse to form the many fins and arches that appear through-out the park.

Not every arch is alike. Experts describe four types. Free-standing arches are the type most people imagine—vertical openings encircled by a layer of rock. A natural bridge is similar but spans a stream or water channel. A cliff wall arch, as the name implies, is attached to the side of a cliff. A pothole arch is an arch turned on its side. I take a brief detour to see one of the most famous pothole arches, an enormous opening high overhead that looks exactly like the toilet seat of a giant outhouse—the aptly named Paul Bunyan's Potty.

If I look carefully as I drive, I can spot buff-colored carvings in the cliffs high above—petroglyphs of human forms, birds, and strange shapes pecked into the dark desert varnish by Native Americans a millennium ago. Once in a while I spot the remains of an ancient granary built into a cliff, but there are no signs of permanent living quarters. Evidently this canyon served only as a hunting ground, not a place of residence.

The wind picks up as the afternoon progresses, first as blustery swirls and eventually as a full-blown gale. At dusk I reach a primitive campsite and pull in for the night. It would be useless to try to light the stove in this wind. I open a can of chicken spread and throw together a sandwich for a simple dinner, then clear enough room in the Jeep to roll out my sleeping bag and retire.

I awake before dawn to a crisp, clear sky. At least for now, the wind is calm. I eat a quick breakfast and head out. My goal is Angel Arch, the largest arch in the park, standing nearly 150 feet high. I've read about it and seen it in pictures, but nothing quite prepares me for the real thing. It is massive, much larger than I imagined, with the distinctive shape of an angel. Her head is turned down in pensive prayer, her wings folded at her back. The arch rests behind her like a fallen halo. I sense something familiar about her, like a distant relative who shows up at your doorstep after decades away. Then I realize I have seen her before. This natural formation is shaped precisely like the figures of angels in the stained-glass windows of medieval churches.

I have gazed into the Grand Canyon, viewed the Mona Lisa, explored Notre-Dame Cathedral. In every case I fought crowds of people doing the

same. Now I stand here alone at dawn, watching shadows drop like cur-
tains as the sun rises to reveal the full beauty of this natural cathedral.
There is no one to share my view. No crowds to battle for the perfect spot.
No humans at all for at least a dozen miles. It is my responsibility, my
duty alone to honor this sacred place today, to represent all mankind. For
a moment I picture the tourists at the Louvre who are even now jostling
to get a brief glimpse of a famous painting. But it is only for a moment. I
have my own responsibility to carry out this beautiful morning, one to be
performed free of distractions. I settle into position, clear my mind, and
absorb the view. It is an assignment I relish. I am in no hurry to depart.

Angel Arch, Canyonlands National Park, Utah

The Three Gossips, Arches National Park, Utah

4

DISCOVERY:
THEN AND NOW

I FIRST CAME to the Slickrock Desert in 1983, together with a young wife and a two-year-old son in a rented recreational vehicle for a two-week trip. I was a veteran camper, but it was Nicki's first time on an extended road trip. We did the usual tourist spots—Grand Canyon, Arches, Canyonlands—staying in motels with civilized showers often enough to maintain family harmony.

I was no stranger to deserts, having grown up in Southern California with parents who were avid rockhounds. My earliest views were shaped by the Mojave and Sonoran deserts—flat, barren, monochromatic lands almost completely devoid of color, with little relief save for the occasional dry wash. On weekends we would head out in search of semi-precious stones—moss agates, fire agates, jasper, rhodonite, rhodochrosite, smoky quartz, amethyst, Apache tears, geodes, petrified wood, opal, ulexite, or any of a dozen other stones the local rock club was excited about at the moment. Our destinations were remote sites with names like Saddle Mountain, Old Woman Mountains, Marble Mountains, Cady Mountains, Red Rock Canyon, Last Chance Canyon, Afton Canyon, Wiley Wells, Devils Playground, Rosamond Dry Lake,

Amboy Crater, or Zzyzx (so named in 1944 by an industrious promoter to assure it would be the last entry in the telephone book). We would hunt for gems by day and sleep under the stars by night, serenaded by the mournful wails of coyotes and scouted by the occasional furtive fox. In the evenings we would build roaring campfires and grill steaks over the flames. Someone would invariably break out a mandolin or harmonica and we would sing the usual campfire songs. Life was good in the only deserts I knew.

Our trip to Utah was a wondrous experience. This was a desert unlike any I had ever seen. Where I was used to low plains of gravel stretching to the horizon, sparsely populated by a few hardy cactuses and inter-rupted occasionally by muddy brown hills, here were yawning chasms and towering buttes in a rainbow of colors. I realized for the first time the deserts I knew from my youth were lowly backwater deserts, the low-rent districts of the kind. This was like a visit to Metropolis, with as much to see as on a stroll down Broadway. The cactuses were still there like vagrants in the shadows, but they were overwhelmed by the mesas and the valleys—nature's equivalent of skyscraper row. My eyes were as wide as a farmer's son's on his first visit to the big city.

Two weeks were hardly enough to absorb the sights, but with a career to manage and a family to raise, several years passed before I could return. In the interim my career took me on business trips to faraway cit-ies on aircraft flying high above the beckoning landscape six miles below. From their windows I would gaze on convoluted layers of fantastic shapes and dream of when I could return.

Eventually I did. It started with surreptitious side journeys on busi-ness trips. When I traveled to Las Vegas, Salt Lake City, or Phoenix for meetings during the week, I would tack on an extra vacation day or two on either side, often saving the company money by flying on off days. By camping out on those days, I had no increased hotel expense. And I could sometimes upgrade my rental car to a 4-wheel-drive SUV through conversations that went something like this:

"Welcome, Mr. Hinch. Thanks for renting from Avertz Rental Cars again. It will be a little while before the micro-mini car your company reserved will be ready for you."

"I'm in sort of a hurry to get to a meeting a fair drive away. I see that Jeep over there looks ready to go. Can I get that?"

"I'm sorry, that's not included in your car class. You would have to pay extra for it."

"That's too bad. I've been thinking about buying a new Jeep just like that, and it would be great to test it out, but my company would never spring for the upgrade."

"Hmmm. Let me see what I can do... Well, it looks like your car won't be ready for another twenty minutes. You're a good customer, so just this once I'll go ahead and upgrade you at no charge. Please drive it carefully."

"Of course, and thanks a lot. I'll be sure to give you a great review in the survey your headquarters sends me."

These side journeys could only touch the periphery of canyon country, but it was a start. Like an invading army, I attacked from multiple angles. A trip to Phoenix added an overnight stop at the Grand Canyon; Las Vegas included a day trip to Valley of Fire; Salt Lake a weekend in Moab. Such trips could offer only brief glimpses of what wonders lay beyond: hoodoo spires, twisted canyons, gaping arches, secret grottos, variegated layers of sedimentary rocks stretching for miles.

And more: an exotic oversized lizard—the Gila monster—prototype for the dinosaurs of 1950s horror movies, found only at the far west edge of the country. An occasional rattlesnake, content to lurk in the shadows but unafraid to deliver a stereophonic warning should you venture too close. Tarantulas, at times so numerous you could drive across their remains on the highway and seldom touch asphalt.

One morning I left my hotel well before dawn and set out in the dark. Driving on a lonely byway in predawn light I was jolted by a sudden movement in the road ahead. As I braked, two, then four, then eight 4-legged bodies rushed past. Bighorn sheep, as evidenced by the spiral horns arcing gracefully like corkscrews from their heads. By the time I could produce a camera they had bounded halfway up a nearby hill.

I needed more freedom to explore, so I bought a durable 4-wheel-drive Mitsubishi Montero (one of the best off-road 4x4 vehicles, sadly now extinct) and began excursions from California, either on my own or with like-minded photographers. As I explored, I came to realize slickrock country is hardly a uniform landscape. The Grand Canyon is as different from Capitol Reef as New York is from New Orleans. A trip through the Escalante canyons traverses a different world from Bryce Canyon. There is much to discover, and even after nearly forty years I have not seen it all. Nowhere near all. But I have plans. It is good to have plans.

❧

THIS LAND IS DESOLATE, but its human history is extensive. Native Americans lived here for thousands of years, although records of their existence are scant. Ruins survive, as do pottery sherds and tools, but if the indelible remnants of their petroglyphs and pictographs tell a story, we have not yet found the Rosetta Stone necessary to decipher it.

The first Europeans known to have reached canyon country were a small group dispatched by the conquistador Coronado in 1540. Coronado's army had stormed a Zuni pueblo in today's New Mexico they imagined to be one of the "Seven Golden Cities of Cibola." They found no riches but

The Watchtower at Desert View, Grand Canyon National Park, Arizona

heard rumors of a large river to the northwest. Coronado sent an expedition of 12 men led by Don Garcia Lopez de Cárdenas to find it. With help from Native American guides, Cárdenas and his men eventually reached the south rim of the Grand Canyon.

The exact spot is subject to dispute. Many scholars believe it to be somewhere near Desert View, not because of any physical or written evidence, but because that was the location of known Native American trading routes. Not everyone agrees. A minority opinion contends the Natives would have known better than to share such secrets. Coronado had already developed a reputation of taking what he wanted by force. The wary Natives might have deliberately led Cárdenas away from the profitable trade routes to a region with no access to the river, in the hope the unwelcome foreigners would be discouraged and never return.

We know this very thing happened later in Coronado's quest. A Native the Spaniards named "the Turk" led Coronado's army hundreds of miles northeast into Kansas in a quest to reach the mythical land of Quivira, where silver and gold were said to be prolific. After many weeks with nothing to show for their journey, Coronado realized he had been duped. The Turk eventually confessed to leading them astray in hopes they would perish, for which Coronado ordered him put to death.

At an overlook far to the west of Desert View, an enigmatic inscription of unknown origin bearing the cryptic words "MONTE VIDEO" carved into the sandstone may have been made by the Cárdenas expedition. If so, it would be convincing supporting evidence, although its origin is far from certain. In any event, I favor the minority opinion for the simple reason it makes sense, and I apparently give the Natives more credit than do many scholars. If this was indeed their tactic, it was spectacularly successful. The expedition departed discouraged, and it was nearly 250 years before men of European descent returned to the area.

When they did return in 1776, it was not to settle but to find the quickest possible way through it. Two Franciscan priests, Fray Francisco Atanasio Domínguez and Fray Francisco Silvestre Vélez de Escalante, led a party of 12 men from their settlement in Santa Fe in search of a route to the missions of California. Domínguez was the expedition's leader, but like every good manager he delegated the labor-intensive tasks to those below him. It fell to Escalante to keep the detailed diary of the trip.* Like every good subordinate, he was meticulous in his reporting, especially about his superior:

> We did not travel today, Father Atanasio was very ill from a pain in the rectum so severe that he was not able even to move.

Escalante's journal does not indicate who or what was the cause of Father Atanasio's rectal discomfort, which was perhaps the first recorded instance of an affliction all too familiar to countless future generations of managers.

The expedition started north through Colorado, then west through Utah. They took a circuitous route, apparently because they were at least as interested in finding Natives to convert to Christianity as they were in finding a route to California. On August 13, Escalante's journal records one of the first sightings of an Ancestral Pueblo ruin by Europeans:

> An observation was made by the sun and we found we were in 38° and 13½' north latitude. Here there is everything needed for the establishment and maintenance of a good settlement in the way of irrigable lands, pastures, timber and firewood. On an elevation on the south bank of the river in ancient times there was a small settlement of the same form as those of the Indians of New Mexico, as is shown by the ruins which we purposely examined.

They progressed slowly through September and October, on occasion helped by friendly Natives. But the journey was much more challenging than they had anticipated. By early November, half-starved, facing severe snowstorms, and nowhere near their goal, they made the difficult decision to turn back. They ended up making a great counterclockwise trek around the Colorado Plateau, returning across the Colorado River at a ford later named Crossing of the Fathers, now submerged under Lake Powell. It

---

* Quotes are taken from Herbert Bolton's excellent article in the 1950 *Utah Historical Quarterly* "Pagent in the Wilderness: The Story of the Escalante Expedition to the Interior Basin, 1776." Used by permission. See Selected References for full citation.

took almost two weeks to find a suitable crossing. Escalante recorded an initial unsuccessful attempt:

> On all sides we were surrounded by mesas and inaccessible heights. There-fore, two men who know how to swim well entered the river naked, carrying their clothing on their heads. It was so deep and wide that the swimmers, in spite of their prowess, were scarcely able to reach the opposite shore, and they lost their clothing in the middle of the river, never seeing it again.

They eventually found a viable crossing and returned to Santa Fe. The mission was not a complete failure, as they conducted an extensive mapping of the region. One outcome of Escalante being the journalist is that it made him far more famous than Dominguez. Among other things, he has been immortalized in the name of a desert, a town, a river, several parks, and numerous commercial establishments throughout the South-west. Other than a single small ruin named after him at the Canyon of the Ancients Visitor Center near Dolores, Colorado, commemorations of Domínguez are scant.

By the early 1800s, individual mountain men were exploring the land. Most had little interest in leaving records for posterity, but one French-Canadian fur trapper, Denis Julien, was prolific. From 1831 to 1844 he carved inscriptions in rocks throughout the area, including several loca-tions along the Colorado and Green Rivers in today's Arches and Can-yonlands National Parks. Always containing his name and the date, they survive today as the only records of his journeys.

The most famous nineteenth century canyon country explorations were those of John Wesley Powell, a one-armed civil war veteran who led expeditions down the Colorado River in rickety wooden boats in 1869 and 1871. His journeys have become legendary, with books written and movies made of his story. Largely because of these accomplishments he went on to serve as the second Director of the U.S. Geological Survey. We will learn more about Major Powell soon.

Powell's trip was not the nation's first official expedition into the region. In 1857 a detachment of 45 men from the US Army Topographical Engineers under the command of Lieutenant Joseph Christmas Ives set out to plot the course of the Colorado River and its tributaries. Their assignment was to determine the river's suitability as a trade route. They began at the river's mouth on the Gulf of California, where they boarded a paddlewheel steamboat and traveled north to a point near today's town of Needles, California. There they disembarked and started overland for the Grand Canyon, guided by the Mohave chief Irataba and several members of his tribe. They eventually reached the rim of the canyon and descended to the river at its junction with Diamond Creek, now part of the Hualapai Reservation. Ives' report back to Washington has become infamous for his dismal opinion of this land:

> The region is of course, altogether valueless. It can be approached only from the south, and after entering it there is nothing to do but leave. Ours has been the first, and will doubtless be the last, party of whites to visit this profitless locality.

Not everyone in his party held such a dim view. The journal of Balduin Möllhausen, a Prussian artist invited by Ives to join the expedition, illustrates the difference between an engineer and an artist:

> My thoughts and glances were absorbed by the sublime scenery, seemingly in wild confusion, but arranged into a beautiful whole by the master's hand.

Today, as we drive in air-conditioned comfort along the paved highway from Grand Canyon Village to Desert View, it is easy for us to disparage Lieutenant Ives for his lack of vision. But he was a product of his time, just as we are of ours. A hundred years from now, our progeny (should the species survive) may well disparage us for driving in air-conditioned comfort along the paved highway from Grand Canyon Village to Desert View, with no thought for the long-term damage our travel was doing to the future health of the planet.

View from South Rim, Grand Canyon National Park, Arizona

Colorado River, Grand Canyon National Park, Arizona

5

DOWN AN
UNKNOWN RIVER

THE NINETEENTH CENTURY was an era of unbridled westward expansion. At the beginning of the century the nation's sixteen states all lay east of the Mississippi. The lands to the west were an unexplored frontier. By the end of the century its forty-five states spanned from sea to sea and the Census Bureau had declared the frontier no longer extant—there were no tracts of land anywhere without settlers.

The transition had not occurred overnight. Even after the Civil War much of the Southwest was still a blank spot on the map. Certainly, some of it had been explored by a few mountain men and trappers, but whatever they learned they kept to themselves. Even government sponsored expeditions such as those led by Joseph C. Ives and John C. Frémont left much of the region unexplored. To the great majority of Americans, the vast wastelands of Colorado, Wyoming, and Utah remained *terra incognita*.

That changed in 1869 when Major John Wesley Powell led an expedition of ten adventurers in four sturdy wooden boats down the Green and Colorado Rivers. Not only was the expedition monumental in itself, Powell knew how to get publicity. He befriended two newspaper reporters who published glowing reports of his exploits. They inspired millions of readers in a country committed to westward expansion, even readers who would never want to be part of that expansion themselves.

Of the ten men who started the expedition, two of them, Jack Sumner and George Bradley, kept detailed journals.[*] Major Powell kept a cryptic journal but followed up several years later with a bestselling book, *The Exploration of the Colorado River and its Canyons*, that has never been out of print. What we know of the journey comes largely from the records of these three men.

Although Major Powell's book purports to be a day-by-day journal of the 1869 expedition, in reality it is an amalgam of events that happened on both this expedition and a second one he led in 1871. There is no doubt the Major knew how to tell a story, even if he had to resort to fictional nonfiction to tell it. He would be neither the first nor the last western author to do so.

But we are getting ahead of ourselves. In a story such as this, it is best to start at the beginning.

ᡐ

JOHN WESLEY POWELL was born in Mount Morris, New York, in 1834 to Joseph and Mary Powell. His early life could hardly have foretold the enormity of his contributions to the understanding of the arid lands of the West. His father was a preacher who named his son after the cleric who founded the Methodist movement. The elder Powell always hoped his son would enter the ministry and was never completely supportive of his scientific interests.

The Powells moved to Ohio in 1838, where their abolitionist views made them unpopular with many locals. After young John Wesley was stoned by classmates, he was taken out of school and tutored by George Crookham, a self-taught scientist. Although together only a short time,

---

[*] Bradley's journal and the last half of Sumner's, both edited by William Culp Darrah, appeared in the *Utah Historical Quarterly* in 1947. The first half of Sumner's journal, once thought lost, was discovered to have been published in the *Missouri Democrat* in 1869 and was reprinted in the *Utah Historical Quarterly* in 1969. Quoted by permission.

Crookham had an outsized influence on the young Powell. Their trips into the countryside to study nature stimulated Powell's interest in such fields as geology, geography, ethnology, archaeology, and history—all of which drove his later life.

Powell's schooling was sporadic. His biographer Wallace Stegner called it the "homemade education" typical of many who lived in the West. In 1846 it was interrupted for four years when the family moved to Wisconsin. There, the young Powell spent full time managing the family farm while his peripatetic father was away preaching. He loved learning and read every book he could get his hands on, especially those on science and history. Despite his limited formal education, by the time he was 18 he had secured a teaching job in Jefferson County, Wisconsin. He quickly discovered he had to become a quick learner to stay ahead of his students.

The schoolteacher's life was only an intermittent one for him. George Crookham's influence had inspired him to want to explore the land. He made several trips in the late 1850s that were warm-ups for his later trips down the Colorado River. In 1856 he rafted down the Mississippi much like Huckleberry Finn. The next year he floated down the Ohio and Missouri Rivers, and the following spring, down the Illinois River. On all these trips he collected specimens of fossils, flowers, shells, and archaeological relics for his personal museum.

In 1860 he was named principal of public schools in Hennepin, Illinois, and in 1861 he was elected secretary of the Illinois State Natural History Society. Whatever he imagined for his future was changed by the onset of the Civil War. An ardent abolitionist, he enlisted in the Union Army as soon as the war began. He entered as a private, but within a few months had been promoted to lieutenant and then to captain, serving on General Grant's staff as an expert on fortifications. Against his family's wishes he took a few days off to marry his cousin, Emma Dean, then returned to duty.

During the Battle of Shiloh in April 1862, his right arm was shattered by a musket ball and was amputated above the elbow. Evidently, the loss of an arm was only a minor inconvenience for him. After recovering he returned to the Army and served three more years, initially as an army recruiter. One has to wonder what was going on in the mind of the officer who thought it would be a good idea to send a one-armed, battle-maimed veteran out to convince raw recruits to sign up. Perhaps Powell had already impressed his superiors with his strong negotiating skills.

Eventually he rejoined the fray, distinguishing himself in several battles in the Vicksburg campaign. At the time of his discharge in January 1865 due to the lingering effects of his amputation, he was commander of the artillery for the 17th Army Corp, with the rank of Brevet Lieutenant Colonel. (As "brevet" refers to an honorary commission for meritorious service at a rank higher than an officer's formal rank, he was always thereafter called "Major Powell.")

Powell returned to teaching later that year when he accepted a position as a professor of geology at Illinois Wesleyan University. In 1866 he moved on to the nearby Illinois State Normal University (now Illinois State University). He was popular with students because he taught as much through field trips and hands-on experience as he did through classroom lectures.

Considering his love of the outdoors, it is no surprise that Powell was soon crafting an excuse for an extended expedition. He started by talking the state legislature into approving funds for a museum operated by the Illinois State Natural History Society, with him as curator. He then convinced the Board of Education in Bloomington that museums need artifacts, and he was the one to lead the expedition to collect them.

Expeditions need financing, and Powell set his sights on getting it. He cobbled together funds from a variety of sources. He got the Board of Education to allocate a portion of the museum's budget for the trip. He convinced railroads to provide free passage in exchange for the publicity. And he undertook his first trip to Washington in search of federal support, where he achieved modest success. The Smithsonian agreed to loan him scientific instruments, and his old commander, General Grant, now Secretary of War, committed to providing the expedition with sufficient rations for a party of 12 men. Clearly, his years in the army had taught him how to plead a case convincingly.

The result was an 1867 expedition of twelve volunteers into the Colorado Rockies to explore a largely unknown land. Joined on the trip by his wife Emma, they climbed Pikes Peak (she is said to be the first woman to do so), explored the Front Range, and gathered specimens for his collection. They accomplished little of true scientific value but gained experience navigating the wild.

While on this trip Powell met two men who would take on important roles in his future. O. G. Howland had been a printer and editor for the *Rocky Mountain News*. Articulate and intelligent, Howland was also an experienced outdoorsman. Jack Sumner was a veteran mountain man and a wilderness guide for well-to-do easterners. By the time Powell left Colorado that fall, the three of them had concocted a plan to explore the last unknown region in the West—the canyons of the Colorado River—the following year.

Upon returning to Illinois Powell divided his time between teaching, organizing his museum collection, and planning his next expedition. He went again to Washington to promote his plan and get what help he could from the Smithsonian and Congress. He argued the knowledge gained from his expedition would surely benefit the entire nation in its westward expansion. Joseph Henry, Secretary of the Smithsonian, was an ardent supporter and lobbied Congress on his behalf. Once again, Powell cobbled together funds from a variety of sources, augmented with his own money where necessary.

The qualifications of his new team were only slightly improved from those of the previous year's expedition. The twenty-one-member Rocky Mountain Scientific Exploring Expedition was a collection of student volunteers, Methodist preachers, amateur scientists, family relatives, and the occasional trained expert. Powell's wife Emma, his brother Walter, his sister Nellie Powell Thompson, and his brother-in-law Almon Thompson all joined the expedition in various roles. George Vasey, their botanist, was already a person of some note in scientific circles, although his most productive years were still ahead of him, inspired in part by his travels with this expedition. To this core team, Powell added a group of mountain men he recruited after he arrived in Colorado.

Powell's 1868 expedition had to serve two masters. His academic sponsors expected it to further explore the Front Range and collect more specimens for the natural history museum. Congress and the Smithsonian expected it to survey the Green and Colorado Rivers. The summer and fall of 1868 were devoted to the first task. They collected numerous animal and botanical specimens, made the first ascent of Long's Peak, and scouted various locations along their planned river trip. Powell met a band of Utes who rekindled his interest in ethnology originally inspired by George Crookham. He spent weeks with the Utes, learning their language and customs. Years later this experience would be a major influence in his decision to direct the Bureau of Ethnology.

The 1868 trip was important for one other reason. Powell spent time with Samuel Bowles of *The Springfield Republican* and William Byers, founder of *The Rocky Mountain News* and Jack Sumner's brother-in-law. The two editors wrote enthusiastic stories of the expedition, with Bowles' reports gaining it nationwide attention.

The second phase of the trip began in early 1869. By then, the Easterners had returned home, leaving behind only the mountain men and Powell's brother, Walter, to form the core of the river trip. While Powell took a train east from Green River, Wyoming to finish preparations (joined by Emma, who would wait out the year at home), the rest of the team spent the winter along the White River.

In Chicago, Powell commissioned a boatbuilder to construct four wooden boats to his specifications. The 16-foot pilot boat, christened the *Emma Dean*, was made of lightweight pine for good maneuverability. The other three, christened *Maid of the Canyon, Kitty Clyde's Sister*, and the inspired *No Name*, were sturdy, 21-foot boats made of oak, with watertight compartments at each end. All would prove challenging to maneuver through rapids and heavy to carry on portages. From Chicago Powell moved on to Washington, where he was only able to negotiate a level of support similar to the year before.

Powell took the Union Pacific Railroad back to Green River. He arrived and had the boats unloaded on May 11, 1869—one day after that line joined with the Central Pacific in Promontory, Utah, to complete the nation's first transcontinental railroad. At Green River he met the rest of the party, and they spent the next two weeks preparing for launch. In Powell's typically conservative fashion, he loaded enough supplies for a ten-month journey, divided equally between the three larger boats.

In the early afternoon of May 24, 1869, a small crowd of locals gathered on the riverbank to see them off. More than a few of those locals probably thought the expedition was doomed and would never be seen again. Everyone had heard stories of thousand-foot waterfalls, subterranean canyons with no way out, and rapids that would drown anyone who tried to run them. No one had actually seen such hazards, but they were sure to exist.

The nine men who joined Powell were a varied lot. Besides Jack Sumner and O.C. Howland, the party was a mix of trappers, vagabonds, and former army veterans: William Dunn, Seneca Howland, Billy Hawkins, George Bradley, Frank Goodman, and Andrew Hall, plus Powell's brother Walter. In his book, *The Exploration of the Colorado River and its Canyons*, first published in 1875, Powell wrote about them. Of Sumner, he said:

> Sumner was a soldier during the late war, and before and since he has been a great traveler in the wilds...When Bayard Taylor traveled through the parks of Colorado, Sumner was his guide, and he speaks in glowing terms of Mr. Taylor's genial qualities in camp, but he was mortally offended when the great traveler requested him to act a doorkeeper at Breckenridge to receive the admission fee from those who attended his lectures.

Of Goodman, a last-minute volunteer, he wrote:

> Goodman is a stranger to us—a stout, willing Englishman, with florid face and more florid anticipations of a glorious trip.

Perhaps the most telling description was that of his brother, Walter, who today would be diagnosed with post-traumatic stress disorder:

> Captain Powell was an officer of artillery during the late war and was captured on the 22d day of July, 1864, at Atlanta and served a ten months' term in the prison at Charleston...He is silent, moody, and sarcastic,

though sometimes he enlivens the camp at night with a song...We call him "Old Shady."

The first few days were relatively easy. They encountered nothing more serious than frequent rain and the occasional broken paddle or grounding on a sandbar. They took time to explore the geology and measure the height of cliffs along the way. Sumner noted in his journal that he stole two bread-pans from a nearby cabin. They began assigning names to features along the river—Flaming Gorge, Beehive Point, Red Canyon—names that persist to the present day, even for features now submerged under reservoirs.

They developed a rhythm for navigating the river's innumerable rapids—many of which would have been called falls on other rivers. Upon first hearing the roar they would land so they could determine what they were about to face. If it were a relatively mild flow, they might choose to run it in the boats. Everyone preferred that approach as being the easiest, but Powell was cautious. He used a method called lining to cross many of the less severe falls. Each boat would be unloaded and ropes tied to its bow and stern. Half the men took the bow line down to the end of the fall while the rest held the stern line. The crew at the stern would lower the boat through the fall until they could no longer hold it, then let go so the bow team could haul it ashore downstream. Finally, they had to lug the thousands of pounds of supplies on foot across rocks to the waiting boat.

Lining wouldn't work in the worst spots. For those, they had to perform complete portages, carrying not only the supplies but also each of the boats overland around the flow.

Throughout the trip their attempts at hunting the wildlife were often unsuccessful. Sumner recorded an incident that brought back disturbing memories for the war veterans among the crew.

> While rounding a bend, we came on a herd of mountain sheep that scampered up a steep, rocky side of the canyon at an astonishing rate. The crews of the freight boats opened up a volley on them that made the wilderness ring, reminding us all of other scenes and times, when we were the scampering party.

Everything changed on June 8th. In the early afternoon while floating through a canyon they named Lodore, they came to a tremendous rapid where they could see "nothing but spray and foam." Powell in the *Emma Dean* signaled for all boats to pull ashore, but the *No Name*, piloted by O. C. Howland and crewed by his brother Seneca and Frank Goodman, was too far out in the current. She struck a rock and spun sideways, crashing into another rock that broke her bow. The two Howlands and Goodman made precarious jumps to safety, but the boat and most of its cargo were lost. The unlucky boaters lost every stitch of clothing except the light garb they were wearing.

The next day they reached the wrecked stern of the *No Name* and recovered all the barometers, several thermometers, a pair of old boots, and quite a surprise to Powell, a hidden cask of whiskey of either two, three, or ten gallons depending on whose account you believe. The crew cheered its recovery but soberly realized a third of their supplies were suddenly gone.

While lining the remaining three boats past this perilous rapid, they discovered an iron bake-oven, several tin plates, part of a boat, and numerous other fragments. While the origin of this wreck has never been firmly established, Powell thought it was a relic from General William Henry Ashley's aborted trip down the river in 1825. (Ashley had been a Brigadier General in the Missouri Militia during the war of 1812 and later a fur trader in Utah.) Given its dark history, they named this stretch of river Disaster Falls.

The mood had subtly changed. Their first portage might have been an adventure but by now, carrying thousands of pounds of supplies by hand around lengthy rapids day after day had become weary. Powell's authoritative, military-style command grated on the men. His insistence that they tarry to take measurements of the land and study its geology even when supplies were short was worrying. And Powell himself may well have blamed Howland for the error in navigation that wrecked the *No Name*. George Bradley captured the prevailing sentiment in his journal entry for June 11: "The Major as usual has chosen the worst camping ground possible. If I had a dog that would lie where my bed is made tonight I would kill him and burn his collar and swear I never owned him."

An incident on June 16th didn't improve the mood. While Powell was out exploring, Billy Hawkins, serving as cook, carelessly built his fire too close to an alcove filled with dead willows. A dust devil swirled through camp and spread burning embers into the thicket. Suddenly everything around the camp was ablaze. The men grabbed all they could, jumped into the boats, and ran them through rapids to escape. Hawkins grabbed the mess kit (what still remained after the loss of the *No Name*) but stumbled and dropped it in the river. From afar, Powell watched everything in astonishment. Later they salvaged a few cups and a camp kettle, but the rest was gone forever.

Things got better once they left the Canyon of Lodore. At the junction with the Yampa River in today's Dinosaur National Monument, they put ashore and rested for several days. The Yampa was a river they had camped on the previous year, and its familiarity boosted their morale. Powell climbed the cliffs, explored the geology, and made astronomical measurements of latitude and longitude. A rock next to their camp returned reverberating echoes of even the "slightest and most varying sounds," so they named it Echo Rock and their camp Echo Park.

Back on the river they floated for several days without serious obstacles. They caught trout for breakfast and geese for dinner. They were serenaded by wolves one evening and again the next morning. Sumner observed, "The whole country is utterly worthless to anybody for any purpose whatever, unless it should be the artist in search of wildly grand scenery, or the geologist, as there is a great open book for him all the way."

They reached the Uinta River on June 28th after making sixty-three miles the previous day and fighting hordes of mosquitoes that evening. They landed at the site of a vague wagon road near where they had camped the previous winter. This was their one chance to connect with civilization during their trip. They spent the next few days writing letters, then sent them off with Walter Powell and Andy Hall to the Uinta Agency more than twenty miles away. The Major followed two days later, along with Billy Hawkins and Frank Goodman.

While there, they learned of the many rumors swirling about their certain demise. One enterprising fellow had even emerged to claim he was the only survivor of the lost expedition. He had told an elaborate story of the disaster, complete with an invented geography and fictitious names of compatriots. He managed to get free meals and train rides east, and even met with Governor Palmer of Illinois, before being exposed as a fraud. The letters delivered to the Agency did much to reassure the public the expedition was safe, at least for the moment.

When they returned to the boats on July 5, Frank Goodman was not with them. The florid Englishman, claiming he had seen enough danger, stayed behind and disappeared forever from history. Apparently, no one was sorry to see him go.

To replenish their depleted supplies Powell brought 300 pounds of flour back with him. It was a meager addition but was all the Agency could spare. He may not have had the funds to buy anything more even if it had been available.

Everyone was happy to get back on the river the next day, but the cheer was short lived. As they passed an island on which someone had planted a garden, they got the idea that "stolen fruit is sweet." Andy Hall cooked up a stew of beets, turnips, and potato tops for lunch, claiming "potato tops are good greens." Soon after, everyone was nauseous and vomiting, rolling around in pain. By midafternoon the worst had passed, and they continued the journey. Jack Sumner wrote in his journal, "We all learned one lesson—never to rob gardens."

The following days they floated down Desolation Canyon, through Coal Canyon (now called Gray Canyon), past the Roan Cliffs, and into Labyrinth Canyon. It was a challenging stretch of rapids, with boats occasionally capsizing and more supplies being lost. But Powell continued his geologic explorations across the cliffs and canyons with typical abandon. At one point he managed to trap himself precariously on a narrow foothold above a sixty-foot drop, clinging to a rock outcrop with his single arm, with no way to recover. Bradley happened to be on the cliff above him, just out of reach. After a moment's thought, Bradley sat down, pulled off his long underwear and lowered it to Powell, who let go of his handhold and grabbed the dangling garb just before he would have tumbled to oblivion.

They left Labyrinth Canyon on July 17 and entered what Powell called "a wilderness of rocks—deep gorges where the rivers are lost below cliffs and towers and pinnacles, and ten thousand strangely carved forms in every direction, and beyond them mountains blending with the clouds." This was the Land of Standing Rocks. Even today, it is one of the most remote regions in the continental United States.

The next day they reached the junction with the Grand (which at that time above the junction was considered to be a separate river from the Colorado below it) and stopped for a few days to rest and explore the land. Their food was running low. The flour had been soaked and dried so many times it had acquired a musty smell. They ended up discarding 200 pounds of the worst of it, leaving them no more than two months' supply, and that only if no more was lost.

On July 20, Powell and his brother Walter climbed the canyon to explore the strange shapes they had passed in the Land of Standing Rocks. They spent the day wandering through a landscape as foreign as if they were walking on the moon, exactly one hundred years to the day before two men on another voyage of discovery became the first to truly do so.

They launched again on July 21, entering what they later named Cataract Canyon. The rapids of Desolation and Labyrinth Canyons paled in comparison to the dangerous white water here, but they were now experienced river runners. Over the next several days they made it through with no problems more serious than an occasional lost oar.

The frequent portages were backbreaking. Bradley, who would rather run rapids because "portage don't agree with my constitution," wrote:

> We know that we have got about 2500 ft. to fall yet before we reach Ft. Mohavie and if it comes all in the first hundred miles we shan't be dreading rapids afterwards for if it should continue at this rate much more than a hundred miles we should have to go the rest of the way up hill which is not often the case with rivers.

On July 28th they reached a muddy stream with an unpleasant odor. Not shown on any map, they decided to give it a name. Dunn, when asked if it might harbor trout, called it a "dirty devil," the name by which it has been known ever since.

The Colorado became noticeably more docile past its junction with the Dirty Devil. They were now floating down Glen Canyon, a peaceful interlude in their journey. They discovered and explored Ancestral Pueblo ruins that had once stood three stories tall. Powell wrote:

> At one place, where there is a vertical wall of 10 or 12 feet, I find an old, rickety ladder. It may be that this was a watchtower of that ancient people whose homes we have found in ruins.... Probably the nomadic tribes were sweeping down upon them and they resorted to these cliffs and canyons for safety....Here I stand, where these now lost people stood centuries ago, and look over this strange country, gazing off to great mountains in the northwest which are slowly disappearing under the cover of night; and then I return to camp.

By now, well more than two months into the journey, nerves were frayed and morale was ebbing. Rations consisted of little more than flour, coffee, and dried apples, on rare occasions supplemented by a successful bighorn sheep hunt. Everyone but Powell wanted to keep pushing on without delay. Bradley's frustration showed in his journal entry for August 2nd, when they laid over in camp for a second day so that Powell could conduct more observations of the landscape.

> In the same camp, doomed to be here another day, perhaps more than that for Major has been taking observations ever since we came here and seems no nearer done now than when he began.

On the river again, Powell attempted to record an eclipse of the sun on August 7. He was thwarted by rain. The rest of the men spent the day repairing boats. According to Bradley, "constant banging against rocks has begun to tell sadly on them and they are growing old faster if possible than we are."

Finally, to avoid a potential mutiny Powell decided to forgo his geology studies and accelerate the remainder of the trip. It was just as well. They were now in Marble Canyon, the most dangerous stretch they had yet encountered. It would not be the worst.

More rapids, more portages. The only saving grace, if you could call it that, was that they now had so little in the way of supplies that it didn't take long to portage them. And the less heavily laden boats rode the rapids higher in the water, allowing them to run stretches they would formerly have portaged. They were now in a race to reach the end before supplies ran out.

They entered the Grand Canyon on August 13th. Bradley observed, "One thing is pretty certain—no rocks ever made can make much worse rapids than we now have." They spent the next several days fighting through one set of rapids after another. On August 16 they reached what Powell later called Bright Angel Creek, a name chosen as a contrast to Dirty Devil Creek.

On August 27, the discontent reached the breaking point. After dinner, the Howlands and Dunn privately informed Powell they had had enough. The next rapid ahead looked insurmountable, and they were done. They would exit up a side canyon to the north and head out cross-country to Mormon settlements. Powell tried to convince them they were within a few days of their destination on the Virgin River, but they were unmoved. Their river trip was finished. Powell agonized over whether to join them but decided to press on. He informed the others, who all promised to finish the trip with him.

The next morning, they ate breakfast in silence. "The meal is solemn as a funeral," Powell wrote. With only six men remaining, he decided to abandon the *Emma Dean* and proceed with just two boats. They gave two rifles and a shotgun to the three departing men and offered some of their rations, which were refused. Howland said he had no fear of finding something to eat. They exchanged copies of the expedition's records with the intent of assuring that duplicate copies went with each team. But in their haste Howland took both copies of some records. Sumner gave Howland his watch to forward to his sister if he did not survive.

Then the six men in the two boats set off down the rapid, while the three departing members climbed the cliffs to watch. Both boats made it through what they later named Separation Rapid soaked but safe. They quickly landed and waited a couple of hours in hope the three would relent and take the *Emma Dean* through, but it was not to be. The two

Howlands and Dunn were gone, having climbed the canyon and out onto the plateau. It was a fatal mistake.

The exact fate of the three has never been conclusively determined. They were apparently killed by the Shivwits soon after reaching the top. Rumors suggest it was because white men were known to abuse Native women, or because they were thought to be prospectors looking for gold who would drive them from their lands. When Powell returned the next year to learn what happened, that is what he was apparently told by the Shivwits he met. But a minority of historians believe the three were killed by Mormons who mistook them for government agents and orchestrated a cover-up afterwards. They point to the fact that Powell had brought Jacob Hamblin, a Mormon who knew the Shivwits, along as translator. According to them, Hamblin had been known to cover up Mormon atrocities in the past and may well have fabricated the story while translating. The weakness in this theory is that Powell was no slouch in understanding Native dialects. And in 1923, an elderly Shivwits warrior recalled a time many years before when three white men came up from the Grand Canyon and were murdered in ambush by a warrior named To-ab and two accomplices. The true story may never be known.

While the three on the plateau were meeting their fate, the remaining six continued down the river. For the rest of the day they fought one rapid after another, capsizing on occasion but emerging unscathed. Bradley, who had always objected to Powell boating on the Sabbath, wrote, "This is the first Sunday that I have felt justified in running but it has now become a race for life. We have only enough flour to last us five days and we do not know how long we may be winding around among these hills."

The next day they reached a valley they recognized as Grand Wash. To their great relief they were now back in known country. The worst was over.

On August 30 they met a few Utes camping along the river but learned little from them. Later that day, they reached the Virgin River and saw several people in the water fishing. They turned out to be Mormons, who "seem far less surprised to see us than we do to see them." Word of the lost expedition had reached the settlers several weeks before, and they had been asked to watch for any fragments that might float past.

The fragments they found turned out to be much livelier than they had anticipated.

Major Powell and his brother left the river there, returning first to Salt Lake City and then home to a hero's welcome. Sumner, Hawkins, Bradley, and Hall continued down the river and into obscurity.

BRADLEY SETTLED IN CALIFORNIA and established a small fruit ranch. In 1885, in declining health he moved to Massachusetts to live out his final days with family. Sumner married and moved to Colorado, then Wyoming and Utah, achieving success as a mining supervisor. He died in 1907. Hawkins became a rancher and Justice of the Peace in Arizona, where he died in 1919. Hall returned to being a stage driver and was killed by robbers in 1882, all three of whom were hanged the following week.

In Washington, Powell's success finally got the attention of the federal government. When he proposed a follow-up trip to create the detailed map he had not completed in 1869, Congress awarded him a $10,000 grant, better equipment, and more support than on his first expedition. And through a fortunate clerical error, he was put under the jurisdiction of the learned Smithsonian Institution rather than the politically-driven Department of the Interior.

This second expedition, conducted in two parts over the years 1871 and 1872, met its objectives. Powell, even though he rode more comfortably in a better boat with an armchair placed high as if it were a king's throne, was along only for parts of it. His interest in river trips had waned, and he found excuses several times to leave the expedition for other business. His brother-in-law, Almon Thompson, became the trip's true leader. To their everlasting dismay, Powell largely left this team and its accomplishments out of his book, ascribing them instead to the 1869 expedition.

Over the coming years, Powell took on an ever-larger role in Washington to influence western policy. He advocated for the sensible opening of the West. He had seen enough to know land-use practices that worked in the rainy East were not practical in the arid lands west of the hundredth meridian. His 1878 *Report on the Lands of the Arid Region of the*

United States, with a More Detailed Account of the Lands of Utah, laid out a plan for land use and farming methods, which if followed, could have prevented the ruin of countless settlers who tried to apply Eastern methods here. But many powerful men in Washington, more interested in personal profit than public good, prevented most of its policies from being enacted. Some things never change.

Powell was not one to be pushed aside. In 1881 he was appointed the second director of the U.S. Geological Survey, a position he held until 1894. Under his leadership he built the Survey into an institution respected the world over. He initiated the goal of creating a nationwide topographical map of the entire United States, which first required him to lay the necessary foundation—new standards for map nomenclature, symbols, and colors, for example. And the Survey's staff contributed much to the advancement of the new discipline of geology. The geologic reports written during his tenure reflect outstanding scientific quality. Many are still referenced today.

Like any person of power in Washington, Powell had his detractors. His proposal for how to manage the arid lands of the West was defeated in 1890, leading him to decide to resign as soon as he groomed his replacement. He chose Charles Walcott in 1894 and transferred to become head of the Bureau of Ethnology, where he served until his death in 1902.

Today, much of the river looks nothing like it did in Powell's day. Dams and reservoirs have tamed large stretches of what was once a wild river. It is still possible to raft down rugged stretches of the Green River through Desolation Canyon or the Colorado River through the Grand Canyon, but the experience is not the same. Technology has improved immeasurably over the last 150 years, and rafting companies that have run the same trip dozens of times know what to expect around every bend in the river. You won't risk life and limb running rapids or break your back portaging supplies around falls. A river trip today is not the same as in 1869, but for most people, it is close enough.

Cliff Palace, Mesa Verde National Park, Colorado

6

THE ANCIENT ONES

HEY SIT TUCKED AWAY in the darkest recesses of dank alcoves, or high on rock walls inaccessible to all but the hardiest climber. Some lie on canyon floors in plain sight for those who know where to look: crumbling structures of mud or sandstone, broken sherds of pottery, arrowheads, stone tools, fading figures etched or painted on the rock—relics of a vanished civilization, silent reminders that people were living here centuries before the first Europeans.

Those people have been gone for seven hundred years, but calling them "vanished" is a controversial claim. Modern Puebloans are quick to say the most recent prehistoric people to inhabit this land did not vanish, they were their ancestors. For reasons not entirely known—prolonged drought, intertribal warfare, disease, or some combination of all—by the year 1300 they had packed up and left slickrock country to form the Pueblos of today's New Mexico, Arizona, and Texas. Evidently it was a rapid departure. In their haste, they left behind perfectly good pottery, tools, sandals, clothing, and in some cases, uneaten last meals. Why the rush? Were they planning to return? No one knows.

The modern Pueblo people may well be descendants of this ancient culture, but the fact remains that those who once lived here no longer do, and they are not coming back. As with more recent ghost towns of the nineteenth century, their relics linger as mute evidence of a time long gone—the hallmarks of a vanished civilization.

Even knowing what to call these ancient people is controversial. Early pothunters led by the controversial Richard Wetherill used the term "Anasazi," a Navajo word translated literally as "Ancient Enemies" but commonly understood to mean "Ancient Ones." The archaeologist Alfred V. Kidder formalized this name at the 1927 Pecos Conference he convened in New Mexico for scientists to "thrash out the various questions of problems, method, and nomenclature" for this ancient culture. Every archaeologist who knew anything about the Southwest was there. In a not-so-subtle comment on the state of the science of the day, in one letter inviting a colleague to the conference Kidder wrote, "we are having a conference of Southwestern field-workers—almost all the grave-robbers will be there and it would be the greatest pleasure to have you."

Modern day Puebloans, especially the Hopi of Arizona (who would rather not be anyone's enemies), object to calling their ancestors by a Navajo name they consider insulting to those ancestors. But the various Pueblos—Acoma, Hopi, Jemez, Laguna, Taos, Zuni, and dozens of others—don't use one common language. They speak in tongues that come from four different language families, with multiple dialects for some families. Words spoken in the native language of one Pueblo might not be understood in another, which is why English tends to be today's common denominator. So, while they may object to the word "Anasazi," they can't agree on a better name. Meanwhile the Navajo insist the name isn't offensive, it just means, "those who came before us."

Within the anthropological community and in popular culture, the terms "Ancestral Pueblo" to describe the culture and "Ancestral Puebloans" to describe the people have gained support as sort of benign alternatives. Some publishers require their authors to use these terms in their books and technical papers, but even here, controversy lingers. "Pueblo" is a Spanish word. If the Navajo word "Anasazi" is insulting, replacing it with a name from a culture that was even more oppressive of those people should be doubly so. And modern Pueblos trace their history well beyond the cliff dwellers of canyon country to other ethnic groups including the Mogollon of New Mexico and the Hohokam of Arizona. Using a name that implies their heritage is limited to ancient Pueblo cultures discounts this broader ancestry.

For lack of a better alternative, I will adopt the term "Ancestral Puebloans" here, although I can't help but think it would be insulting to those ancient people, were any still around to be offended. Rather than honoring them with their own identity, it implies their only purpose in life was to serve as forebears of modern Pueblos. Consider this analogy. I live in California. I am descended from pioneers who lived in Missouri and Wisconsin. Would those pioneers be happy to be called "Ancestral Californians" rather than "Missourians" or "Wisconsinites"? I think not. Unfortunately, we don't know what, if anything, those ancient people called themselves.

In the high-tech world, when faced with problems such as this we pay branding companies enormous sums to invent new words to serve our needs. Those ancient people are long past the ability to hire a branding company, but the idea is intriguing: create a simple name that establishes their unique identity without being insulting. Here's an example. In recognition of their status as the "ancient ones," invent a word like "Ancienti," with a suitable exotic pronunciation like "AHN-say-EN-tay." It would pay homage to their status as ancestors, wouldn't favor the language of one modern Pueblo over another, wouldn't be insulting, and wouldn't be an unmanageable mouthful. I'm sure a representative group of modern Pueblo people (let's leave non-Indigenous archaeologists out of it) could agree on an even better alternative. Of course, they could still come back and say, "We like 'Ancestral Pueblo' best," but at least it would then be their own decision, not something foisted on them by well-meaning outsiders.

❧

THE ANCESTRAL PUEBLO culture was only one of several to inhabit this region before the arrival of the first Europeans. As long as 13,000 years ago, a nomadic people archaeologists call Paleoindians lived here during the late stages of the last ice age. At the time, southern Utah was a plateau of grasslands and conifer forests, the domain of gigantic herbivores such as mammoths, mastodons, camels, and sloths, and of vicious carnivores such as saber tooth cats, short-faced bears, and dire wolves.

Early hunters found plenty of game in this lush landscape, although little evidence of those hunters remains today. At a few places like Clovis, New Mexico, excavations in the 1920s and 1930s uncovered bones of extinct bison and mammoths that had stone points embedded in them. Called Clovis points, these oblong, fluted spear points are distinctive of the time. In the Slickrock Desert, the only evidence of Paleoindians comes from a few surface finds of Clovis points or the similar but slightly more recent Folsom points.

We really don't know much about those people. For decades, museums have pictured Paleoindians as fearless hunters of big game who engaged in ferocious battles with their prey—battles in which some hunters survived while others were hurtled to their deaths by angry mastodons. Impressive, but possibly not true. Recent research suggests that while they certainly hunted big game (perhaps older animals that were easier to kill) they were less foolhardy, subsisting on a greater variety of plants, fish, and small mammals than originally imagined.

About 8,000 years ago the climate turned warmer and drier. This was the beginning of what archaeologists call the Archaic period. The big game animals, victims of climate change and over-hunting by humans, soon went extinct. Humans, too, needed to either adapt or follow the same path. To survive, a new Southwestern culture emerged, one the archaeologist Cynthia Irwin-Williams in 1973 called the *Oshara Tradition*. It embraced a wider range of foods and a more seasonal mobility.

As diets expanded, the tools of the trade (what archaeologists call "tool kits") changed. Clovis points, best suited for taking down large animals, disappeared. They were replaced by stone tools better suited for smaller game: dart points, knives, scrapers, snares, and nets. Baskets, milling stones, and other tools associated with a diet based heavily on plants became common. The first limited ventures into agriculture apparently occurred about 3,000 years ago.

Although evidence is rare, archaeologists have learned enough from a relatively few completed excavations to be able to draw at least a general picture of the Archaic culture. In the earliest centuries of the era, these people continued the nomadic traditions of earlier Paleoindians. They lived in caves or natural rock shelters and moved to new locations with the seasons—wintering in lower elevations and following ripening nuts and berries to cooler mountain climates in the spring and summer. They may have returned to the same series of campsites year after year.

The men hunted deer, pronghorn, and bighorn sheep using handheld spears and a new tool, the *atlatl*, a stick that was used to throw those spears with considerable force. They used snares to trap rabbits and other small mammals. The women harvested nuts and seeds, using stone mortars to grind them into powder before cooking. Meals also included various plant roots and stalks, augmented with pads from the prickly pear cactus.

Beginning about 5,000 years ago, the climate turned wetter and cooler. As plant and animal populations grew, there was less need to migrate with the seasons. This middle age of the Archaic period was a time of larger, more stable villages that may have included the first pithouses— semi-permanent living quarters consisting of shallow, circular depressions in the ground with vertical wooden posts supporting thatched roofs covered in mud. Taking a lesson from their counterparts in Mexico and Central America, the people learned to grow crops of corn and squash, although they preferred the ease of harvesting wild plants whenever possible. This was also a time of increased trade with neighboring cultures as far away as the Pacific Coast.

About 3,000 years ago, the climate again turned warmer and drier. During this late stage of the Archaic period wild plant and animal populations declined, forcing people to depend even more on cultivated corn, squash, and beans. As food sources dwindled, people may have turned to the spiritual world for help. Religious leaders known as shamans—individuals who supposedly have the power to influence harvests by communicating with supernatural beings through dreams, trances, and visions—grew in power.

Certain styles of rock art are believed to be evidence of shamanistic influence. The haunting, ghostly figures painted on rock walls at places

like Sego and Horseshoe Canyons are typical of what archaeologists call
the Barrier Canyon style, after an earlier name for Horseshoe Canyon.
Life-size anthropomorphic figures whose heads resemble skulls with enormous eye sockets may represent the dead. Elongated bodies lack arms
or legs, possibly because they are wrapped in funeral blankets. Often
found far from likely habitation sites, the remoteness of their locations
suggests they were associated with sacred rituals. Shamans on vision
quests may well have painted these figures while under the influence of
hallucinogenic stimulants.

The age of these pictographs is subject to debate, but Polly Schaafsma,
a leading expert on Southwestern rock art, believes they may be at least
three thousand years old. While it is not possible to perform radiocarbon dating on pictographs without damaging them, the few tests that
have been run on naturally dislodged scraps are consistent with that
age. She also points out that Barrier Canyon art never includes weapons such as the bow and arrow, which didn't appear in the Southwest
until after A.D. 200. And in sites where Barrier Canyon art coexists with
Ancestral Pueblo or Fremont art, it is always underneath, indicating it is
older. Finally, some pictographs sit high on canyon walls that are nearly
impossible to reach today but would have been readily accessible several

Pictographs, Barrier Canyon Style, Sego Canyon, Utah

thousand years ago, before centuries of erosion lowered streambeds to their current levels.

By about 700 B.C., the Oshara Tradition had evolved, possibly because of intermixing with other cultures from the Great Basin to the west and the Great Plains to the east. This was the beginning of the Ancestral Pueblo era.

This is a good time to take a brief detour to explain the jumble of formats archaeologists use to express dates. The method most of us know is the concept of B.C. (*Before Christ*) and A.D., (*Anno Domini*) based on the date Christians recognize for the birth of Christ. But using any kind of metric derived from the beliefs of a single religion is an anathema for a scientific discipline practiced throughout the world. The simplest alternative is to substitute the generic term, *Common Era* (or *Current Era*), for the transition point. In this approach, B.C. is replaced by B.C.E. (Before Common Era) and A.D. by C.E. (Common Era). It removes the reference to the birth of Christ but otherwise the dates are identical.

Since the development of radiocarbon dating in the late 1940s, an alternative approach expresses age based on how old an object was at the time it was dated. Dates expressed this way are referred to as B.P. (Before Present). Since the "present" changes every year, archaeologists have standardized on the year 1950 as the reference point. For dates thousands or tens of thousands of years ago, the differences are manageable. It's more of a challenge for recent dates. For example, the date of the Declaration of Independence, A.D. 1776 (which is also 1776 C.E.), would be 174 B.P. Needless to say, B.P. is primarily used for dates far earlier than those of modern history. Some archaeologists aren't consistent even when publishing peer-reviewed technical papers. In one paragraph they may give a date as "3,000 B.P." and in another talk about something that happened "3,000 years ago." Are those the same? Who knows? I will take the easy way out and use the layman's format, B.C. and A.D., here.

The earliest era of the Ancestral Pueblo culture is known to archaeologists as *Basket Maker*, further divided into two stages. Most archaeologists call these stages *Basket Maker II* and *Basket Maker III*, using the confusing nomenclature adopted at the 1927 Pecos Conference. Some prefer a less confusing nomenclature, the redundant *Basket Maker* followed by *Modified Basket Maker*, but these names don't seem to have gotten much traction. (I guess calling them *Early Basket Maker* and *Late Basket Maker* would be too mundane.)

You might be wondering what happened to *Basket Maker I*. The Pecos Conference actually did define a Basket Maker I stage even though no evidence has ever been found for it. But Basket Maker II seemed too advanced not to have a predecessor. In 1945, the archaeologist Harold S. Gladwin summarized the situation with a pointed insight:

> Basket Maker I...can best be described as one of those mental abstractions for which modern science is famous. In just the same way that an astronomer recently decided that there ought to be one more planet to account for the aberrations of those which are visible, so the conferees at Pecos agreed that there should have been a Basket Maker who was no more than a hunter. The chief difference between the astronomer and the conferees is that the astronomer found his planet—the archaeologists are still hunting their hunter.

Basket Makers lived in pithouses and as you would expect, made extensive use of woven materials for items such as baskets, sandals, and robes. The two stages of the Basket Maker era lasted about 1400 years, differing primarily in the size of their villages and their level of dependence on agriculture. People of the Basket Maker III stage beginning around A.D. 500 lived in larger villages and were more dependent on agriculture than their ancestors, which meant they were less mobile as they tended their crops. This was when the atlatl began to be replaced with the more powerful bow and arrow. Evidence suggests they had a rather limited diet of corn, beans, and squash, supplemented with wild nuts, berries, and meat from small mammals. While they domesticated turkeys, it was primarily to use their feathers in robes and ornamentation. Turkey bones left over from meals don't show up in middens until much later, in the Pueblo II stage. Nor do fish, reptiles, or amphibians, and birds only rarely. They kept dogs as pets, not as sources of food.

After A.D. 750 things began to change. Living quarters evolved away from subterranean pithouses into above-ground rooms constructed using *wattle-and-daub* (also known as *jacal*) construction. Vertical wood pillars served as the structural elements, infilled with brush or sticks and sealed with a coating of mud. This was the beginning of what the 1927 Pecos Conference called the Pueblo era. The Pecos Conference divided the centuries before the great migration of the thirteenth century into three stages. In the *Pueblo I* stage from about A.D. 750 to 900, wattle-and-daub architecture was predominant, but basketry began to be replaced by clay pottery. *Pueblo II* (A.D. 900 to 1150) was when stone masonry became dominant and pottery more elaborate. The first multi-story great houses appeared at places like Chaco Canyon and Aztec Ruin by this time. The *Pueblo III* stage (A.D. 1150 to 1300) was the time of large cities built into the sides of cliffs, with artificial methods for distributing water.

The old pithouse didn't disappear, it evolved, too, into a specialized room known as a *kiva*. By the Pueblo II stage the kiva had become a separate room used by a single family for both domestic and ritual functions. Similar to kivas used by the modern Hopi, it included a hearth, draft deflector, ventilation opening, and a hole in the floor called a *sipapu* that represented entry to the spirit world. The first great kivas, often more than fifty feet in diameter, appeared during the later stages of Pueblo II and on into Pueblo III. These appear to have served as community centers for spiritual events—the pre-Columbian versions of football stadiums. Cities like Pueblo Bonito in Chaco Canyon had multiple great kivas within their boundaries. While their exact function is unknown, based on our knowledge of kivas used by modern Pueblo cultures, it may have been that only men were permitted to enter. Women may have congregated in their own subterranean structures the anthropologist Jeannette Mobley-Tanaka has called *mealing houses*, where they ground corn and prepared meals for the rituals conducted in the great kivas.

Archaeologists continue to use the Pecos Classification scheme today, nearly 100 years after its creation, even though it is generally agreed to be an imperfect solution. For example, in 1927 Chaco Canyon was assigned to the Pueblo III era because its large, multi-story buildings were thought to be contemporaneous with the cliff dwellings of Mesa Verde. Subsequent tree-ring dating has shown the structures of Chaco Canyon to be a hundred or more years older than those of Mesa Verde.

Chaco Canyon is now classified as Pueblo II, even though its architecture is far more advanced than the Pecos Classification defined for that period. The anguish of archaeologists was evident nearly as soon as the scheme was adopted. Our old friend Harold S. Gladwin wrote:

> It is true, of course, that every archaeologist at one time or another has shown the Pecos Classification to be all wrong—but after 16 years I find that those who make the loudest protests still use its terms when trying to define the period of a ruin.

His comments are just as valid today as they were in 1945.

WHILE THE ANCESTRAL PUEBLO culture was flourishing south and east of the Colorado River, the Fremont culture (named after the Fremont River, in turn named after the explorer John C. Frémont) flourished to the north and west of the river, extending into northern Utah, eastern Nevada, southern Idaho, and the far southwest corner of Wyoming. For decades, archaeologists have debated how this culture should be defined, where it came from, and where it went. While the Fremont showed some traits similar to the Ancestral Pueblo (notably in agriculture and city-building), most archaeologists consider it to be a separate culture. But coming up with a set of parameters to define it has been elusive. The archaeologists David B. Madsen and Steven R. Simms, writing in the *Journal of World Prehistory* in 1998, summarized the frustrations by observing, "The dominant view is that the Fremont can be anything we want the Fremont to be." Madsen and Simms lamented their inability to come up with any kind of cohesive definition for the Fremont, writing in prose quite lyrical for a technical paper, "we must stress that we use 'Fremont' as a generic name for an archaeological construct, which, we suspect, fails miserably in defining a people, who, like the landscapes of the Intermountain West, are not easily described or classified."

Material items such as buildings, projectile points, and pottery have not been helpful in assigning a unique identity to the Fremont. They are either too similar to those of other Southwestern cultures or too vari-able from site to site to be useful. Archaeologists have had to resort to a "behavioral" model, which rather vaguely defines the Fremont as an imperfect blend of foragers and farmers. Based on limited research into Fremont rock art, this may be a better way to define them. In her book, *The Rock Art of Utah*, Polly Schaafsma writes, "The Fremont tradition is characterized by the presence of a distinctive type of dominating anthro-pomorphic figure with a large head and a broad-shouldered, basically trapezoidal torso." It often includes elaborate necklaces and complex headgear. Petroglyphs in Capitol Reef National Park along Highway 24 through Fruita are typical of the Fremont style. The divots in those petro-glyphs are the result of nineteenth-century cowboys using them for target practice.

Petroglyphs, Fremont Culture, Capitol Reef National Park, Utah

Writers in the popular press like to imagine the Fremont disappeared without a trace, as if they were beamed away from earth by alien beings. It makes for entertaining reading but it's simply not true. Evidence indicates that like the Ancestral Pueblo, the Fremont migrated south by the year 1300. One possibility is that they are the ancestors of today's Hopi. This could help explain why the various modern Pueblo cultures speak vastly different languages. Each may have come from a distinctly different origin.

Reading about Ancestral Puebloans is one thing, but to really get a feel for them you need to get out and pay them a visit. It's time to do that.

Spruce Tree House, Mesa Verde National Park, Colorado

Doorways, Pueblo Bonito, Chaco Culture National Historical Park, New Mexico

7

CITIES OF STONE

T HE SKIES ARE CLEAR and the road is dry this February day as my daughter, Juliana, and I drive toward a pinnacle city of Ancestral Pueblo civilization at Chaco Culture National Historical Park in New Mexico. Juliana is studying for a degree in anthropology with an emphasis on archaeology. After spending the summer on an expedition digging four-thousand-year-old mummies in Egypt's Valley of Kings, she wants to see what ancient cultures closer to home look like. As for me, I never turn down an opportunity to explore remote canyons of the Southwest.

Of course, calling Chaco Canyon "remote" is a bit of a stretch unless you are comparing it to the tourist-laden sites at the more famous national park of Mesa Verde. There, you can vacation in total comfort, staying at a deluxe lodge or a full-service campground. You can eat meals at a first-class restaurant served by students recruited from around the world to spend their summers waiting tables. It's a far cry from a week in a tent alone in the wilderness, and I love it every time I go. Not every trip to the Slickrock Desert needs to be to the back of beyond.

Like many other theme parks, at Mesa Verde you'll need to make advance reservations and join a tour group to see the most popular cliff dwellings at Cliff Palace, Balcony House, or Long House. What you, along with about forty or so others will see under the guidance of a knowledge-able ranger are impressive ruins totally devoid of any remaining relics. I've seen pictures of what Mesa Verde was like in the days before its rubble was excavated and its relics hauled away more than a hundred years ago. It would have been a humbling experience to trundle through that rubble when it still harbored pots, clothing, food, and the occasion-al human bone. Still, visitors to Mesa Verde today learn a little about those ancient people and with luck, may come away with an increased understanding of the need to preserve these irreplaceable components of American history.

At the other end of the spectrum are isolated sites in places like Cedar Mesa or Comb Ridge. Far from the nearest road, out along winding trails through rock-strewn canyons, and not nearly so imposing as the big cities of Mesa Verde or Chaco Canyon, some archaeologists consider these to be where the "hillbilly cousins" of the city dwellers lived. Here, you can still view occasional pottery sherds, desiccated corn cobs, and other relics of prehistoric life. In the most remote corners, tucked away high in alcoves far from prying eyes, an explorer who is extremely lucky may discover an intact pot, a wooden staff, or a dusty sandal. Whatever you find, remem-ber everything is protected by federal law, so leave it as you find it.

Sadly, the extent of these relics diminishes every year as ignorant or devious visitors ignore federal law and surreptitiously carry away any-thing they can get away with. The worst offenders have been known to sneak power saws into the wilderness so they can cut out and carry off entire panels of petroglyphs from canyon walls.

Ransacking such as this has been going on since settlers first discov-ered this country in the late nineteenth century. Legions of pothunters made healthy livings scouring the landscape, collecting artifacts, and selling them for handsome profits. The most famous was Richard Weth-erill, the cowboy who discovered Cliff Palace at Mesa Verde, Keet Seel at Navajo National Monument, and many other sites. He has always been a controversial figure. While professional archaeologists of the day dismissed him as nothing more than a lowly pothunter because he profited by collecting and selling artifacts (often to museums), he excavated more carefully and took better notes than many of those professionals. He ran a trading post at Chaco Canyon for years before transferring title at no charge to the Interior Department after the creation of Chaco Canyon National Monument. Wetherill was shot to death in 1910 by a Navajo who owed him money. He and his wife, Marietta (who lived until 1954), are buried together at a small memorial near Pueblo Bonito.

By the dawn of the twentieth century professional archaeologists were aghast at the rate at which artifacts were disappearing. Faced with the prospect that most of those objects would soon be lost to science forever, they took their concerns to Washington. The Antiquities Act of 1906 was passed by Congress and signed into law by President Theodore Roosevelt primarily to prevent the further loss of such relics from federal lands. But that's a story for a later chapter.

These thoughts are far from our minds as Juliana and I bounce along a rutted dirt road toward our destination. The contrast with Mesa Verde is immediately apparent. There, it's a vacation at a five-star resort. Here, it's a trip to the outback. By design, there are no concession stands or restaurants here. No gas stations or hotels. There aren't even any paved roads into this park, only dirt roads that may become impassable after rains. The official park website warns that "some of the local roads recommended by map publishers and GPS devices are unsafe for passenger cars." As I relax in the passenger seat I'm thankful that as usual, we are riding in a four-wheel-drive SUV, this one conveniently rented from an unsuspecting company in Albuquerque. With luck, we will return it in nearly as good a condition as when we picked it up.

We are fortunate today. At an elevation of 6,200 feet, wintertime temperatures around Chaco Canyon often hover near freezing. It's not much more than that now, but at least it's sunny. Patches of snow beside the road remind us that the weather this time of year could have been much worse.

After twenty miles of rough dirt road, we come to pavement just as we approach a modern stone monument designed to imitate the eroded wall of an ancient pueblo. A rectangular brown sign set into the wall announces:

CHACO
CULTURE
NATIONAL HISTORICAL PARK
WORLD HERITAGE SITE

We have arrived.

అ

UNESCO, the arm of the United Nations dedicated to promoting world peace "through international cooperation in education, the sciences, and culture," designated Chaco Canyon a "World Heritage Site" in 1992. Their proclamation states, "Chaco Canyon, a major centre of ancestral Pueblo culture between 850 and 1250, was a focus for ceremonials, trade, and political activity for the prehistoric Four Corners area." The UNESCO designation covers not only Chaco Culture National Historical Park, but also Aztec Ruins National Monument and several associated sites. Juliana and I are about to enter a world-class relic of prehistoric civilization.

We start at the Chaco Canyon Visitor Center. It is typical of those you'll find at many national parks: a small, rectangular structure with a flat roof and a pillared entrance, painted a medium tan to blend with its surroundings. Inside is a reception desk, auditorium, park store, museum, library, and office space for employees. Outside is a small picnic area under the shelter of a wooden ramada. According to SMPC Architects of Albuquerque, the visitor center was designed with a pueblo character in mind. It received the NAIOP Design Excellence Award of Merit for public buildings in 2012.

We pay our entrance fee and take a quick glance around, but it's the ancient pueblos, not the modern one, we are here to see, so we are soon on our way. The main park road is an elongated 9-mile loop, shaped like the eye of a sewing needle. It passes many of the great houses—Una Vida, Hungo Pavi, Chetro Ketl, Pueblo del Arroyo, Pueblo Bonito—and the great kiva at Casa Rinconada. Hiking trails lead to more distant sites at Kin Kletso, Casa Chiquita, Penasco Blanco, Pueblo Alto, and Tsin Kletsin.

I'm immediately struck by another contrast with Mesa Verde. There, the pueblos are built into hollows in walls high above canyon floors—the classic cliff dwellings the general public associates with Ancestral Pueblo culture. Here, there are no cliff dwellings. The pueblos are sprawled out conventionally across the canyon floor like modern cities. It turns out cliff dwellings came into being only near the end of the Ancestral Pueblo era, in a time of strife when protection from marauders was paramount. (Why else would you build your home on the side of a cliff? Imagine trying to raise a two-year-old in such a dangerous environment.) By the time this kind of protection was needed, Chaco Canyon had already been abandoned.

We stop at the halfway point and get out to explore. Pueblo del Arroyo, Kin Kletso, and the largest great house, Pueblo Bonito, are within reasonable walking distance. We start by exploring Pueblo Bonito. Its skeleton-like remains rise from the floor of the canyon like the ruins of a bombed-out city from World War II. In aerial views, its many kivas resemble wartime bomb craters. But this 800-year-old relic has tumbled from the hand of nature, not man. The fact that even portions of it remain

Pueblo Bonito – photo by Paul Reed, Courtesy Archaeology Southwest

standing after nearly a millennium is testament to the engineering skill of those long-ago architects.

Built in the shape of a pregnant half-moon, Pueblo Bonito's crumbling walls are what remain of a four-story building (or a *four-storey* building, for those of you who live in England like my son, Greg, and his family). It once included over 700 rooms and at least 35 kivas arranged in a semicircle that opens onto a broad plaza. A wall running precisely north and south divides it into two halves, with a great kiva on each side of the boundary. Juliana's trained eye spots several areas of modern restoration I would have otherwise missed.

As we enter rooms through doorways in walls three feet thick, I'm intrigued by the size of these doorways. In photographs, they seem majestically imposing. Stand beside one and you realize those people must have been small—the doorways here are barely four feet tall.

I'm also intrigued by the techniques the ancient architects used to construct this great house. Despite living in a region known for natural arches, they seem never to have discovered the power of the arch when used in construction. Unlike the sturdy, keystone-capped arched doorways of medieval European cathedrals, these doorways have flat tops with wooden beams

Doorways, Pueblo Bonito, Chaco Culture National Historical Park, New Mexico

laid horizontally to support the stone masonry above them. It seems precarious, but after standing for 800 years they have proven their durability.

One might wonder where the timbers for these beams came from. It took a lot of logs to construct all the great houses along this road—over 240,000 beams according to archaeologists who apparently have counted them. Many are species of spruce and fir found only in high-altitude forests. There are no such forests nearby today, nor were there any back then. They appear to have come from the Chuska Mountains, 50 miles to the west. But without knowledge of the wheel, how did those people transport them from that distant forest to Chaco Canyon?

That is just one of the questions that keep Chaco scholars awake at night as they ponder the questions of antiquity while staring groggily at the ceiling. Scientists are often at their most productive while in that nebulous state somewhere between being asleep and awake. I can relate. I came up with the idea for my first patent near the end of an 11-hour flight to Tokyo, exhausted but unable to sleep in my cramped, coach-class seat, reduced to pondering the questions of technology while in a netherworld of consciousness. That patent may not have made either my employer or me rich, but at least it earned me the right to fly business class on future trips to the Orient. I can only hope archaeologists receive similarly worthwhile rewards as compensation for their sleepless nights.

There is plenty to keep them awake. Take Pueblo Bonito, for example. What exactly was it, and how many people lived there? With 700 rooms, you'd think it was the Ancestral Pueblo version of a Hyatt Regency Hotel. But most of those rooms were sealed off with no easy access. Some scholars think the sealed rooms were used as storage for grain and other staples, accessed infrequently and designed to keep rats, mice, and other varmints out. Others think they started as living quarters, but as the structure grew over the decades they were sealed when newer rooms were built in front of them. At least some of the sealed rooms were used as burial chambers for what was almost certainly a noble class of citizens—people who were buried along with turquoise and other precious artifacts, and whose bones don't show the wear and tear typical of laborers who spent their days grinding corn or constructing stone buildings.

As Juliana and I stroll through the ruins of Pueblo Bonito, Pueblo del Arroyo, and Kin Kletso, I'm amazed by the architectural and engineering skills that went into their design and construction. Skills that, by conventional wisdom, would be beyond the abilities of a Stone Age society that didn't know about the wheel or have a written language. I'm convinced there is more going on here than can be explained by conventional wisdom and vow to investigate.

CHACO CANYON remains an enigma despite being one of the most studied archaeological sites in North America. In 2018, when *Archaeology Southwest Magazine* published an issue devoted to Chacoan archaeology, over forty archaeologists authored or co-authored articles. These same archaeologists spend countless hours every year debating fundamental questions about the Chaco era. Were the great houses built strictly for ritual ceremonies or were they also living quarters for hundreds of people? Were the small circular structures really kivas, and if so, how were they different from the great kivas? Were the features that look like fragments of a road network connecting central Chaco Canyon (what archaeologists affectionately call *Downtown Chaco*) to other sites really roads or did those "roads" serve a different purpose? How much influence did the people of Downtown Chaco have on people living at great houses in outlying areas a hundred or more miles distant? Where did the food to feed Chaco's inhabitants come from—was it grown locally or imported from many miles away? Why was Downtown Chaco largely abandoned over a hundred years before the great migrations of the thirteenth century? There are more than enough questions here to keep an army of archaeologists awake at night for the foreseeable future.

Part of the challenge is that structures like Pueblo Bonito were built over several centuries by multiple generations of people using a variety of construction techniques and no master plan. What Pueblo Bonito looked like in A.D. 900 was vastly different from what it looked like in A.D. 1150. Materials were frequently reused, so a timber's tree-ring date may have no relation to the year the room where it currently resides was built.

(Tree-ring dating, developed for archaeology during the 1920s, matches variations in the patterns of rings in a log of unknown age to those of trees whose age is known to accurately determine the year the unknown log was cut down.)

Archaeologists generally agree that Pueblo Bonito and the other great houses of Downtown Chaco played an important role in the broader Chaco culture, but exactly what role is subject to debate. The classic view is that the Ancestral Pueblo culture was similar to that of today's Pueblos—an egalitarian society with no class hierarchy; everyone was equal. In this view, Downtown Chaco served as a ritual center to which people from the outlying regions made religious pilgrimages. Otherwise, the outlying great houses were independent towns outside the direct control of any Downtown Chaco empire.

Steve Lekson, retired Curator of Archaeology at the Museum of Natural History, University of Colorado, Boulder, has never been one to shy away from stirring up controversy. He has spent a good portion of his life studying the ancient cultures of the Southwest (and raising the hackles of other archaeologists while doing so). He considers this classic view to be bunk, promulgated by "racist" nineteenth century archaeologists who believed Indians* were savages incapable of creating an organized system of government. He says that over the decades, this view became so embedded in the academic curriculum that it was never questioned. But according to him, it is wrong.

I'm listening to a podcast interview in which Lekson claims the twelve great houses of Downtown Chaco served as the capital of a 60,000 square mile, tightly governed empire of 200 other great houses stretching from near the Mexican border to as far north as Far View House in Mesa Verde—a classic city-state similar to those of the Mayan and Aztec cultures in Mesoamerica. He offers several observations as justification.

---

* The question of what term to use for these people is the subject of ongoing debate. Within their culture, "Native American," "American Indian," and "Indigenous people" all have proponents and detractors. Many consider "Indian" when used alone to be derogatory, although some say they want to be called "Indian" without including "American." Most prefer that we use the name of their tribe, so that is what I do when I know it. I avoid using the term "Indian" except when quoting historical references or people who have used that term in what I quote.

First, the great houses throughout the region share a similar construction method that is characteristic of the Chaco era. Walls are built using core and veneer masonry consisting of an inner layer of rubble sandwiched between outer layers of finished stones. The resulting walls are far thicker than necessary for structural rigidity, suggesting that great houses were built not only to be functional, but also to be impressive. (Lekson doesn't mention it, but the massive walls may also serve as a primitive air conditioner that stabilizes indoor temperatures by absorbing heat during warm days and releasing it on cold nights.)

Second are what appear to be roads connecting the various great houses to each other, all leading to Downtown Chaco. Where two of those distant great houses would otherwise not be visible to each other you will often find raised stone towers at intermediate locations visible to both. These could well be signal towers. Whether great houses could communicate with each other using Morse-code-like signals, Lekson doesn't say. I could imagine them being lit continually. As long as the fires were visible, everyone could sleep soundly knowing all was well in the world—sort of an early version of "we'll leave the light on for you."

Another point is that the various great houses are surrounded by clusters of "unit pueblos," single-family dwellings of 4 to 5 rooms plus a small kiva. According to Lekson, these would have been where the "working class" people lived while the elites lived in the great houses. He also points out that to build cities the size of those in Chaco Canyon, it would have taken a highly organized workforce that included architects, engineers, logistics experts, construction workers, and probably a standing army that collected taxes.

This last point rings true to me. I've managed many large, multi-person projects of several-year durations. They don't just happen by magic. You need a solid hierarchy of leadership with the knowledge and skill to direct workers effectively, with consequences for those who don't follow directions. Even today, with college-educated architects and engineers, buildings still occasionally collapse, as evidenced by the 2021 Champlain Towers Condominiums tragedy in Florida. The legacy of Chaco Canyon flies in the face of the idea that these people were "savages."

The notion that the Chaco culture had a more hierarchical class structure than twentieth century archaeologists assumed is widely accepted today, but the idea that Downtown Chaco served as the capital of a large, geographically dispersed empire is not. The Spring/Summer 2018 issue of *Archaeology Southwest Magazine* included a debate between Lekson and Barbara J. Mills of University of Arizona, Jeffery J. Clark of Archaeology Southwest, and Carrie Heitman of University of Nebraska–Lincoln. The three contend there is little evidence that Chaco ever fielded garrisons or a standing army, or that there was a single "king" of the empire. They believe the evidence better aligns with the concept of a "house society" modeled after that developed by the Anthropologist Claude Lévi-Strauss to describe the feudal societies of medieval Europe. In this view, individual great houses served as lords of their own domains without answering to any higher authority. They could still share ideas, but the success of any individual house society was not dependent on the others.

Regarding the question of a Chaco "road network," more than one Ph.D. candidate has made this a subject in a doctoral dissertation. Some archaeologists believe that what appear to be roads leading to Downtown Chaco may not all be "roads" in the classical sense of something used for transportation. For one thing, they go straight up and over obstacles, rather than around them—hardly conducive for transporting any kind of material goods. For another, they are not continuous. They show up as isolated segments separated by broad gaps. While erosion could have cause some of these gaps, others appear never to have been built. And when the Bureau of Land Management surveyed these roads in the 1980s, their discoveries were surprising—the roads appear never to have been used. Compared to nineteenth century trails that have been heavily compressed due to use, Chacoan roads show hardly any compression at all. The BLM described them as "overbuilt and underused." While some roads may have been used for transportation, many appear to have served a purely ritual function—paths for deities to travel?

Chaco Canyon was largely abandoned by A.D. 1150. Why, and where did the people go? It appears they moved sixty miles due north to where they probably should have lived from the beginning: along the Animas

River at a site now called Aztec Ruins National Monument. It had all the water and fertile pastureland that Chaco Canyon lacked. Some people may have moved on to Mesa Verde, which became the dominant society about this time. But the age of the Ancestral Pueblo culture was already closing. Increased conflict between groups through raids and armed conflict forced people to seek protection in cliffs and alcoves. The coup de grâce seems to have been a multi-decade drought that began in the middle of the thirteenth century. By the end of the century the Ancestral Pueblo cliff dwellings, great houses, and kivas had been completely abandoned. Later indigenous people who came to the region—Utes, Paiutes, Navajos, and Apaches—avoided the ancient dwellings they believed to be haunted by malevolent spirits.

As Juliana and I head out from Chaco Canyon for our return to civilization, we agree it's impossible to really understand the Ancestral Pueblo culture from a visit to only one site, no matter how important that site might have been to the culture. It would be like trying to understand the entire American nation just by visiting New York City. Archaeologists spend entire careers studying Southwestern prehistory and still don't have all the answers. Did the family who lived in that isolated house with the bannisters far down Collins Canyon in Grand Gulch really feel any allegiance to rulers in faraway Chaco Canyon? Or were they like the prohibition moonshiners who hid out in the remote outback to get away from revenuers bent on extracting liquor taxes?

We may never know. All I can do is visit more sites and draw my own conclusions. I've explored ruins at both ends of the spectrum, from the small, isolated unit pueblos throughout Cedar Mesa and Natural Bridges to the large cities of Mesa Verde and Aztec Ruins. But there are many more to see: Salmon, Keet Seel, Betatakin, Hovenweep, Canyon de Chelly, Butler Wash, Mule Canyon, Road Canyon, Lowry, Moon House—the list goes on and on. I may never find answers to all the questions of Ancestral Pueblo culture, but the journey to try could keep me busy for decades to come.

Kiva, Pueblo Bonito, Chaco Culture National Historical Park, New Mexico

Church Rock, Utah – Photo by David Lee Thompson

8

ROAD TO RUINS

THE ROAD NORTH from the tiny town of Monticello to the bustling city of Moab cuts through typical southeastern Utah scenery. US Highway 191 is a well-maintained, two-lane thoroughfare that includes passing lanes often enough to satisfy all but the most impatient drivers as they follow a never-ending parade of slow-moving trucks, trailers, buses, and motorhomes.

From Monticello, elevation 7,070 feet, the highway descends gradually for 50 miles to Moab, elevation 4,026 feet. The initial stretch traverses a flat, sandy desert sparsely populated with sagebrush, juniper, and the occasional pinyon pine. The snow-covered slopes of the Abajo Mountains dominate the western sky while those of the La Sal Mountains loom far ahead on the northern horizon. Approaching Moab, the road descends through juniper covered slopes into Spanish Valley, a broad, flat plain walled on either side by two-hundred-million-year-old cliffs of Navajo Sandstone. Numerous points of interest fly past during the fifty-minute drive, some obvious but many not.

One of the first lies fourteen miles out of Monticello. An isolated pedestal of Jurassic sandstone known as Church Rock rises two hundred feet above the barren desert floor, its three distinct sedimentary layers apparent to even a casual observer. The dark brown, fine-grain sandstone of the Carmel Formation, laid down in a marine environment, forms its base. Above that is a thick layer of bright yellow Entrada Sandstone, the fossilized remains of windblown sand dunes. At its top, a dollop of frosting called the Moab Tongue of the Curtis Formation, remnant of the ancient Sundance Sea, decorates the outcrop.

While Church Rock may be vaguely reminiscent of a cathedral, legend says it got its name for a distinctly different reason. In the 1930s the area was home to a religious cult called "Home of Truth." According to local lore, the congregation had the grand idea of hollowing out the inside of the monolith to serve as a church. Believers point to a small cave cut into the side of the rock as the beginning of that excavation.

Mrs. Marie Ogden, the spiritual leader of the cult, was a widow from New Jersey. Born in 1883, she married a successful insurance executive and became prominent in Newark society, where she served as president of a local women's club. When her husband died in 1929, she took it hard. In her grief she turned to religious mysticism and traveled throughout the country preaching an occult set of beliefs.

In Boise, Idaho, she claimed to have had a revelation telling her to establish a religious colony somewhere in the West. Her persuasive powers must have been considerable, for she was able to convince nearly one hundred Boiseans to turn everything they owned over to her, forsake alcohol, tobacco, and red meat, and follow her to a commune in the high desert of southern Utah. The band eked out a meager living for a few years in a remote spot called Dry Valley until Ogden's fanaticism got the better of them. After one of the members, Edith Peshak, died of cancer, Ogden claimed the corpse would come back to life. In preparation, she had it washed in a salt solution three times a day to await its resurrection.

Even in an isolated outpost like Dry Valley, this stretched the limits of credibility. Word got around, newspapers throughout the country published sensational stories, and eventually local officials paid the colony a visit. After an investigation they decided that since the corpse was now mummified it posed no health hazard, so the widow Ogden could keep it. At the time, Utah had no law requiring the dead to be buried, and officials considered it akin to the many Native American mummies that had been extracted from caves and kept by people in the area. But as time passed and the mummy continued to deteriorate, most of Ogden's followers became disillusioned and drifted away.

A second investigation two years later found no trace of the body. Ogden admitted to a reporter that by then the body was "too dilapidated for Mrs. Peshak to reinhabit." One former member claimed it had been cremated long before. Even after the cult disbanded, Ogden stayed on and ran the county's only newspaper, the *San Juan Record*, until 1949. Eventually she moved to a nursing home in Blanding, where she died in 1975. Apparently, her time with the cult was something she preferred to forget. When the *Record* interviewed her for a full-page story published on May 30, 1963 in celebration of her 80th birthday, she made no mention of her time with Home of Truth.

You can still see the dilapidated remains of the colony along Utah Route 211 as you head toward the Needles District of Canyonlands National Park. A few miles west of Highway 191, look on the left for a gate with a weathered sign proclaiming, "Marie's Place." Numerous wooden shacks lie scattered across the land, the last remnants of the failed colony.

And what of that cave cut into the side of Church Rock? It was carved not by Ogden's disciples but by a local rancher a full decade later to serve as a storage area for cattle feed.

ॐ

MANMADE CAVES ARE COMMON in this part of Utah. Twenty-five miles north of Church Rock lies another—a popular tourist destination whose name is blazoned on a cliff beside the highway in letters twenty feet tall: HOLE N" THE ROCK. This 5000-square foot hollow in the side of the cliff once served as a home and diner.

Hole N" The Rock is the legacy of Albert and Gladys Christensen. Albert's parents homesteaded the 80-acre site in a one-room cabin in the 1920s. With four sons and three daughters, living quarters were cramped, so the boys spent much of the year camped out in tents. At some point Albert's father got the idea of enlarging a natural rock alcove as a space for the children. When Albert inherited the property, he continued the excavation with help from his brother, Leo. Over a 12-year period beginning in the early 1940s they extracted fifty thousand cubic feet of sandstone to create a subterranean home.

By 1945 the space was large enough for Albert and his wife, Gladys, to open Hole N" The Rock Diner at the front of the cave. (Gladys steadfastly refused to correct the erroneous punctuation in the name.) It was frequented by miners and cowboys, not all of whom had money to pay for their meals. In that case, Albert was happy to have them work off their debt by helping with excavations. Before setting off the next charge of dynamite he would ring a bell to warn diners it was time to hold onto their plates.

Albert had a pet donkey, Harry, who helped carry rubble from the excavations. When Harry died, Albert decided to try his hand at taxidermy. From personal observation I can attest that his results were less than spectacular, but he wasn't discouraged. Today, along with several other specimens the forlorn equine continues to greet visitors who take a 12-minute tour of the cave.

Albert died in 1957 and Gladys in 1974. Gladys' son from an earlier marriage, Hub Davis, had no interest in continuing its operation, so he sold the property. Although the diner closed years ago, the current owners have maintained the home close to its original state and added a gift shop and petting zoo. The cave, now uninhabited, is open for tours most days. With its carved rock architecture supported by strategically located sandstone columns, this residence seems more suited for Fred Flintstone than Fred Astaire. But there's another spot off Highway 191 north of Moab where Fred Flintstone would be even more at home.

THE TRACKS I SEE IN THE SAND tell an age-old story. The mighty beast had been moving northeast at a lumbering gait, foraging for food while scanning for danger. The danger it feared was lurking in the background: a deadly predator trailed by several smaller scavengers. The predator was limping, possibly from an earlier encounter with its prey. Hunters of large animals, whether they be lions taking down elephants or Paleoindians taking down mammoths, risk their lives for every meal. These tracks show that the lumbering beast made a sudden sharp turn to the right, possibly when the predator struck. What happened after that, I can't tell. The tracks end as the encounter begins. But it's likely the predator was victorious on that warm summer day one hundred and fifty million years ago.

The tracks I am exploring are at the Copper Ridge Dinosaur Trackway, a Jurassic-era remnant of life along the coast of the ancient Sundance Sea. Experts who have studied these tracks have concluded they were made by dinosaurs, although the exact details of the encounter are only guesses. The lumbering beast was probably a sauropod, most likely *Camarasaurus* or *Diplodocus*. The predator was a theropod, most likely an *Allosaurus*, whose bones are so common in Utah it has been named the state dinosaur. Its limp is evident from the unequal spacing of its foot impressions—the stride of its right foot is five feet, while that of its left is four.

I'm amazed these tracks even exist. It takes special conditions to preserve footprints in the sand for millions of years. First, the animals would need to be traversing sandy tidal mudflats that were wet enough to form distinct impressions of their feet but not so wet as to quickly let those tracks slump away. Next, warm, dry air would need to harden the tracks before wind or water could destroy them. Then, the tracks would need to be filled by secondary sediments of slightly different composition blown or washed into them. Finally, the tracks would need to be buried deep in the earth long enough to allow heat and pressure to turn the sand into sandstone. At Copper Ridge, all these factors came together to preserve the tracks I see today.

Within paleontology, a discipline called ichnology is devoted to the study of fossilized footprints, trackways, burrows, and similar trace fossils. Until recent years, most paleontologists gave little thought to the scientific value of trackways—the series of footprints ("tracks") made by a moving animal. That changed in the 1980s, when academic papers began appearing more often in scholarly journals. When I started researching the subject, it quickly became evident that one name appeared as author or co-author on nearly every paper: Dr. Martin Lockley, Professor of Geology at the University of Colorado Denver.

Dr. Lockley is a Welsh paleontologist, now retired, who earned his doctorate at Birmingham University in England and started his career studying Paleozoic marine invertebrates, primarily clam-like brachiopods, in Glasgow, Scotland. When he accepted an offer in 1980 to move to the United States and teach geology at the University of Colorado, he knew there were no marine fossil sites anywhere nearby, so he would have to broaden his interests. His entrée into trackways began almost accidentally when a student invited him to check out some tracks in a coal mine in the southern part of the state. What he saw kindled his interest, and he discovered it was an overlooked aspect of the science. When he and his student documented the site, they instantly became trackway "experts."

Over the course of his career, Dr. Lockley has become the world's foremost expert on fossil trackways across all geologic ages, far beyond the multitude of tracks found throughout the American Southwest. In 2020, the government of the Republic of Korea honored Dr. Lockley with their Presidential Citation for his many contributions to research on trackways in that country.

Dr. Lockley showed that fossil trackways are uniquely able to indicate the size, weight, gait, and even the speed of the animal that made them. Exactly what animal that was, though, is difficult to determine. It is possible to get some idea by comparing the shape of a footprint with the fossilized foot bones of animals found in sediments of similar age, but it isn't exact. Different animal species can make very similar tracks, and tracks from the same animal can look very different depending on whether it had been running or walking. So, tracks are assigned not to specific animal species, but to separate *ichnospecies*. The tracks of the sauropod at Copper Ridge have been assigned to the ichnospecies *Brontopodus*, and those of the theropod to *Hispanosauropus*.

When the Copper Ridge site was first discovered in 1989 by Linda Dale Jennings Lockley (the name Lockley seems to have a corner on the market for fossil footprint discoveries), such trackways were thought to be exceedingly rare. In the intervening years, even more impressive trackways have been found throughout southern Utah. Just a moderate walk from Copper Ridge is another, the Dinosaur Stomping Grounds, a broad expanse of sandstone with over two thousand individual footprints of sauropod and theropod dinosaurs. It is the largest single collection of tracks in Utah.

One of the most recent finds lies just to the west of Highway 191 south of the Moab Airport. The Mill Canyon Dinosaur Tracks were discovered accidentally by a jeep enthusiast in 2009. This site from the Cretaceous Period includes over 200 tracks of sauropods, ornithopods, dromaeosaurs, ornithomimids, and crocodiles. The BLM has erected a wooden boardwalk to make it easy for people to view these tracks without damaging them.

꙰

WHERE THERE IS SMOKE there is fire, and where there are dinosaur tracks there are dinosaurs. Not together, unfortunately—tracks are almost never found with bones of the dinosaur who made them. But the sediments of the Colorado Plateau are thick with bones, if you know where to look. The family-friendly sites tend to lie near Highway 191 outside the edges of the Slickrock Desert—places like Dinosaur National Monument in the far northeast corner of Utah and the Cleveland-Lloyd Dinosaur Quarry 80 miles north of Green River, Utah.

Dinosaur National Monument is the prototypical example of a monument created to protect a dinosaur quarry. (Well, if you dig deeply enough, you'll discover its original purpose was to protect the Carnegie Museum's ability to extract and sell bones from that quarry, but that's another story.) It was established in 1915 as an 80-acre site to "preserve the outstanding fossil resources at the dinosaur quarry north of Jensen, Utah." Its charter was expanded to over 211,000 acres in 1960 to protect paleontological and archaeological sites throughout the river corridors of the Green and Yampa Rivers.

The historic quarry is now sheltered inside a massive exhibit hall, where an entire wall of fossil-bearing sandstone has been prepared to partially expose hundreds of bones from at least 11 dinosaur species.

When I first visited in the early 1990s, you could watch paleontologists as they continued to expose new bones. Excavations largely ended by 1999, and the emphasis today is on preserving what is there.

The Cleveland-Lloyd Dinosaur Quarry, centerpiece of the 850-acre Jurassic National Monument created by Congress in 2019, is home to the densest collection of Jurassic-age bones of predatory dinosaurs anywhere in the world. Over 11,000 bones from at least 74 individual dinosaurs have been excavated here over the years. Well over half of those bones come from the fierce carnivorous dinosaur, *Allosaurus*, and many of those from juveniles. No one is quite sure why. The quarry does contain skeletons of herbivores—*Camarasaurus*, *Stegosaurus*, and *Camptosaurus*. One theory is that these prey animals became stuck in a muck-filled water hole, drawing the carnivores to the prospect of an easy meal. Inexperienced juveniles may then have become mired in this natural "predator trap" similar to how Ice Age mammoths and saber tooth cats became trapped in California's La Brea Tar Pits. But this is by no means certain. It is just one of many competing theories.

Jurassic National Monument is a bit off the beaten path and the last dozen miles are over rough dirt roads, but it welcomes tourists. The Cleveland-Lloyd Visitor Center hosts a mounted *Allosaurus* skeleton, and the nearby quarry often permits visitors to view excavations in progress.

The Slickrock Desert's most intriguing scientific research is being conducted on a high plateau far from busy highways. At elevations of well over 6,000 feet across its full 60-mile length, the Kaiparowits Plateau is, quite literally, the high point of Grand Staircase-Escalante National Monument. This triangular-shaped mesa is bounded by the Straight Cliffs to the east and the Cockscomb to the west. Between these two grand escarpments lies a broad expanse of late-Cretaceous sediments sliced by numerous creeks and canyons: Wahweap Creek, Nipple Creek, Last Chance Creek, Paradise Canyon, Surprise Canyon, Mudholes Canyon, Sunday Canyon, Monday Canyon, to name a few.

Over the last twenty years, paleontologists here have unearthed fossils from twenty-five species of dinosaurs found nowhere else in the world— exotic dinosaurs, the Frankenstein monsters of dinosaur land. Dinosaurs like *Kosmoceratops*, a *Triceratops* relative known as "the horny-est dinosaur" because it sprouted a frill of 10 horns hanging like bangs across its forehead. Or *Utahceratops*, another horned dinosaur with an enormous frill rising like the mainsail of a clipper ship. Or *Gryposaurus*, the largest known dinosaur of Utah, an enormous member of the duckbill family (more correctly called the *hadrosaur* family) over 30 feet long. It was here on the heights of the Kaiparowits Plateau that Dr. Alan Titus, then the monument's paleontologist, made the discovery of a lifetime.

Dr. Titus is another paleontologist who was attracted to the science by invertebrates—in his case, ammonites. He earned his B.S. in geology from University of Nevada Las Vegas, his M.Sc. from University of Arkansas, and his Ph.D. from Washington State University. As a trained geologist, Titus is an expert on rock. Which apparently explains why in his spare time, he plays lead guitar in a rock band called *Mesozoic* (chosen because it means "middle life," like someone having a midlife crisis). Not surprisingly, the band specializes in songs from their school years in the '70s and '80s.

When President Clinton created Grand Staircase-Escalante National Monument in 1996, Titus was teaching geology at Snow College in Ephraim, Utah. Like many Utahns, he was initially upset by the proclamation. He had been taking his students to Grand Staircase on fossil hunts, and that would now be prohibited. But his mood changed once he realized the monument was dedicated to scientific research including paleontology, and there would be ample opportunities to be a part of it. Before long he was the monument's paleontologist, out in the field making numerous discoveries. None of those were more significant than the one he made on a stormy day in July 2014.

Alan's day had not started well that morning. He and two assistants, MJ Knell and Katja Knoll, had been waiting in a remote stretch of the plateau for a team of volunteers who were supposed to help with an excavation project. But storm clouds in the distance and heavy rain the previous night worried the volunteers. They felt the weather was too uncertain to risk getting stuck on a flooded dirt road miles from civilization, so they decided not to come.

Threats of rain don't concern experienced field paleontologists. If you only went out in perfect weather, you'd never get anything done. Upset, Titus decided to take a walk to soothe his frustrations.

That stretch of plateau was prime fossil hunting land. Its low buttes of naked sandstone were dotted only intermittently by junipers and sagebrush. It was the kind of place where, if you looked carefully, you could spot fossils lying exposed on the ground. Titus had been there before but hadn't found much of interest—just a few turtle shells and bones. But that day was different. Recent rains had exposed fresh sediments and new possibilities.

As he scanned the landscape, Titus spotted a series of dark shapes emerging from the buff-colored sandstone. He recognized them as an ankle bone from an adult tyrannosaur. He called his assistants, who helped him unearth dozens of bones from at least two individuals—an adult and a juvenile. The more they dug, the more Titus realized they were exposing a massive bone bed unlike anything he had seen before.

When he returned to the BLM office and told his colleagues about his discovery, he was met with skepticism. Titus had a reputation for being enthusiastic about nearly everything he found. Half in jest, his former lab manager said, "Every site you discover is always 'Rainbows and Unicorns' all the time"—using a slang term for something so amazing it couldn't possibly be true. But his field assistant jumped to his defense, proclaiming, "This site is, in fact, Rainbows and Unicorns!" The name stuck, and the Rainbows and Unicorns Quarry, often abbreviated as RUQ, is its official name in peer-reviewed scientific papers.

Over the next seven years, Titus led expeditions that collected over 1300 specimens from five individual tyrannosaurs and a multitude of other animals. These included aquatic species of alligators, turtles, rays, sturgeons, and bony fish, along with invertebrates such as gastropods and bivalves. Terrestrial species, in addition to the tyrannosaurs, included bones from a single raptor and two hadrosaurs.

One of the most obvious questions was, why did all these tyrannosaurs end up together? Tyrannosaurs had always been viewed as solitary predators. Did they all die together, or was this some sort of "tyrannosaur graveyard" where individuals came to die? And tyrannosaurs are land animals. Why were they found in a river environment? Titus convened a team of nine experts from institutions around the world to analyze the find. Using techniques ranging from geochemistry to sediment analysis to taphonomy, they came up with an answer. In April 2021 the Bureau of Land Management held a press conference to announce the results of their work.

The COVID-19 pandemic had been raging for over a year, so the press conference was conducted by video conference. Titus, wearing a mask typical of the day, was seated in his laboratory. Katja Knoll, also masked, was standing nearby, ready to hand him sample bones on request. Joining remotely were team members Dr. Celina Suarez, Professor in the Geosciences Department at the University of Arkansas, and Dr. Joseph Sertich, Curator of Dinosaurs at the Denver Museum of Nature and Science. These four did an admirable job of explaining their work to a nontechnical audience. It was a convincing story.

On a warm summer day seventy-six million years ago, these five tyrannosaurs of the species *Teratophoneus curriei*, ranging in age from 4 to 22 years and probably all from a single family, were congregated along the channel of a river, possibly planning a coordinated attack on the hadrosaur. But torrential rains caused a massive flood that drowned them all and washed their bodies downriver into a jumbled pile at the edge of a lake. Flood kills such as this are a common cause of large animal mass mortalities—they happen even today. To illustrate that point, in the paper they published in the scientific journal *PeerJ*, the team included a photo showing well over a hundred cattle that had drowned in a flood in Queensland, Australia. Their carcasses had been swept by the raging waters into a massive pile along a floodplain, much like what may have happened to the bodies of the tyrannosaurs.

Finding an entire family of doomed tyrannosaurs together runs counter to the established view of these beasts as lone predators. It suggests they hunted in packs much like wolves or lions, which would have been a frightening scenario for the herbivores of the day.

Not every paleontologist agrees. The predominant objection is that tyrannosaurs' brains were too small to have the intelligence necessary to collaborate on hunts. In his presentation, Titus countered that objection with an example of how a modern dinosaur—the Harris's Hawk of the Sonoran Desert—does exactly this. These birds raise their young communally, hunt in packs, share in kills, and practice a division of labor where some birds serve as sentries while others go on the ground to flush the prey. This reduces the risk to any individual bird and allows the pack to hunt larger animals such as jackrabbits that would be difficult for one bird alone to kill. The Harris's Hawk has accomplished all this even though its brain—a true bird brain—is much smaller than that of a tyrannosaur.

Titus also points out this is the third similar tyrannosaur mass mortality site discovered in North America, the other two being in Canada and Montana. A single mass mortality site might be the result of chance, but three sites suggest there is more in play here than just luck.

In an interview with a reporter from the journal *PeerJ*, Titus laid out his vision for future work. So far, the evidence supporting the theory that tyrannosaurs hunted in packs has primarily been based on geological arguments. There is much more to do on the biological side. Were these individuals really all from one family, or had the flood washed lone animals spread out across large distances into a single pile? Further chemical and isotope analyses of the bones could show whether they were all living in the same eco-space and eating the same foods.

Another lingering question is exactly how the animals died. Although drowning in a flood seems to best fit the evidence, other less likely causes haven't been completely ruled out—neurotoxins in the water or death by wildfire, for example. (Charcoal from burned wood was found at the site but appears to have come from a fire long after the animals' deaths.) There are enough unanswered questions to keep a team busy for years to come.

The Rainbows and Unicorns Quarry may well stand out as the high point of Dr. Titus's career. At the press conference, he said, "I consider this a once in a lifetime discovery…I probably won't find another site this exciting and scientifically significant during my career."

But don't rule it out. Like all scientists who abhor absolutes, he quickly offered an optimistic qualification: "Although who knows, I could get lucky."

Hispanosauropus footprint, Copper Ridge Dinosaur Trackway, Utah

Fallen Roof Ruin, Cedar Mesa, Utah

9

INTO CEDAR MESA

HIGHWAY 191 IS THE ROAD to more than just manmade caves and dinosaurs. The highway from Monticello to Bluff is one segment of the *Trail of the Ancients*, designated by the US Department of Transportation as a National Scenic Byway to highlight the cultural and archaeological history of the Four Corners region.

Trail of the Ancients is not a single road, but rather a 900-mile spider web network of paved and dirt roads across Colorado, Utah, and New Mexico. It passes many of the Southwest's most notable archaeological sites. A side route through Arizona is not yet an official part of the national scenic byway but has been named one by the state.

It would be nearly impossible to drive the entire route on a single trip, although I suppose some people have done it. I've driven most of it, spread out across multiple trips over several years. I'm sure I drove blindly past many points of interest along the way, not all of them prehistoric. (Galloping Goose Railcar & Museum, how did I miss you?)

Cortez, Colorado, is the unofficial center of the Trail. It is the gateway to Mesa Verde National Park and Canyon of the Ancients National Monument. Lowry Pueblo and Hovenweep National Monument are each less than an hour's drive away. Crow Canyon Archaeological Center, a few miles from the center of town, conducts extensive research and public education on a number of Indigenous cultures.

Trail of the Ancients explores much of a region that was once the home of the Ancestral Pueblo culture. It's easy to imagine this as having been one monolithic culture, but in reality, it had at least six distinct subcultures, what archaeologists call traditions. Just as sociologists recognize the lifestyle of Southern Californians to be different from that of rural Montanans, archaeologists recognize differences in Ancestral Pueblo traditions by differences in geography, pottery, architectural styles, and social organization. From west to east, the major traditions are the *Virgin*, named after the Virgin River through western Utah and eastern Nevada; the *Kayenta*, named after a trading post in the far northeast corner of Arizona; the *Little Colorado*, along the river in Arizona of the same name; the *Mesa Verde*, centered on Mesa Verde National Park and its surroundings; the *Chaco* around Chaco Culture National Historic Park; and the *Rio Grande*, along the Upper and Middle Rio Grande River in New Mexico. A smaller subculture of the Kayenta known as the *Tusayan*, thought to be ancestors of the modern Hopi, is found near Petrified Forest. Finally, the *Cibola* tradition stretching across eastern Arizona and west central New Mexico seems to have been a composite of both Ancestral Pueblo and Mogollon cultures.

Way down in the southeast corner of Utah, hidden among pygmy forests of juniper, pinyon pine, sagebrush, and prickly pear cactus, lie the remnants of an Ancestral Pueblo culture that doesn't readily align with any of the major traditions. Pottery sherds found among ruins suggest strong Kayenta and Mesa Verde influences, but surveys show clear evidence of Chaco-style great houses. Even the Virgin tradition is represented in some of its recovered relics. This high plateau—Cedar Mesa—seems to have lain at the intersection of several traditions whose influences varied greatly across the centuries.

There were no large cities in Cedar Mesa. Even the few verified great houses are small compared to those in Chaco Canyon. Hikers and backpackers come here to explore the photogenic single-family ruins built into the walls of its umber canyons—canyons with names like Fish Creek, Owl

Creek, Mule, Bullet, Slickhorn, Johns, and the granddaddy of them all, Grand Gulch. Archaeologists, though, say that many more people once lived on the mesa top than in its canyons—not in impressive Pueblo-era ruins like those tucked into canyon walls, but in the low pithouses of Basketmaker times. Many of these remnants are little more than a few scattered rocks from ancient foundations hidden among the junipers—hardly of interest to backpackers but fascinating to archaeologists.

Researchers have studied Cedar Mesa for decades. Bill Lipe, Professor Emeritus at Washington State University, and R.G. Matson, Professor Emeritus at the University of British Columbia, began the Cedar Mesa Project field studies in 1972. The official project ended in 1975, but it inspired ongoing research by numerous others, much of which has been documented in the Cedar Mesa Project archives at Washington State University. In over 100 technical papers, slide show presentations, charts, and graphs, a story emerges of more than thirteen thousand years of human history.

The earliest eras are represented by only a few relics: a light scatter of Paleoindian Clovis points on Lime Ridge at the southeast edge of the mesa, a few Archaic-era points found among Pueblo-era relics. These may have been "collectors items" cherished by their finders similar to how modern collectors cherish nineteenth century arrowheads.

Cedar Mesa's Ancestral Pueblo settlements flourished in the Basketmaker eras from the late B.C. era through a period known as the Grand Gulch phase from A.D. 200 to A.D. 400. Populations waxed and waned over the following centuries. From A.D. 400 to A.D. 650 the mesa seems to have been completely abandoned. People returned to the mesa top in the late seventh century, followed by another decline a century later. Populations on the mesa top grew again in the 1100s, culminating with a retreat to the defensively superior cliff dwellings deep in the canyons by the thirteenth century.

By then, people were already migrating south. Discouraged by constant intertribal warfare and marginal harvests, they were drawn to the Pueblo communities of southern Arizona and New Mexico to seek a more stable lifestyle. A great drought from 1276 to 1299 seems to have put the final nail in the coffin of Ancestral Pueblo habitation in Cedar

Mesa. It wasn't the end of all civilization there—by the 1400s Utes, Paiutes, and Navajos had migrated onto the mesa, but their lifestyles were
vastly different. Utes and Paiutes were mobile hunters who left little
evidence of their existence. Even the Navajo, who were less mobile farmers, didn't build cities of stone. Their log hogans were sized for single
families and rarely survived over multiple centuries. The ruins of the
Ancestral Puebloans remain the most extensive relics of pre-Columbian
civilizations.

ॐ

ON A WARM OCTOBER DAY near the turn of the millennium I set out to find
one of the secret sites of Cedar Mesa, a Pueblo III-era ruin known as Moon
House. It was rumored to be the largest and most unusual site on Cedar
Mesa, with dozens of rooms hidden away on the side of a canyon behind
an outer wall like the wall of a castle. Supposedly, there was nothing else
quite like it in all of Ancestral Pueblo land.

David Roberts had written about Moon House in his book *In Search
of the Old Ones* several years earlier. Even though he hadn't published
exact directions, he had woven an intriguing tale. I knew that before long,
throngs of people would be hiking to Moon House like pilgrims to Mecca.
I wanted to be one of the first of those pilgrims.

Roberts hadn't been the first to write about Moon House. In 1989, William Bloomer, an archaeology student under Lipe's guidance at Washington State, published his master's thesis titled *Moon House: A Pueblo III
Period Cliff Dwelling Complex in Southern Utah*. Bloomer started with
the work others had done over the previous two decades and added his
own original research, including several months of on-site work. It was
the definitive scientific analysis of the site, and you can still read it today
in the online archives of the Cedar Mesa Project. But Bloomer's thesis
is a tedious read, even for someone like me who has written plenty of
tedious prose himself. It received little notice outside the archaeological
community, and Bloomer soon moved on to other areas of the profession.
It was Roberts's book, not Bloomer's thesis, that introduced Moon House
to the general public.

At the time the Internet was still in its infancy, and I hadn't been able to discover much about Moon House online. I knew it was in Cedar Mesa, and I eventually discovered the name of the canyon it was in—McLoyd's. I gathered an assortment of USGS topographic maps for the Cedar Mesa region and spread them out on the table. Initially, I was discouraged when it became obvious McLoyd's Canyon was not labeled on any of the maps, but logic eventually prevailed. I noticed that all the other canyons did have names. There was only one of any appreciable size that didn't. It seemed to be the only possible candidate. Trusting largely to faith, I decided to head out and see if I was right.

From Moab, Cedar Mesa is a two-hour drive. You first head south along Highway 191 to Blanding, then west on Highway 95, then south again on Highway 261—the road that cuts directly across the center of the mesa. That much I knew. From there, it was a guess. The unimproved road I thought passed nearest the likely canyon was a four-wheel-drive route labeled "Mormon Trail" on maps. It was the route blazed by the original Hole-in-the-Rock Mormon settlers back in 1879 (we will learn more about them soon). Of the two possible ways to reach it, I took the one that looked less challenging and shifted into four-wheel-drive.

The single-lane road was deeply incised into the top of the mesa and lined everywhere with trees. It would have been nearly impossible for two cars to pass, but thankfully, I didn't encounter any other vehicles as I wound through the dense pinyon-juniper forest. Although it is called Cedar Mesa, not a single cedar grows naturally anywhere on it. Blame the name on the Mormons. As their 1879 expedition sliced through the forest, they mistook the fragrant junipers for cedars and named the mesa after a nonexistent conifer.

Beneath the signature trees lay an understory of sagebrush, saltbush, Mormon tea, prickly pear cactus, yucca, and a number of shrubs and grasses I didn't recognize. Wildflower blooms had long since peaked and faded, making the drive less colorful than had I been there in springtime. As I traveled over hill and dale, I caught occasional glimpses of two isolated buttes looming side-by-side far in the distance—the features that would years later lend their name to Utah's newest national monument, the Bears Ears.

I was meandering across the face of the mesa without a clear idea of where I was going. In truth, I wasn't sure the canyon next to my chosen route was McLoyd's. And with all the trees blocking my view, I couldn't even see it from my car. Eventually I decided I had driven far enough. It was time to find the edge of the canyon and do some reconnaissance. I spotted a faintly rutted track heading away from the road in the general direction of the canyon. It looked wide enough for my SUV, so figuring this was as good a place as any to explore, I turned and bounced along until the last remnants of the track disappeared.

Now it was time to get out and hike. My pack was already loaded with camera gear. It had just enough room for a few snacks and what I thought should be enough water. I heaved it over my shoulders and began the trek along a vague footpath, but whether it had been made by man or was a simple game trail I couldn't tell. The trees of this pygmy forest were typically only twenty to thirty feet high. Although not nearly so tall as those of forests in the Pacific Northwest, they were dense enough to prevent me from seeing ahead for any distance.

Suddenly I emerged from the forest onto bare slickrock. A few more feet and I was at the edge of the canyon, staring down into the abyss. There, on the canyon's opposite wall far below, nestled under three bulbous slickrock outcrops, was the object of my journey. A nearly solid manmade rock wall punctuated by only a few small windows stretched for many yards across a broad expanse of undercut sandstone that reminded me of a cave. At the wall's edge I could see what appeared to be structures hidden behind it. To the right sat more structures not protected by the wall. In all my explorations I had never seen anything remotely like what I was now seeing. This was Moon House. As I scanned the canyon, I saw that even though it was a sunny Sunday, the place was deserted. There would be no other pilgrims here today.

Moon House might be the biggest ruin in Cedar Mesa, but it was nothing like the city-size ruins at places like Cliff Palace in Mesa Verde or Pueblo Bonito in Chaco Canyon. Moon House might have had twenty or more rooms, but most of those appeared to be small granaries or storage rooms. There may have been only enough living space for one extended family.

I was anxious to explore the ruin, but first I had to get there. With little in the way of a trail down the steep edge of the canyon, it was a dangerous 400-foot descent. An accident here would be disastrous—one of the known dangers of my penchant for hiking alone.

At one point I came to a sheer six-foot drop. It was evident I was not the first to pass this way. A neat pile of rocks had been stacked at the base of the drop as a sort of landing pad to reduce the gap. But whether it was a recent addition or a relic left behind by the ancients I couldn't tell. I surveyed the ground, saw not a single body of any previous hiker sprawled about, and decided to trust my luck.

I laid face down, lowered my tripod over the edge as far as I could, and let it fall. It tumbled the remaining few feet to the ground, making a dull thud as it landed. Then using a short length of strap, I slowly lowered my pack. When it reached bottom, I let go and it toppled onto the ground.

Now I was committed. Either follow the gear or retreat in defeat. The answer was obvious. With my stomach pressed against the slickrock, I carefully lowered myself toward the landing, feet dangling in midair. After only a brief moment of panic my toes touched the rock pile and I was safely down. The worst was now over. I would worry about how to get back up later.

I scrambled down the remainder of the rock wall, crossed the canyon floor, and climbed twenty feet to the base of the ruin. I tried to imagine what it would have been like for ancient raiders to attempt to storm this fortress, to dash up the exposed sandstone bluff while their opponents, safely ensconced behind the wall, launched arrows from well-positioned openings. It may never have happened. Like today's thieves who bypass locked cars for unlocked ones, the ancients may have bypassed Moon House in search of easier pickings. But if not, the slickrock I was now climbing would have once run red from the blood of the attackers.

The outer wall was solid from the base of the cave to its roof—almost certainly a defensive redoubt. To enter, I had to crawl through a single rectangular opening barely tall enough for me to fit. A series of sandstone slabs served as primitive steps to the entrance. Once in, I began to explore.

I walked along a wide hallway separating the outer wall from a row of rooms tucked against the rear wall of the cave. Construction techniques for these rooms varied, using both wattle-and-daub and several styles of masonry. The rooms were evidently built over an extended period using different techniques.

Along the top of several walls was a broad band of white paint topped with a sequence of small white dots running the length of the band. Inside one room, the band was decorated with what appeared to be pictographs of the phases of the moon. Although of unknown significance, these were the features that gave Moon House its name.

The more I explored, the more I was convinced this structure was built for defense. Numerous small rectangular portholes (known as "loop holes") in the outer wall, most near eye level, would have been ideal for launching arrows at attackers. But not every archaeologist agrees. Not all of the loop holes are in locations that would be useful for defense, although I haven't heard of any convincing alternative explanations.

Most of the rooms were surprisingly small. I later learned that archaeologists think only five rooms at Moon House served as habitations, and those for perhaps a total of only twenty to thirty people. The rest showed no evidence of the soot-covered walls typical of living quarters. It is believed they served as storage areas for grain and other staples—enough space for as much as five years' worth of food for the inhabitants.

Why so much storage? Archaeologists aren't sure. Bloomer, in his thesis, reports on two possibilities. The first is that the residents had lived through enough years of drought to recognize the importance of stockpiling plenty of supplies. The second is that Moon House may have been a "regional storage" location serving a population far broader than the few direct inhabitants—sort of an early version of an Amazon distribution warehouse.

I explored the ruins in awe, studying the features that once made this a home: eight-hundred-year-old fingerprints still impressed in mud walls; eight-hundred-year-old timbers spanning gaps in a ceiling; an eight-hundred-year-old polychrome pictograph of a snake. The afternoon passed far too quickly, and the sun was setting far too soon. If I was going to get back to the rim of the canyon before nightfall I needed to be on my way.

The ascent was tiring, but I made it safely. I turned to look one final time at the storied ruins before I departed. At my age I knew it was unlikely I would ever be here again. There were too many other places on my list to visit.

Today, the experience at Moon House is far different from when I was there. The pilgrims came in such numbers that the BLM finally had to initiate policies to protect the site. In 2016, Moon House was included in the proclamation President Barack Obama signed to establish the 1.35-million-acre Bears Ears National Monument. Even after Trump gutted the monument, reducing it by 85 percent to a mere 200 thousand acres (since restored to its full extent by President Biden), the land around Moon House was retained as a tiny, isolated outpost within it. You now need a permit to go there, and the BLM awards permits for only twenty people per day. The parking area has been improved and the trail is now cairned, although it is still a challenging hike. What else has changed I wouldn't know. As I predicted, I've never been back. But the memories of that long ago trip remain as fresh to me today as the day I was there. They will nurture and inspire me for the remainder of my life.

Moon House, McLoyd's Canyon, Utah

Moon House Interior, McLoyd's Canyon, Utah

Peek-a-Boo Gulch, Grand Staircase-Escalante National Monument, Utah

10

FORMS OF NATURE

THE SLOT CANYONS of the Slickrock Desert—deep, narrow cracks through solid slabs of sandstone—have a special draw for photographers. In the depths of a slot, light swirls around the contours of the rock, attenuating the blues and radiating warmth. In the deepest of the gorges the light casts an intense purple glow. A dedicated photographer can spend hours wedged between walls three feet apart and a hundred feet high searching for just the right composition.

But slot canyons can be deceptively dangerous places. Some extend more than 50 miles, forming an unbroken channel of solid rock walls, a sort of natural aqueduct. A cloudburst many miles away can send a wall of water roaring through the chasm, washing away trees, rocks, and any hikers unfortunate enough to be in the way. The sky overhead may be cloudless blue, giving no hint of the distant downpour. When the torrent arrives, the victims have no way out. No way except down the slot, carried along by the flood, crashing endlessly against the walls until their battered corpses wash onto sandbars many miles away.

Numerous deaths have occurred in flash-flooded slot canyons. A few examples. In 1961, four Boy Scouts and their leader were swept away while exploring the Narrows in Zion National Park. In 2016, another group of seven experienced hikers were killed while exploring nearby Keyhole Canyon. A flash flood through Antelope Canyon in northern Arizona in 1996 swept 11 hikers to their deaths. Only their guide survived. A year earlier, a torrent through Utah's White Canyon caught 13 hikers in a narrow stretch presciently called the Black Hole. Miraculously, only one died. Unaware of that tragedy, a few years later I clambered through the Black Hole and marveled at the sight of full-size trees wedged precariously into crevices twenty feet overhead.

These facts vaguely percolate the thoughts of four photographers as we peer down into Coyote Gulch and its slot canyons—Peek-a-Boo, Spooky, and Brimstone—two hundred feet below. We have come to photograph the slots. We arrived last night after driving thirty miles down Hole-in-the-Rock Road, a rough unpaved byway out of Escalante, Utah in Grand Staircase-Escalante National Monument. We set up camp well off the road, with glorious views westward to the straight cliffs of the Kaiparowits Plateau, an imposing escarpment five miles away and 3000 feet above. This morning we awoke to a line of gray clouds building over the Kaiparowits. This is cause for concern. Slot canyons are no place to linger if rain is imminent.

The four of us huddle: Dave, the idea-man of the group, with enough maps, guidebooks, Internet printouts, and hearsay inputs to lead an expedition into darkest Africa, always throwing out ideas for the next site to visit before we've even gotten to the current one; Mark, the most athletic of us (nearly opposite of Dave, his mantra is, "just tell me where to go and when to be there"); Pete, an energetic sexagenarian, the jokester of the group; and me, the serious one, all business. All of them are better photographers than I, but none of them rub it in.

I pull out my scanner and tune it to a weather broadcast. Thirty percent chance of rain in the Lake Powell region. Worrisome, but the discussion is quick.

"I don't like the looks of those clouds."

"Don't worry, this isn't monsoon season. That ended in September, a whole month ago. Besides, Coyote Creek has only a short drainage. If it rains ten miles from here, we won't see it."

"I came a long way to photograph these slots. I don't want to turn back now."

"I'm hungry. Let's eat breakfast and get going before the light changes."

"Come on Steve, don't be a wimp."

I'm outnumbered. It may be a foolish decision but after a quick breakfast we pack our gear and prepare to head down the cliff.

When we arrive, the trailhead is deserted. From the canyon rim we can look out over a hundred square miles of humps and hollows. We sign the guest register—four people, day hiking, estimated six hours duration. Then down we go, down into the abyss. Overhead, clouds continue to billow. Soon after we reach the canyon floor, it begins to sprinkle.

YESTERDAY'S DRIVE along the 62-mile-long Hole-in-the-Rock Road closely followed the route of the original trail blazed by Mormon settlers in 1879-80 on their way to establish settlements in the San Juan region of southeastern Utah. Miners and stockmen from Colorado had been inching westward, and the area was known as a hideout for criminals. Church leaders were anxious to lay claim to the land so it could be opened for settlement. This meant driving away the outlaws and developing friendly relations with the Indigenous cultures (although stories of subsequent atrocities suggest this latter objective was never accomplished).

Silas S. Smith was appointed leader of the expedition, comprised of 250 men, women, and children in groups that convened from such points as Cedar City, Oak City, Paragonah, and Parowan. A preliminary scouting expedition explored two possible routes, concluding that the northern route, roughly following today's Highway 89 from Panguich north to the future Interstate 70, then east and south past Moab (at the time an abandoned settlement) to the San Juan, might be possible. But it would have meant traveling many months over a distance of more than 450 miles to get to a point only 200 miles away. Relying more on rumor than reconnaissance, Smith decided to take a shortcut southeast from Escalante, cross the Colorado River, and continue on to the San Juan. He estimated the journey would take no more than six weeks. It took six months.

The travelers convened during October and began the trek in November. They were quickly hit with early snows, and the livestock soon ate most of the available grass. Smith realized the venture was underfunded and would take much longer than expected, so he headed to Salt Lake City to lobby for more money and supplies. Conveniently, he ended up staying there all winter. It fell to his second-in-command, Platte De Alton Lyman, to lead the expedition.

One traveler wrote that the trip from Escalante down the trail now known as Hole-in-the-Rock Road was "the roughest country I ever saw a wagon go over." Twenty-three-year-old Elizabeth M. Decker called it "nothing in the world but rocks and holes, hills and hollows." But compared to what lay ahead, this was the easy part. At the rim of Glen Canyon, expedition members gazed down a two-thousand-foot chasm to the Colorado River far below. Imagine approaching the Grand Canyon for the first time, needing to find a way to cross it with wagons and livestock. Theirs was a similar challenge.

Undaunted, they discovered a narrow crevice extending down to the river and spent several months blasting and chiseling to widen it enough for the wagons and stock to descend. Wagons were securely roped and lowered using teams of men and oxen to control their descent. People climbed down on their own and livestock were carefully guided. The crevice they carved came to be known as Hole-in-the-Rock.

A wide-eyed Elizabeth Decker wrote of the descent in a letter to her parents:

> If you ever come this way it will scare you to death to look down it. It is about a mile from the top down to the river and it is almost straight down, the cliffs on each side are five hundred ft. high and there is just room enough for a wagon to go down. It nearly scared me to death. The first wagon I saw go down they put the brake on and rough locked the hind wheels and had a big rope fastened to the wagon and about ten men holding back on it and then they went down like they would smash everything. I'll never forget that day.

Once down, they built a wooden ferry to cross the Colorado and spent more months navigating the nearly impenetrable maze of cliffs and canyons on the east side. Heading vaguely east across Grey Mesa, they cut a dugway over the Clay Hills and then skirted the north side of a great canyon they named Grand Gulch. When they reached Comb Ridge, they turned south, eventually cutting a pass over the southern end of the ridge and naming it San Juan Hill—eighteen years before Theodore Roosevelt's charge up a more famous hill of the same name. Throughout the journey they were plagued by snowstorms and dwindling supplies. Livestock died for lack of food, but the company pressed on.

From San Juan Hill they circled north, then east, finally coming to a promising spot along the San Juan River. Although short of their original goal at Montezuma Creek, it was good enough. Exhausted, they founded a town and named it Bluff City. The post office later simplified it to Bluff to avoid confusion with Council Bluffs, which was already nicknamed Bluff City. Amazingly, not a single member of the expedition died along the way, and two children were born. After such a perilous journey, Hole-in-the-Rock trail quickly fell into disuse.

಄

THERE IS NO EVIDENCE the pioneers entered the slot canyons we now explore, and there would be little reason for them to do so. They had more pressing matters at hand. But we have no towns to found or outlaws to evict so we explore, each going his own way. Photographers are peculiar in that they prefer to work alone, sharing their precious views with no one. We carry two-way radios to stay in touch, but it is doubtful they will work in the confines of narrow slot canyons.

I reach Peek-a-Boo Gulch amid light rain and discover the entrance requires a dangerous climb. I am about to skip it when Pete appears and says he found a way to enter it by circling around from the top. He leads me along a faint trail to the access, where Mark is already waiting. The first thing we need to do is lower our camera bags down. I happen to have a rope, something I salvaged from under a seat in my car after years of neglect. Mark ties it around a juniper and scrambles down. He waits at the bottom as we lower the bags one by one, untying the rope each time and sending it back up for the next one. When that's done, Pete climbs down. I follow, picking my way carefully. Thankfully the juniper is sturdy and the ancient rope remains intact.

When I reach bottom, Pete and Mark are already gone, so I begin to explore. As I move forward the canyon continues to narrow. I can reach out and touch both sides of its sinuously sweeping walls. Rain pools make for occasional obstacles, but by placing my back against one wall and my feet against the other I can wedge myself across, like a crab scuttling sideways. It doesn't occur to me to question why so many pools of water are even there.

Eventually I extrude myself from the last convoluted swirl, jump over a large pool, and reach solid ground. Along the way I set up my camera and make photographs in several places, although in these pre-digital days I am using a 4x5-inch view camera, so I can only hope they will turn out well. Making photographs with a view camera is a complicated process, and any of a number of things done wrong can ruin them. Alas, you won't know it until the film is developed days or weeks later.

My next stop is Spooky Gulch, an even more convoluted swirl. In places the slot is so narrow it is difficult to squeeze through even without camera gear. If I were any larger, I couldn't fit. I stash my gear and continue on without it. I will pick it up on the way out.

Navigating the slot is a challenge. There is little light and few firm footholds. The slot descends down into oblivion, with no sign of a bottom. A slip here could break a leg and require a difficult extraction. I inch forward by pressing hands and feet against opposite walls and cautiously moving ahead. After a few minutes I am convinced there are no interesting photo opportunities here and retreat in defeat.

I spend a few more hours exploring and photographing both Coyote and Brimstone gulches, but by noon the rain is increasing. We reach each other on the radios and reluctantly agree it is time to leave. We climb to the rim and retreat to our vehicles just as a sudden downpour pelts the cars. For half an hour it reverberates against their metal shells like an echo chamber. Overhead, flashes of lightning illuminate the darkened sky. A protracted roar and a muddy torrent in the canyon below tell us we evacuated the slots not a moment too soon.

By mid-afternoon the storm has passed and the clouds begin to clear. It is time to move on. We have other destinations to reach, other canyons to photograph, before this trip is over. We shake the water off of our tents, pack up the rest of our gear, and throw it into the cars to dry out later. The mood is somber. No one speaks of how close we came to disaster.

Devil's Garden, Grand Staircase Escalante National Monument, Utah

Delicate Arch, Arches National Park, Utah

11

TROUBLED ICONS

OUR NATIONAL PARKS. Scenic wonderlands. Pristine landscapes where human presence is only transitory. Wilderness havens where beleaguered city dwellers can escape and rejuvenate. The Pulitzer Prize winning author Wallace Stegner called them "the best idea we ever had," a quote repeated by Ken Burns in his documentary series, *The National Parks: America's Best Idea.* Stegner may not have originated the phrase—Burns attributed it to him but Stegner himself gave somewhat dubious credit to Lord James Bryce, the early twentieth century British ambassador to the United States who seems never to have said it. Regardless, the idea has become embedded in popular culture. For decades, loading the kids into the car for their first visit to a national park has been a rite of passage for countless American families.

Today, this pilgrimage has become an arduous undertaking. When the clan arrives brimming with excitement, they join the multitudes on roads teeming with vehicles and trails overrun with families pushing strollers, preteens screaming, teenagers texting, couples embracing uninhibitedly. At some of the most heavily trafficked parks you won't even be allowed in without advance reservations. In the words of Edward Abbey, an unending stream of visitors has turned America's national parks into America's national parking lots.

My own feelings for the national park system are decidedly mixed. The parks are undeniably beautiful, and the rangers who manage them are dedicated. But when I venture into the wilderness, I do so to get away. Away from cell phones. Away from social media. Away from throngs of people. Today, that is a rare accomplishment in a national park.

Whatever the original intent, national parks have evolved into sacrificial altars meant to satiate a god called the general public. Places designed to attract humans like yellowjackets to a picnic. Like lumberjacks to a forest. They stand like once-proud mansions that after years of neglect, reflect only a shadow of their former grandeur.

It's not a new problem. As far back as 1912, Lord Bryce voiced his opinion of letting automobiles into Yosemite National Park: "If Adam had known what harm the serpent was going to work, he would have tried to prevent him from finding lodgment in Eden; and if you stop to realize what the result of the automobile will be in that wonderful, that incomparable valley, you will keep it out." But the idea of creating national parks was still new, with many well-known and vocal detractors. Proponents realized it might not survive without an abundance of visitors. Lord Bryce's words went unheeded.

The state of Utah hasn't helped the problem. Although tourism numbers had been steadily rising, the Office of Tourism decided it wasn't enough. In 2013 they launched a massive ad campaign called "The Mighty Five." Through billboards, magazine ads, television spots, social media, and building wraps (including one 240-foot-tall behemoth on Wilshire Boulevard in Los Angeles) they promoted the state's five national parks.

The campaign was enormously successful. It has been credited with increasing visitation to the parks by half a million people each year. To parks that aren't equipped to handle the influx. On some holiday weekends, the wait to enter Canyonlands may be an hour long. At Arches, rangers close the gates to prevent further entry. Visitors from around the world who came because of the ad campaign are turned away as if they were bums seeking a handout.

I have come to accept this. Let the multitudes flock to these icons so they don't overrun the diminishing number of other wilderness locations known only to an adventurous few. Locations where you can still head out for a week at a time, by foot or by vehicle, and not see another soul. Locations where, as Ansel Adams said, you can revel in "the clear realities of Nature seen with the inner eye of the spirit."

And where are these secret locations? You won't learn of them here. The places I share are those already well known. To find the true secret locations you will have to get up from your easy chair and venture out to explore. Down rough unpaved backroads, down lonely foot trails, or out where there is no trail at all. The best I can hope for is that by sharing my experiences, you will be inspired to make your own journeys into the little-known wilderness. Or absent that sense of adventure, that you will at least advocate for the preservation of such regions for future generations to enjoy. And if, during your explorations, you do discover some of these secret places, resist the temptation to broadcast your finds. No posts on social media, no photographs in calendars, no stories in books or magazines. Save that urge for places already known. Let others discover these sites the way you did. Today, only a small fraction of original wilderness remains. Don't dilute it further.

And what of the national parks? They may seem to be on life support, but don't be quick to write them off. It's still possible, with enough advance planning, to venture away from the crowds and into solitude. At such places as Horseshoe Canyon or the Needles District in Canyonlands. Along the Burr Trail through Capitol Reef. At Pueblo Bonito in Chaco Culture. In a raft drifting along the San Juan River in southern Utah. Or to the pinnacle objective for all dedicated adventurers, down into the twisted canyons and towering spires of the Maze District of Canyonlands—the most remote region in the lower 48 states. Don't even attempt it without an experienced guide and at least two durable four-wheel-drive vehicles.

৵

I HAVE COME to one of those places. It doesn't matter which one, it could
be any of them. I parked my car in a lonely pull-out at the side of a road,
loaded my backpack with supplies, and headed out across undulating
waves of sandstone. There is no trail here, and I don't need one.

The backcountry permit in my pocket says I must camp at least one
mile from the road, but I plan to go much farther. The hike shouldn't be
hard. Today's spring weather is mild, and while the afternoon sun warms
the rock, it doesn't radiate the kind of stifling heat that will come later in
the year. Tonight, it may drop below freezing. Clouds to the west portend
a chance of rain or snow tomorrow.

Noise from traffic on the distant road, intermittent even when nearby,
fades into silence as I continue my trek. I have seen no one since I started.
As the sun drops lower in the sky it is evident I will be alone here this
evening. Just the way I like it.

Although "alone" is a relative term. While I am the only human in
this neighborhood, there are everywhere signs of life. Rock wrens chirp
in the distance. A lizard scurries away as I approach. Bees flit about
a nearby brittlebush brimming with yellow daisy-like flowers. Insects
scuttle across the ground on important business known only to them. A
cottontail rabbit bounds away from an imaginary predator. High above, a

Biological Soil Crust, Arches National Park, Utah

lone turkey vulture, iconic symbol of the west, soars on ethereal currents. It is arrogant to say I am alone.

My travel takes me across naked slickrock and sandy washes. Where possible, I avoid the pockets of crunchy, black crust that in times past, was called cryptogamic, cryptobiotic, or microbiotic soil. Today, the preferred term seems to be *biological soil crust*. Whatever you call it, it is a delicate community of living organisms that can take centuries to form and seconds to destroy with a single poorly placed footprint.

Biologists tell us that cyanobacteria, one of the oldest forms of life, is the dominant component of this crust, which may also contain lichens, mosses, and other bacteria in varying amounts. In many places, the crust can cover as much as 70 percent of the land. When young, a crust appears flat and brown, but over the decades it grows into bumpy black spires. During the long dry months its organisms remain dormant, but with rain, they spring into action. Cyanobacteria begin migrating through the soil, leaving behind polysaccharide filaments, a sort of natural sugar. The sticky residue acts like a glue to cement the grains of soil together. Lichens and mosses make their contribution through root-like structures called rhizines and rhizoids that further bind the soil.

Well-established biological crusts are essential to the desert ecosystem. They control erosion and trap water where it can filter into the ground. They also extract nitrogen from the air and secrete it into the soil where plants can absorb it. Researchers who earn their living studying the subject have found that disturbing a crust by walking or driving over it can reduce its efficiency as much as 90 percent. It can take 20 years for a disturbed crust to begin to recover, and then only if it hasn't already been blown away by the wind. And so I plod carefully, walking around the black pinnacles wherever I can. But it is not always possible, and I apologize to the crumpled masses when I can't avoid them.

The sun is setting behind a distant range of hills. As usual in the desert, the temperature is falling rapidly as the glowing orb descends. It is time to set up camp. I have two choices. I can camp on the hard slickrock or down in the sandy washes. Ordinarily I would pick the softer sand, but the uncertain weather forecast makes the decision for me. I have no desire to be caught in a flash flood should a rainstorm arrive tonight. I pick out a flat spot on the slickrock well above the likely waterline and unpack.

My first task is to erect my tent, an optional add-on I packed only because of the forecast. It is the lightest freestanding model I could find. With no place to drive stakes in the sandstone, I resort to gathering rocks heavy enough to weigh down the tent corners. Hopefully this will be sufficient to keep it from blowing away should the storm arrive.

Next, I prepare dinner. I have never been one to turn trailside meals into culinary events. I always have more interesting things to do. Usually I am out photographing the landscape until well after sunset. Today, even without a camera I prefer to "revel in the clear realities of Nature," watching without distraction the brilliant sunset as it fades to gray. When the last of the sky's vermillion glow has waned, I prepare my standard fare: a freeze-dried backpacker's meal of chicken à-la-King mixed with two cups of boiling water. Simple, nourishing, and as long as I don't feast on it every day, should allow me to live long enough to enjoy many more such sojourns.

The night sky is brilliant with stars. For a city dweller, the silence is eerie, haunting, intriguing. Without any modern distractions, I have time to think, to contemplate the wonders of the universe. I watch as one tiny point of light glides slowly, silently across the dark sky from west to east before suddenly disappearing. An otherworldly UFO? No, just an artificial satellite orbiting high over the earth, reflecting the sun. When it entered the earth's shadow, the reflection blinked out.

As I admire the view, a rapid yipping in the distance is answered by a cacophony of barks. A coyote pup who momentarily lost sight of the pack was quickly ushered back. The noise fades as quickly as it arose, and the eerie silence returns.

I am tired from the hike. After taking care of the final necessities I unroll my sleeping bag and clamber into bed, soon to dream surreal dreams.

❧

IT SEEMS to be morning. The hour when it is not quite light but not quite dark. A strange noise floats in from the distance, a low moan that reminds me of tree branches rubbing in the wind. But there are no trees here, and from what I can tell from inside my tent, very little wind. As I listen, even more distant moans come wafting in.

I poke my head out to a cloudless sky. It is well below freezing. There will be no rain or snow this morning. And then I see two eyes peering at me from across a low wash, two more in the middle distance, and several more beyond that. Cattle. They probably wandered in from some nearby range. The beasts have no regard for park boundaries, nor do they care about ecology. I try to explain the finer points of biological soil crusts, but their blank eyes suggest my lecture is beyond their ability to comprehend.

The cattle are as surprised to see me as I them, and they move slowly away. They may not have seen another human for months, if ever. They conclude it is time to put distance between themselves and this strange presence. Not trained in handling bovids, I am happy to see them go.

It is time for breakfast—my usual fare of freeze-dried scrambled eggs and ham. But in the icy air my butane-fueled backpacker's stove sputters and struggles to stay lit. It is a poor choice for cold weather. I have to warm the canister inside my jacket so it will stay lit long enough to boil water.

After breakfast I clean up around camp and begin packing. Much as I would like to stay another night, this has been a temporary side

Desert Pronghorn

journey on what, for tax purposes, is a business trip. It's a five-hour drive to Salt Lake City, and I need to be there tomorrow for an important industry event.

I've done it again. "Important" is a relative term. The rock wrens care nothing about my schedule. Nor do the lizards, the bees, the insects, the coyotes, the cottontails, or the solitary turkey vulture, still soaring high overhead, waiting patiently, quietly, for events that are sure to unfold. The junipers, the agaves, the canyons and the mesas will be here long after I and everyone now alive have ceased to exist. It is arrogant to say my minuscule event is important.

The trek back to my car is uneventful. I am in no hurry. Several times I take side journeys to explore unknown canyons. At one point I see a white flash as an animal disappears in the distance—a desert pronghorn, the famed antelope of western ballad. Neither deer nor antelope, it is the sole surviving member of an otherwise extinct family of ungulates. Unlike deer, the pronghorn has horns, not antlers. And unlike true antelope, its horns are branched, not single point. It is the fastest animal in North America, clocked at speeds up to 65 miles per hour. It can happily cruise along at 30 miles per hour for many miles at a time. It has no close relatives anywhere on earth. It may be distantly related to goats, and some experts think its closest living relative may be the giraffe. I bid it farewell as it dashes quickly out of sight.

By noon I am back at my car. I dust off the usual layer of dirt from my clothes, brush away a stray scorpion, load the vehicle, and depart, heading vaguely west and north toward civilization. I delay the inevitable by driving secondary roads, even dirt roads, where possible, rather than superhighways.

Eventually I arrive at the gleaming metropolis. Vehicles swarm the roads like ants scurrying about a drowning nest. Overhead, a steady stream of swept-wing mechanical insects alight nearby to disgorge scores of tiny parasites. Though I have not yet mentally made the transition from wilderness, I have physically returned to civilization.

My journey to slickrock country has been but a brief interlude in a busy life—a necessary interlude, a vital counterpoint to the din of the masses. Even a single day helps remind me of what is really important in life. But it is not enough. It is never enough. I am already planning, scheming, waiting to return. Five hours away, a lone turkey vulture is waiting, too.

Burr Trail, Capitol Reef National Park, Utah

Poison Spring Canyon, Cedar Mesa, Utah

12

BEYOND THE MIGHTY FIVE

I N MY CORPORATE LIFE I once worked for a German manager based out of our European headquarters in Stuttgart. After one visit to my office, he decided to take a week off to drive from California to Denver through the heart of canyon country. Armed with directions I had given him for the best sights to see, he headed out. Some weeks later when I asked him how it went, he said it was an interesting experience, but after hours and hours of boring scenery one he would never want to do again.

We need more people like that in this world.

My German friend was an exception. The Utah Office of Tourism's Mighty Five campaign has put Utah's national parks on the bucket list of every European tourist who comes to the United States. It's done the same for visitors from the Far East. Stroll along any of the trails of the Mighty Five—Arches, Bryce Canyon, Canyonlands, Capitol Reef, or Zion—and you'd be hard pressed to tell what country you are in. Conversations in French, German, Italian, Japanese, or Chinese are just as common as those in English.

A 2020 analysis titled *Marketing, congestion, and demarketing in Utah's National Parks*, published in the journal *Tourism Economics* by Tatiana Drugova and a team from Utah State University, found that "Arches, Bryce Canyon, and Zion National Parks currently suffer from excess demand." Using the kind of advanced statistical analysis worthy of a doctoral dissertation, they showed that over a 3-year period, the campaign's impact has been to increase annual visitation by 500,000 people per year.

No kidding! Scientific analysis is interesting, but you don't need a Ph.D. to know Utah's national parks are overcrowded. Nothing beats first-hand observation through boots on the ground. Visitor complaints, not academic analyses, are what get administrators' attention. And the complaints have been many. The tourist onslaught, with its crowds of people, mounds of roadside trash, and hourlong lines of cars entering the parks, is only part of the problem. Restaurants have interminable waits; grocery stores are cleaned out of staples; housing prices in Moab and Springdale have soared, putting them out of reach of the locals those towns need to staff the stores, restaurants, schools, police departments, fire departments, hospitals, hair salons, barber shops, visitor centers, gas stations, and all the other businesses frequented by visitors and residents alike.

What is Utah's Office of Tourism doing to deal with the problem? Simple: they put together a "demarketing" program to try to relieve the congestion at the Mighty Five—not by telling people to stay away, but by telling them about all the other great places they should also go. Having filled the national parks to the brim, the Office of Tourism now wants to do the same to all the other scenic wonders in the state. Little-visited areas like Goblin Valley, Kodachrome Basin, Cottonwood Canyon, and Natural Bridges are now prominently displayed on their website. About Cedar Mesa, they say: "For adventurers with a love of solitude...this area has it all." How long do you think that solitude will last once frustrated visitors from Zion or Bryce Canyon read those words?

You might claim the Office of Tourism has only been doing what they were supposed to do: increase visitation (and thereby tourist revenue) throughout Utah. What better way to do that than by promoting

Utah's national parks? One apologist, responding to the complaints, claimed that tourism officials "were vilified because they were so successful."

Rightly so. The idea may have been sound, but the execution was terrible.

I know a little about marketing. For several years in my high-tech career, I served as the director of a 100-person marketing department for a $300 million/year product line. Later, I took on the role of general manager for an entire business—the corporate equivalent of a private company's CEO—to manage not only sales and marketing, but also manufacturing and new product development. That job showed me how important it was for marketing not to act on its own. For a business to be successful, marketing must coordinate with the other functions. If marketing sells many more products than manufacturing can produce, the result will be scores of unhappy customers—customers who switch to competitors. If the Office of Tourism sells many more people on the idea of visiting a park than it can reasonably accommodate, the result will be scores of unhappy tourists—tourists who never return and tell their friends to stay away, too. As baseball great Yogi Berra said, "Nobody goes there anymore. It's too crowded."

Let's look at how the campaign should have been run, starting with some basic premises.

A well-designed marketing campaign needs four components. First, it must have a clearly defined set of objectives that spell out exactly what it is supposed to achieve—not in vague generalities but in measurable results. Second, it needs a defined set of actions that will be taken to achieve those objectives. Third, it needs explicit metrics that will be tracked to measure the campaign's success. Finally, it needs a contingency plan kept in reserve, ready to be pulled out only if the objectives aren't being met. The Mighty Five campaign doesn't seem to have put much thought into any of those components.

What were the campaign's objectives? I doubt they were to "pack the parks with visitors like sardines in a can." According to the campaign's creative team, they were driven by this theme: "Five national parks. One epic vacation. Only in Utah." A noble goal, but is that enough to drive a whole marketing campaign? Not a chance. That's not an objective, that's a tagline. How do you measure success? Is a ten-percent increase in visitation enough? Is twenty-five percent too much? Nobody seems to have asked that all-important question. You can't optimize a campaign around nonexistent goals.

At least as important was the need to include park administration and local town officials in the planning process to get their support and to determine what the parks could handle. Nobody seems to have done that. Leave a creative team to their own devices, give them a nearly unlimited budget, and they will shoot for the moon. That's what happened here: TV commercials, magazine ads, posters on transit buses and taxicabs, giant billboards hung from the sides of buildings, and enormous hallway wraps placed in metropolitan transit centers. Who cares if you would have been able to fill the parks simply by advertising in a select few cities around the United States? Don't stop there, plaster the message across Europe and Asia, too. If a little is good, a lot must be even better.

The metrics? Again, take a look at what the creative team tracked: $2 billion in new visitor spending, $338 in new revenue for every dollar spent on the campaign. And oh yes, perhaps the most important metric for a creative team, several prestigious awards at travel industry trade shows. Nothing about the quality of the visitor experience or the ability of the parks and nearby towns to absorb the influx. That was somebody else's problem.

Which brings us to the contingency plan. A good contingency plan doesn't just say what you will do if a campaign isn't working, it should also address what to do if it's working too well. In my own career, on rare occasions our marketing campaigns were so effective we were selling products far faster than we could build them. That meant we needed to adjust the plan. Scale back marketing while we built up manufacturing capacity; meanwhile, have the marketing team work on the customer satisfaction message.

If you measure a marketing team only by how many orders they get, they will keep working on getting more. Who cares if customers are upset because they can't get their products or tourists are upset because the entry lines are too long? That's somebody else's problem.

In the high-tech industry, you can always build new factories to increase manufacturing capacity. In Utah, you can't add more national parks. Well, you could, but neither the Utah legislature nor the environmental community would let you. The legislature abhors the idea of giving the National Park Service control over more of their precious landscape. Environmentalists abhor the idea of seeing more of that landscape suffer the same fate as the Mighty Five.

If the visitor experience deteriorates, you need to come up with ways to fix it. One way would be to increase admission fees to the parks. That's what airlines do with ticket prices when more people want to fly than aircraft have room to accommodate them. That's a bad idea for parks, which are supposed to be equally accessible to all Americans. Raise prices and you end up discriminating against lower-income families.

Another possibility is a quota system. When you want to visit one of the Mighty Five, go online and put your name into a lottery for a chance to win one of a restricted number of daily admission passes. That's how it works for private individuals who want to raft the Colorado River or visit certain canyons in Arizona. But the kind of multi-year waits typical for rafters would be inconceivable for people who just want to visit a park. And as we saw when the first COVID-19 vaccines arrived, unscrupulous members of the upper class would undoubtedly try to offer large sums of money to buy passes from lower-income people who won them. There'd be a thriving black market and you'd still need to be rich to visit a park.

Zion has already implemented a policy in which private automobiles are prohibited from the main roads for much of the year. You see the park from the windows of a shuttle bus, getting on and off at designated stops—an experience eerily reminiscent of riding the Disneyland Railroad around the perimeter of the theme park. The same approach is being considered for Arches. While it reduces traffic on the roads, it just moves the problem. Hourlong lines of automobiles are now replaced by hourlong lines of tourists waiting to board the buses. And if you miss the last bus of the day? Good luck, it's an eight-mile walk to your car.

Without any better ideas, the Office of Tourism has turned to demarketing campaigns—first the "Road to Mighty" followed by the "Red Emerald." The messages are similar: you are welcome to visit the Mighty Five, but here are a bunch of other places you should also think about going. Will it work? The jury is still out. It just might be that a global pandemic does more to stem the tide of visitors than anything done by the Office of Tourism's creative team.

By now, you are probably wondering, "so, what's the answer?" In this fast-paced world, everyone wants an immediate solution. But good solutions take work—work that hasn't yet been done. The answer is, "follow the process." Start by agreeing on the objectives. How many visitors per year is the right answer? How do you want them distributed across the year? Get inputs from the key stakeholders: the park administrators who must deal with the influx and the elected officials from the nearby towns who must accommodate the crowds. You don't need to go much beyond that—the park administrators should represent the needs of the park, the elected officials that of the locals. Once you know what you want to accomplish you can figure out the best way to do it. It's idiotic to roll out a marketing campaign designed to attract a million more visitors a year to parks that can only accommodate a tenth of that increase. It's not necessary to stop all advertising, just scale it to a level consistent with the goals. This will give park administrators and local officials the insight they need to get ready for the campaign. Do all that and you can give visitors an enjoyable experience while keeping the local tourism industry happy.

At this point a cynic might say, "That's fine, Steve, but you've just written a book that will do exactly what you are advocating against: encourage more people to visit southern Utah. How do you justify that?"

Well, first, I promise that if my book sells enough copies to drive tourists to Utah at anywhere near the rate the Mighty Five campaign has done, I will immediately take it out of print. It's a promise I undoubtedly won't need to worry about. Books have been written about this area for over fifty years—creative nonfiction like *Desert Solitaire* by Edward Abbey or *Wind in the Rock* by Ann Zwinger, and photography books like *Utah* by David Muench or *In the Land of Moab* by Tom Till—books that have had far more impact than mine ever will. In all those years, southern Utah was never overrun with more tourists than it could handle. It took the Mighty Five campaign to do that.

An advertising campaign has but one goal: get more people to visit the parks. Books have a broader appeal. Sure, by reading a book you might be inspired to visit, but even if you never do you will have learned about the region. (How many people decided to become whalers just because they read *Moby Dick*?) Books are a better match to what southern Utah now needs than any multi-country, multimedia advertising campaign.

Enough about that. I come to the Slickrock Desert to get away from my day job. It's time to get back to nature. Preferably beyond the Mighty Five.

PLACE NAMES IN UTAH reflect the pioneers' fascination with the morbid side of life, probably because in such a harsh land, they had to confront it regularly—names like Death Ridge, Death Hollow, Box Death Hollow, Little Death Hollow, Deadman Point, Dead Horse Point, Deadhorse Canyon, Poison Canyon, Poison Spring Canyon, Poison Spider Mesa, and the generic Death Canyon. It's only natural I should want to visit one of those inspiring spots.

Fellow photographer Dave and I leave our wives back at the motel in Escalante and head out to a destination well off the beaten path, down a meandering byway in no hurry to get anywhere, past the red sands of Steep Creek Bench, the golden-leaved cottonwoods of The Gulch, the auburn bluffs of Long Canyon, and the juniper-lined palisades of the Circle Cliffs. At an unmarked, rough dirt road we turn south for a dozen miles to an empty parking area little more than a wide spot beside the road. The hike through Little Death Hollow begins here. We head out under blue October skies, with cottonwoods at the crest of their yellow autumn glory.

"Little Death Hollow" is a conundrum. Is it possible to be "a little dead" like being "a little pregnant?" According to the French, it is. Their phrase *la petite mort* is often used to describe a feeling of "little death" after sexual orgasm. It is tempting to imagine the canyon being named because it was once a place of rapture rather than terror, but in such a harsh land I know how unlikely that would be.

For the first mile the trail crosses a nondescript sandy wash surround-ed by groves of cottonwoods filled with shimmering yellow leaves. Even though Dave is carrying a heavy medium-format film camera with mas-sive tripod and extra lenses, he is already well ahead of me, anxious to reach the more interesting defile of the canyon. A retired schoolteacher, he has plenty of time to practice his craft. His color prints are of profes-sional quality. Some hang prominently in galleries. Mine hang promi-nently in my living room.

As usual, I lag behind, the result of too many hours sitting idly behind a desk. Today I carry a lightweight 35mm SLR rather than my bulky view camera (soon to be replaced by digital), but even so, I am no match for his level of energy.

Tomorrow we will meet up with two more photographers, Mark and Pete. Together with our wives, we will spend the next few days exploring the areas around Escalante, Zion, and Bryce Canyon. Dave and I met a day early to do this warmup hike. I definitely need it.

As I cross a gully, I hear a caterwauling off the trail ahead. Dave has found something.

"Hey Steve, get over here, I think I've found a dinosaur bone."

I weave through the brush to a stretch of salmon-colored sand where Dave is standing. The photogenic red rock towers that had drawn him to this spot loom in the distance. At his feet I see a bleached white bone half buried in the sand.

I'm an electronics engineer by training, which means I've never had to take a biology course in my life. I wouldn't know a clavicle from a femur. Everything I've learned about anatomy I picked up outside a classroom. But I do know something about fossils, having spent a little time on digs in Utah, Nevada, and Wyoming. I'm not impressed. "Uh, I don't think that's a dinosaur fossil, Dave, it looks more like a bleached cow bone."

He looks crestfallen. "You don't think it's a tyrannosaurus leg bone? Pull it up and look."

I think it's my leg bone that's being pulled. "I don't think it's even a fossil. Besides, the formation around here is the Navajo Sandstone. That would make it Jurassic, not Cretaceous. It couldn't be Tyrannosaurus, but it could be Brontosaurus."

Dave knows more about fossils than he lets on. "Steve, didn't you know Brontosaurus is an obsolete name? The person who found the first one back in the 1800s called it Apatosaurus. I forget who that was, but since that was its first published name, that's its official name today."

I apparently know more than he does. "But Dave, recent published work has shown that Brontosaurus is indeed different from Apatosaurus, and it's been classified as its own species again."

Dave objects. "Ah, but not every paleontologist agrees with that paper, so the jury is still out."

I've reached the limit of my paleontological expertise. "Well, it doesn't matter anyway because that is neither Brontosaurus nor Apatosaurus. I'm pretty sure it is a cow bone. You going to take a photo?"

The alleged cow bone doesn't interest him. "No, I'm going to head on up the canyon. See you later."

I stay behind to frame several compositions, then follow his lead. The canyon opens wide and gradually narrows, although not to the point of becoming a true slot canyon. It will do so farther up, but at our rate of travel we will not reach that stretch before we need to turn around. The stream bed is dry, but the sight of numerous golden yellow cottonwoods attests to water below the surface. Jumbled vegetation wrapped around the tree trunks tells a story of raging torrents at certain times of year. Scattered throughout the wash are jet black shards of rock that look out of place in the orange sand—fragments of petrified wood typical of those found throughout the Slickrock Desert.

For the next few hours we explore the narrowing canyon, setting up cameras and tripods here and there like budding Ansel Adamses. I can't claim to have made anything spectacular, but it is a good warmup for the coming week. As we head back to the car, we agree there are only so many photographs you can make of yellow cottonwoods against orange cliffs and blue skies before you go numb.

When we return to the motel, Pete, Mark, and Mark's wife Marcy are already there, enjoying drinks around the bar with Nicki and Dave's wife, Grace. Pete's wife decided to stay home, so the seven of us find a nearby restaurant for dinner, then retreat to our motel to share portfolios of recent prints and plot out the trip. The next two days we will explore around Escalante, then head over to Bryce Canyon and Zion. We'll start by camping out and end up at lodging we have booked near both national parks. We claim it's to humor our wives, but secretly we look forward to warm beds and hot showers just as much as they do.

Next morning we rise early, scarf down breakfast at a nearby diner, and head out. Our first stop is Devils Garden, a convoluted series of hoodoos and arches just off Hole-in-the-Rock Road. It's perfect for a few hours of exploration and photography. After lunch we take a primitive dirt road to Egypt—the cliffside escarpment, not the North African country—where we spend the afternoon toting cameras through eroding slickrock ledges that apparently reminded pioneers of a Sahara Desert they had probably never seen. Then its on to a primitive campsite for the night.

Evening around the campfire. Dinner is finished, cleanup complete. We are enjoying a bottle of Sonoma County merlot Nicki and I brought along to share, although I occasionally glimpse Pete taking a swig from a flask that undoubtedly holds something stronger. Dave tosses several more logs onto the fire. It erupts to warm and brighten our immediate surroundings, but in so doing turns everything beyond an inky black, isolating us from the very outdoors we have come to enjoy. We could just as well be astronauts encased inside a tiny spacecraft, hurtling toward a distant planet through the blackness of space.

The conversation grows with the flames. We talk about old times, good times, and times of little consequence in the larger scheme of life. Pete, as usual, entertains us with a never-ending series of lame jokes, spurred, no doubt, by the liquid from his flask. Overall, a pleasant way to pass an autumn evening. The weather has been good, with sunny skies framed by the occasional white cloud. Now, as evening eases into night, the temperature is dropping rapidly. The conversation slows, like a tired grandfather clock on its last ticks before stopping. We say goodnight and retire to our beds.

I have cleared enough room in the back of the SUV to roll out two sleeping bags. It's not the Ritz Carlton, but it will have to do. I appreciate that Nicki is game for it, at least for a couple of nights. We'll be upgrading to a motel soon.

By dawn, I am up boiling water for my standard camping breakfast: a packet of freeze-dried backpacker's ham and eggs, boxed orange juice, and instant coffee. Nicki wanders over with a skeptical look. "What's that?"

"Breakfast."

"Hmmm."

I'm not helped by the aroma of bacon and fresh-brewed coffee wafting over from Mark and Marcy's camp nearby. I turn to stir the boiling water into the packet and when I look up, Nicki is gone. I find her with Mark and Marcy, a plate of bacon and eggs in one hand, a cup of steaming hot coffee in the other. Clever girl. She gives me a contented look. "Camping is not so bad."

I eat my breakfast in silence directly from the packet.

Over the next three days we scour the landscape for photographs like coyotes stalking jackrabbits. We again explore around Escalante before settling in for another night of camping. Then it's over to Bryce Canyon, where we join a hundred other photographers recording the sunrise from Inspiration Point. By evening we are at Zion, and the next morning out for more hiking and photography. We avoid the shuttle buses by driving the Zion-Mount Carmel Highway to a trailhead east of the road's namesake tunnel. From there, we hike through canyons flush with autumn colors and even more flush with autumn hikers. The contrast with the isolation of our first two days is striking.

Finally, it's time to depart. We say our goodbyes and promise to meet again next year. Mark and Marcy head north to Idaho, Dave and Grace to Southern California, and Pete to Washington.

Nicki and I are not quite ready to head home. We have one more thing to do, something to be done far from prying eyes, preferably at an isolated spot with a spectacular view. Nicki unfolds a paper map and studies it intently. She tosses out a series of intriguing place names—Mollie's Nipple, Towers of the Virgin, Poverty Flat, Halfway Hill. We decide to turn off the highway at an unnamed dirt road that has interesting possibilities.

The so-called road turns out to be rougher than we had expected. We bounce along cautiously, and at one spot I discover the limitations of my newly purchased SUV. Although advertised as being off-road-capable and having a high ground clearance, its bumper projects well forward of its front wheels, giving it a rather anemic ability to climb sharp hills—something known in the trade as the vehicle's "angle of approach." When we cross a small gully, the front bumper hits the rising slope at the far edge of the gully before the wheels can get there to climb it. For a moment we are stuck, but with effort I am able to back away.

I get out to survey the situation. The sensible thing to do would be to gather up enough rocks and juniper branches to construct a crude ramp. But rocks are heavy and juniper branches scarce. I decide on a quicker solution. I climb back in, shift into low, and gun the engine to lurch forward over the formidable obstacle. We hear a loud grinding sound as the air dam under the front bumper scrapes along the ground, but forward momentum carries us up and over, and we continue on our way. I give Nicki a quick glance and notice her eyes seem wider than usual and her face more pale. But she soldiers on without complaint.

The next obstacle is more of a challenge. We come upon a herd of cattle spread out across the road and surrounding lands. Most of the herd gives us disinterested stares, but one angry bull resents our intrusion. He stands in front of us defiantly and begins to charge. For a moment I feel like John Wayne in the movie *Hatari!*, driving a speeding Land Rover while an angry rhinoceros crashes against its side, thrusting its deadly horn dangerously close. Fortunately, this bull's horns are shorter. He turns out to only be bluffing and backs off as we speed away. Nicki seems more excited than panicked.

Another mile down the road we come to an overgrown four-wheel-drive track heading toward a distant hill not marked on the map. The track doesn't appear to have been used in years, but the sagebrush growing within it seems low enough to drive over. We agree this looks like an ideal spot—isolated but with grand views in every direction across miles of multicolored desert. I turn onto the track and bounce over the shrubbery to the hill, where we stop and prepare for the hike to its crest.

A steady wind is blowing, so we put on jackets. I open the rear passenger door and extract a simple wooden box from under the seat. I have carried it before, but I am still struck by how heavy it is for its size. Then we are on our way, box in hand, to the top of the hill.

The box contains the cremated remains of my brother, Harlan, who loved the desert as much as I do. It was his refuge from the troubles of ordinary life, a place to recover and reenergize. We have come to disperse his remains across this land he loved.

At the top of the hill, the wind blows even more fiercely. We scan the landscape, gazing across crags and valleys, rocks and cactuses, all the way to the horizon—a beautiful but lonely land far from civilization, well matched to his personality. We say a few solemn words and I cast him to the winds. The gusts carry his ashes high into the air, spreading them across the miles to everlasting freedom. After a few minutes we return to the car and then to civilization. We christen the previously unnamed peak "Harlan's Hill." I doubt the US Geological Survey will add it to their official list of place names.

Cow Bone, Little Death Hollow, Utah

Marching Men, Arches National Park, Utah

13

WIND AND WATER

I T IS NOT SUPPOSED TO RAIN in the desert. Deserts are hot, dry, forbidding places where the sun blazes incessantly and where forlorn inhabitants peer furtively from under rocks or bushes, waiting endlessly for relief that never comes. Just my kind of place.

By definition, a desert gets less than 10 inches (250 mm) of rain a year. Moab, Utah, averages even less, much of that coming during summer thundershowers. It is not unusual to watch clouds billowing overhead, rain streaking thickly from their underbellies, only to see it evaporate before it ever hits the ground—a phenomenon meteorologists call *virga*. For the denizens of a parched, sunbaked land, it makes for a special kind of torture.

With that in mind, I was expecting only sun for my ascent into the high canyons of Arches National Park on what should be a warm spring day. Even when I learned rain was forecast, I imagined it would only be a light sprinkle. What I got was a deluge.

I rose before dawn, downed a quick breakfast, and headed out in the dark. My objective was the sandstone cliff of Delicate Arch to catch the first rays of morning sunlight. From there, I would spend the day

exploring remote canyons down rough dirt roads. My plans were unstruc-
tured, amorphous, ready to change as the day unfolded.

By dawn, clouds obscured the sky, blocking the sun and casting a dull
gray light. Cold winds whipped through the alcoves at Cove of Caves,
through the mirror windows of Double Arch, and past the tenuous spire
of Balanced Rock. As I pulled into the Delicate Arch parking lot, snow
was falling in the distant La Sal Mountains.

Hiking to Delicate Arch is a bit like entering Disneyland and trekking
down Main Street to Sleeping Beauty's Castle. You start from a parking
lot only slightly smaller than the one at the theme park, pass the requisite
restrooms, and then join Disney-sized crowds on the 3-mile roundtrip,
500-foot climb to the arch. When you get there, you will probably be one
of a hundred people swarming like gnats around the 65-foot-tall, 60-foot-
wide span. In peak season when the parking lot is full you won't even be
allowed access. Even on the day I arrived, with a rainstorm imminent,
I was not alone.

It didn't used to be that way. When I hiked this trail in the 1990s,
I encountered only a few others along the way. I could take photos of
the arch without a single person in view. That all changed when Utah
started promoting "The Mighty Five" campaign. Now, like many others
I can only lament the good old days—not all of which were quite as good
as we like to remember.

Early settlers would be astounded at how this land has evolved. For
them, it was a desolate wasteland where mere survival was a chore. At
the beginning of the trail to Delicate Arch stands a stark reminder of
that distant past—a one-room cabin built from native cottonwood and
juniper logs, a dugout root cellar, and a nearby corral. On older maps it
is called Turnbow Cabin after Marvin Turnbow, who lived there in 1929
and helped the U.S. Geological Survey map the region. Edward Abbey
told Turnbow's story in his classic book, *Desert Solitaire*.

Unfortunately, Abbey didn't get the story quite right. It's not really
his fault; when *Desert Solitaire* came out in 1968, little was known of the
history of the cabin, and over the years what tales there were of early
settlers had been jumbled together. But in 1971, seventy-three-year-old
Esther Stanley Rison arrived at the park with stories and photos of her

life there as a young girl long before Turnbow bought the land. Esther's grandfather, John Wesley Wolfe, was the settler who built the cabin.

John Wesley Wolfe was born in Tennessee in 1834 (some sources say 1829). By the time the Civil War broke out he was living in Ohio. Despite his Southern heritage, he joined the Union Army to fight against slavery. He entered Ohio's Seventeenth Independent Light Artillery Battery in 1862. Over the next year, he fought in numerous battles across Arkansas and Mississippi. During the Siege of Vicksburg, he was severely injured when a cannon fell on his leg. The injury left him unfit for service and he was discharged by order of the War Department in June 1863.

His leg bothered him for the rest of his life, and he never again walked without a crutch. By 1888 his leg was so painful (he may also have had tuberculosis) his doctor gave him a stern warning. Unless he moved to a drier climate, he would be dead in 6 months. Shaken, John took his doctor's advice and moved west. But his wife, Lydia, was adamant. She would never take her children to such a wild and untamed country. Only his oldest son, 16-year-old Fred, agreed to come with him.

Their first stop was Colorado, but by 1898 they had moved to Utah. Like others who came to Utah for the solitude, John and Fred settled in an isolated landscape far from civilization. Their main connection with the outside world was Thompson Springs, a stop on the Denver & Rio Grande Railroad a full day's wagon ride north. The tiny town of Moab was a similar distance to the south.

Access to a reliable source of water was essential, so they established their small cattle ranch along the brackish waters of Salt Creek. They dammed the creek to irrigate patches of squash, pumpkins, corn, and melons, but had to get drinking water from a freshwater spring (still shown on topographic maps) three-quarters of a mile away. Why so far? A look at the topo map suggests the answer. The spring emerges from the side of a cliff up a narrow canyon. The cabin sits at the edge of a level stretch of shrubland ideal for grazing cattle. Evidently, living close to the cattle took priority.

Summers were hot and dry, winters cold and snowy. When it did rain, it could come down in torrents. One year, Wolfe's first cabin was washed away in a flash flood. As for the incessant wind, Wolfe wrote, "Sometimes a sudden sandstorm threatens to blow our cabin down." But the dry air served him well, and the pain in his leg slowly improved.

In 1906 Wolfe convinced his daughter, Flora, along with her husband, Ed, and their two children, 7-year-old Esther and 5-year-old Ferol, to come live with him. Arriving at a tiny shack with a dirt floor, Flora found the living conditions intolerable. She insisted they needed better accommodations, so John, Fred, and Ed built the sturdy cabin that still stands. It wasn't much larger than the old one where John continued living, but at least it had a wooden floor.

Though the children flourished in their remote outpost, Flora found it a meager and lonely existence. Within two years, she moved her family to a small house in Moab. John and Fred eventually joined them, and by 1910 John had sold the ranch and moved east with the family, first to Kansas and then to Ohio, where he died in 1913. Though the ranch passed through several owners before becoming part of Arches National Monument in 1938, the name of its original inhabitant has finally been restored.

I BEGAN THE TREK to Delicate Arch under overcast skies. The trail passed Wolfe's cabin and crossed the bridge over Salt Creek, then stretched across a sandy dry wash and up onto the slickrock. Rock cairns marked the way, but even without them the path over the slickrock was obvious, worn into the sandstone by millions of hikers before me.

I was only mildly enthusiastic about this hike. The weather was dubious, the trail was already crowded. I'd been here before, so I wouldn't see anything new. Today wouldn't be a good one for photography. I pressed on more because I felt I should rather than because I was inspired. A nagging thought kept rattling through my brain: should I continue?

And then the decision was made for me. A blinding flash and a roaring thunderclap followed by a wave of rain told me it was time to turn back. Exposed slickrock is no place to loiter during a thunderstorm. I remembered a time long ago when I found myself alone atop the barren tundra of a fourteen-thousand-foot mountain in the middle of a thunderstorm, sur-rounded by lightning, overcome by altitude sickness, and barely able to move, a full six miles from my car. How I made it back alive is a story for another time. But I had no desire to ever repeat such a horrid experience.

I beat a hasty retreat to my vehicle, encouraged other to do the same, and drove to Panorama Point. I ate lunch in the driver's seat while watch-ing waves of rain roll across Devils Garden to the north. Far down a drenched four-wheel-drive road at the end of Salt Valley, the minarets known as Marching Men stood nearly obscured by clouds. It was a fasci-nating afternoon, but it made for dull and uninspired photography.

The rain eventually stopped late in the day and the sun poked ten-tatively through the clouds. I raced along the road, stopping at various points for photos—Garden of Eden, Petrified Dunes, Courthouse Towers. Sunset was vague; clouds to the west obscured the sky, but the rain was gone. For at least a little while, the denizens of the desert had a welcome relief. Tomorrow the water would be gone.

DESPITE THE ARIDITY, it is water, not wind, that has most sculpted this landscape. You may not believe it while standing on a slickrock outcrop with sand from gale-force winds stinging every exposed surface of your body, but it is a scientific fact. Think of windblown sand as nature's sand-paper. As every woodworker knows, sandpaper is used for finishing work, not bulk removal of material. For that you use a power saw. In canyon country, water is nature's power saw.

Water erodes the landscape in several ways. Geologists use the term *fluvial processes* to describe erosion by streams and rivers. Water by itself carries significant erosive power, as anyone who has seen the results of a rainstorm on the soil of a newly planted garden will attest. Even more erosion comes from rocks and sediments that abrade the riverbed as they are washed downstream. Flash floods are particularly powerful, combin-ing both effects in a single muddy torrent. The tortuous canyons of the Colorado River and its tributaries are canyon country's most obvious examples of the power of rushing water.

Water also erodes through a *freeze-thaw cycle*. Water is one of the few liquids that expands when it freezes, putting enormous pressure on whatever is holding it in. That's why exposed water pipes can burst in freezing weather. Imagine the weight of a full-size city bus squeezed onto a surface the size of your thumbprint and you will have an idea of how much force frozen water can exert. Slickrock has little chance against rainwater that wicks into cracks during the day and freezes at night. The rock-strewn talus slopes scattered at the base of cliffs throughout the landscape are often the result of this process.

A third way water erodes is through *chemical weathering*. Pure water is essentially inert; the minerals dissolved within it are the culprits. One of the most common dissolved minerals is halite—common table salt—found throughout canyon country. Others such as pyrite and even carbon dioxide from the atmosphere or from decaying organic matter dissolve in rainwater to form solutions of weak acids that slowly erode the rocks.

At this point, I should apologize to any professional geologists in the audience. They make a distinction between *erosion*, which involves transport of material from one place to another by wind or water, and *weathering*, which does not. And they use yet a third term, *mass wasting*, for movement by the force of gravity. The differences are sometimes subtle. If gravity causes acidic rainwater to roll downhill and dissolve rock as it goes, is it weathering, erosion, or mass wasting? If you're seeking a degree in geology, you should probably have an answer. If not, just call it erosion.

Wind is the other major influence on this landscape. And, yes, geologists have a handy name for that, too—*aeolian* (or *eolian*) *processes*—after Aeolus, the Greek god of the winds. Wind erodes in two ways. First is through a process called *deflation*. Blowing wind carries away loose particles of dust and sand, leaving behind a hard surface known as desert pavement. Second is through a process called *abrasion*. As those particles of dirt and sand are carried along by the wind, they scour the surfaces of whatever they strike—nature's sandblaster.

You now know everything you need to know to understand how the fantastic shapes found throughout Arches National Park are formed.

Well, almost. You also need to know something about rocks.

Geologists tell us the earth is composed of three basic types of rock: *igneous, sedimentary,* and *metamorphic.* Igneous rock originates in the molten magma deep within the earth. It consists mainly of silicate materials and water vapor, making it lighter than the surrounding rock. It rises and pushes up the rock above it on the earth's surface (called *country rock* by geologists). As it does, it cools and solidifies. It can intrude onto the surface one of two ways: either violently though a volcanic eruption or quietly through erosion of the rock layers covering it. While volcanic eruptions get all the publicity, most igneous rock has been exposed through erosion. In canyon country, the Henry and the La Sal Mountains are two examples of enormous igneous intrusions called *laccoliths* that solidified below the surface and pushed up the country rock as they rose. Over millions of years, much of that country rock has eroded away, exposing the igneous rock of the laccolith.

The second type of rock, sedimentary rock, is the result of that erosion. It forms one of two ways. *Detrital sedimentary rock* such as sandstone is composed of loose debris held together by some sort of natural cement. In canyon country, the cement is most often calcium carbonate—the mineral seashells are made of—dissolved in water and deposited in the sand by ancient seas and rivers. When the waters retreated, the calcium carbonate remained, hardening into a natural cement that locked the grains of sand in place.

Chemical sedimentary rock like limestone consists entirely of the hardened remains of minerals that were once dissolved in water. As heat and pressure from overlying rock layers drove the water out, the minerals solidified—not unlike the dingy brown scale that grows in a toilet that is seldom cleaned.

Although sedimentary rock makes up only a tiny portion of the total volume of the earth, it is the most common rock at the earth's surface—a broad, thin, layer of particular interest to scientists because it is what contains the fossilized records of the earth's history.

The third type of rock, metamorphic rock, is almost unknown in canyon country. It is any type of rock that has been altered by heat, pressure, or chemical reactions. Shale, for example, is a relatively soft sedimentary rock that consists primarily of silt and clay. Bury it deep underground where it is subject to enormous pressure, add heat from deep within the earth, wait long enough, and you will discover it has changed into a much harder metamorphic rock called slate. Similarly, the sedimentary rock limestone, when subjected to immense heat and pressure, transforms into the much harder metamorphic rock, marble.

Sedimentary rock is the bedrock of canyon country. In Arches National Park, it is primarily exposed as sandstone. Being little more than grains of quartz sand held together by calcium carbonate cement, sandstone is particularly susceptible to chemical weathering.

Sandstone is found throughout the world, but the arches so common here are rare elsewhere. What is so special about southern Utah? One word: salt. Three hundred million years ago, long before the first layers of sandstone were laid down, southern Utah was covered by a shallow sea in a depression that scientists call the Paradox Basin. Over time, fault movements along the edges of the basin cut the sea off from the larger ocean. In the warm climate the water slowly evaporated, leaving behind a layer of salt. Eventually the sea returned before again retreating, depositing another layer of salt in its wake. Geologists have found at least 29 cycles of seawater evaporation in the Paradox Basin, with an accumulated salt thickness of many thousands of feet—all of it now buried deep beneath layers of sandstone.

By the end of the Triassic Period 200 million years ago, all of this salt had been covered by sandy deserts thousands more feet thick. Salt is not a solid. Push down on it and it oozes like toothpaste squeezed in a tube. The weight of these sediments caused the salt to flow in ways that buckled the overlying sandstone into a series of ridges and troughs—the beginning of the rows of sandstone fins from which today's arches derive. Over the eons, more cycles of flooding and evaporation built up layer after layer of wrinkled sandstone. By the close of the Cretaceous Period sixty-six million years ago, the seas were gone for good. It was now time for rain and wind to do their part.

In such an arid country, it may seem unlikely that water could have much impact on exposed sandstone. But the calcium carbonate cement within it dissolves in acid, even the very weak carbonic acid formed by carbon dioxide in rainwater. Sandstone is porous. Given enough time, even infrequent rains percolate through cracks in the rock and dissolve the cement. Small differences in the distribution of the cement cause it to weather unevenly. Windblown sand does a final polish, leaving behind the fantastic shapes of fins, gargoyles, pillars, and arches so unique to this land.

The park's arches form almost exclusively in a layer of reddish-orange sandstone several hundred feet thick that geologists have named the Entrada Sandstone. During the Jurassic Period 160 million years ago, the Entrada Sandstone was a broad series of sand dunes lying along ancient beaches and tidal flats. If you look carefully, you can still see the outlines of those fossilized dunes preserved in the rock—a phenomenon called *crossbedding*. Over time, as water levels rose and fell to cover the dunes in ever more layers of sediments, the cement hardened and turned the dunes to sandstone. Flowing salt buckled it into the rows of fins and troughs we see today.

Mildly acidic rainwater then dissolved that cement, releasing loose grains of sand that collected in the troughs. The wet sand at the base of the troughs retained water longer than the bare rock above it, causing the sandstone to dissolve upward from the bottom of the troughs. Eventually a small hole opened in the base of a fin and grew with time. Ice and gravity also did their part. Strips of sandstone under stress broke off to relieve the stress, leaving the remaining rock in the shape of a natural arch—the strongest shape in nature.

All of this knowledge comes from the work of geologists—academics who straddle a fine line between white-collar and blue-collar work. College educated but often out in the field rubbing elbows with hard rock miners and oil field roustabouts, they aren't entirely comfortable in either world. But in a way, you have to envy them. They've found a profession that lets them get paid for camping out a hundred or more nights a year. They bounce along in four-wheel-drive vehicles over rough roads, fly in helicopters at company expense, fight off snakes, mosquitoes, cougars, and bears, and don't worry about bathing for days on end.

I've known a few geologists in my time, including a friend from college who worked in the oil exploration industry. He regaled us with exciting stories of summer jobs that included harrowing encounters with grizzly bears in the oil fields of Alaska. He once said it was a great career for a single guy, but he wasn't sure how compatible it would be with marriage. Sadly, he never got to find out. Only a few years after graduation, he and a colleague were killed in the crash of their small plane while on assignment for their employer in Utah. But every profession has its hazards.

EIGHT A.M. on a blustery spring morning. I'm sixteen miles west of Bluff, Utah, standing at the rim of a canyon overlooking the San Juan River eight hundred feet below. A series of cliffs to my left, in various shades of gray, brown, buff, and red, drop off to a low valley that runs north as far as I can see and disappears in the distance. The valley is Comb Wash, a thirty-mile-long gash in the earth that follows an ancient fault line. On its eastern edge rise the sharp bluffs of Comb Ridge—a nearly impassible five-hundred-foot-high wall stretching for a hundred miles from near Kayenta, Arizona to just west of Blanding, Utah. Comb Ridge is a monocline, a tilt in the earth whose sharply raised western edge forms the impenetrable sandstone cliffs I now see, and whose eastern edge slopes gently downward like an enormous skateboard ramp.

Comb Ridge was formed at the end of the Cretaceous Period during the collision of two continent-sized tectonic plates: the Farallon Plate moving eastward under the Pacific Ocean, and the North American Plate riding over the top of it. Tremendous pressure from the collision of these two plates buckled rocks across the landscape of the entire West. At Comb Ridge, it tilted the rock along an existing fault as if it were a stack of plywood sheets lifted on one side. The result was a sharp ridge or hogback along the edge of the fault and gently sloping land toward the east. Comb Ridge runs almost perpendicular to the San Juan River, which was already there and cut through the ridge as it was rising.

Beside me is Professor Gary Gianniny, Chairman of the Department of Geosciences at Fort Lewis College. He has brought a group of twelve of us here for a tour of the geology around the San Juan River. It's an area he knows well, having conducted extensive studies of the limestones in this area. Over the next few hours, he will lead us down those red and gray cliffs and back up as we explore layers of sediments representing a hundred million years of the earth's history.

Gary is living evidence that being a married geologist doesn't have to be a contradiction in terms. I know this because he has just introduced us to his wife, Dr. Cynthia Dott, a respected professor of biology herself. She will be joining the hike and offering her own perspective as we explore.

As you might expect of people who spend a lot of time outdoors, Gary and Cynthia are physically fit. The rest of us range from twenty-some-things to septuagenarians, and health-wise we are all over the map. One young lady recently completed a thousand-mile solo hike through canyon country and could probably outpace anyone. Others look like they rarely get outdoors. I'm somewhere in the middle.

Except for a short stretch at the outset, our descent over the escarp-ment will follow no trail. We will be scrambling over gullies, boulder fields, and loose scree as we get up close to the geology. The 600-foot descent over the first two miles is not what worries me. It's the climb back up I'm dreading. I chastise myself for not getting more exercise in

Comb Wash and Comb Ridge, San Juan County, Utah – Photo by Tom Bean

preparation for this trip but am relieved to know I probably won't be the last one back.

At the moment we are looking down on a giant meander of the river, a seven-hundred-foot deep, mile-wide loop that is missing only one thing: the river itself. The San Juan long ago took a shortcut by punching through a thin wall of the meander, leaving this former oxbow loop abandoned. I can't help but be reminded of an enormous pandemic-era baseball stadium where the bleachers are empty and the athletes are no-shows. We turn away from this stark feature and head over to the slopes on our left.

As we cross a layer of reddish gray sediment, Gary provides commentary. "We are walking on one of the very last limestones of a marine environment. This is the Honaker Trail Formation and is of Pennsylvanian age," he says, emphasizing the word, *Pennsylvanian*. He picks up a loose rock and asks, "Anyone know what these little circles in the rock are?"

No response.

"These are relatives of starfish. They are called crinoids. They lived on stocks made of stacked layers of bagel-shaped pieces of calcium carbonate. When they died, the stocks broke apart and left these calcium carbonate rings. This rock is probably ninety percent fragments of crinoid stems."

Gary shows us other fossils in nearby rocks. He points to an oval-shaped feature with what looks like a spring lying along one side. "This is a cross section of a critter kind of like a clam, but not a clam, called a brachiopod. This spring-like hinge line is indicative of it being a brachiopod."

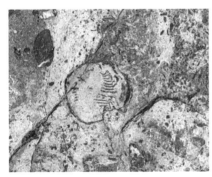

Brachiopod, Honaker Trail Formation   *Rhizolith, Halgaito Formation*

He then points to a series of vertical stripes in the limestone. "These are almost certainly clam burrows. If any of you have ever floated down the San Juan River below Grand Gulch you can see this exact same layer with these exact same clam burrows."

He points to layers of red sandstone well down the slope. "Those red layers down there are where we are heading. Notice the difference. The limestone of the Honaker Trail Formation is from a marine environment. Those red sandstones were formed in a land or terrestrial environment. They are of Permian age," he says, emphasizing the word *Permian*. "When we get to the red layer, we will see more plant fossils."

Something doesn't seem right about what he says, but as I pick my way through the rough, boulder-strewn slopes, I'm more worried about staying upright than processing his comments. Eventually the incongruity emerges from the fog of my distracted mind. If the Honaker Trail Formation where we are now standing is of Pennsylvanian age, it was laid down almost 300 million years ago—50 million years before the first dinosaurs. If those red sandstones down below are of Permian age, they are at least 25 million years younger. And Gary says that as we continue to descend, the rocks will keep getting younger.

I'm perplexed. One of the fundamental concepts of geology is something called the law of superposition. It says that for undisturbed sedimentary rocks, younger rocks always overlie older rocks. The farther down in the layers you go, the older the rocks will be. If I believe Gary, the farther down we hike, the younger the rocks will get. Have we entered some crazy house of mirrors?

Gary explains the discrepancy by saying the rock layers have been lifted and tilted. It doesn't exactly make sense to me, but it will have to do for now. Later, when I get back home and do more research, the answer becomes obvious. It has to do with the collision of those two mighty tectonic plates, the Farallon Plate and the North American Plate.

Initially, the sedimentary layers were flat, with younger layers overlying older layers as you would expect. But the tectonic collision pushed up a region across southern Utah like an enormous bubble—a feature called the Monument Upwarp. This upwarp was fairly flat across its center, but at its eastern edge—Comb Ridge—the layers curved sharply downward as they followed the curve of the bubble at about a 50-degree angle. Over time, the top layers eroded away, exposing older rock on the upwarp's flat surface and the younger layers across its downward sloping eastern edge. The outcome of this erosion is clearly visible in aerial photographs.

When we reach the red layer, Gary stops again. "Now we are at the next youngest unit. In this red rock, see these black and gray regions?" He points to several long, narrow, sinuous black stripes in the rock surrounded by gray sheaths. "That's where plants were growing when these sediments were deposited in the Permian. Their roots grew in the sediments, and around their roots, calcium carbonate was deposited. We call these rhizoliths. The black parts are the roots. The gray areas are the calcium carbonate. You can find this in modern soils as well. What's really cool here is that some of these roots were eaten by insects." He passes around a rock with burrow holes where ancient larvae ate the living roots, leaving behind the indelible relics of a 250-million-year-old dinner.

We take a break to have lunch and recuperate for the return climb. As we feast on prepared deli sandwiches, the discussion turns to the subject of climate change. Gary points out that climate change has been going on since the beginning of time. "We know that greenhouse gases are driving what's going on right now, but if we look on larger time scales—100,000 years, 40,000 years—it turns out there are aspects of the earth's orbit around the sun and how our planet wobbles that change our susceptibility to developing ice on the planet. The 100,000-year periodicity relates to how elliptical our orbit is around the sun, and the 40,000-year periodicity relates to how tilted the axis of the earth's rotation is. Right now, the tilt is about twenty-three-and-a-half degrees, but it changes from about twenty-one to twenty-four-and-a-half-degrees, and that changes the intensity of the seasons and how likely we are to build glaciers."

Gary says these aren't the primary reason for today's climate change. It is clearly due to the influence of man. "What we are seeing right now is radically different from what we have seen in the past. The rates of warming are much higher than almost anything we've seen before—except for maybe a few instances like, oh, say, the biggest extinction in the history of life."

I perk up. I know he is talking about the boundary between the Permian and the Triassic periods, the beginning of the age of dinosaurs. I ask if the Permian extinction was larger than the Cretaceous extinction, the event that killed off those dinosaurs. "Yes, definitely," he replies. "On the order of 96 percent of marine species went extinct at the end of the Permian, compared to about 76 percent at the end of the Cretaceous. The Cretaceous was dramatic because of the dinosaurs being wiped out, and it was probably induced by getting whacked by an asteroid. The Permian extinction appears to be associated with a spike in greenhouse gases."

Geologists don't agree on the cause of that spike. Some argue for a catastrophic event like an asteroid impact. Others argue for gradual processes such as enormous quantities of sulfur dioxide and carbon dioxide being released into the air from increased vulcanism. The oceans would have absorbed much of those emissions, creating an acidic environment deadly to sea creatures. Current evidence suggests the extinction happened quickly, perhaps over just a few thousand years. But we may never get a definitive answer. Having occurred 250 million years ago, almost all of the evidence necessary to answer this question was probably destroyed long ago.

The hike back to our cars is about as I expected—hot, steep, tiring. But Gary takes breaks to point out more geology often enough that even the most out-of-shape of us makes it back without incident. It's been a rewarding experience, and everyone agrees we wouldn't hesitate to do it again. Then we climb into our cars and head out in various directions—Bluff, Page, Salt Lake City, Durango. I point my car north on Utah Highway 191 for the two-hour drive to Moab and the next stage of my journey. I try not to think about the greenhouse gases my vehicle is emitting along the way.

Mi Vida Mine, San Juan County, Utah

14

THE FUEL FOR
ARMAGEDDON

CLOUDS TO THE EAST darken the sky as I drive a lonely side road across a barren plain. Rutted dirt tracks meandering to places unknown are a common sight along Utah highways. Most travelers don't give them a second thought, but there are those who gaze on such a road and wonder, "Where does it go? Who put it there? Why?" All leading to the ultimate question, "Why not head over there and find out?" I count myself as one of those.

Usually, I let my journeys of discovery take me where they will: "Which way should I turn at that next fork in the road? Does it really matter? Either direction will lead to adventure." But today, those questions are irrelevant; I have a specific objective in mind.

I have seen no one since I turned off the highway five miles back. My Honda Pilot cruises along confidently at forty miles an hour, with no need for four-wheel-drive. It is a much better ride than the dirt roads I usually explore, and for good reason. Although seldom maintained today, this road still bears evidence of the asphalt paving that once spanned its entire route. That is why I am here—not because of the asphalt but because of where it leads.

In another three miles the road climbs a line of hills. Early spring snow covers shaded stretches of the road, and now, as I weave through the slush, I'm thankful I have a high clearance SUV that knows how to optimize torque across all four wheels. Near the top I pull into a slight clearing and park. It is doubtful anyone will drive past while I am here, but by force of habit I pull well off the road. I clamber out and trudge across a low wash. The morning air is brisk, with a slight but steady wind. I tug my jacket a little tighter, pull my hat more firmly on my head.

As I reach a broad, flat ledge extending from a cliff, a pair of ravens sweep low across the sky. An ill omen? Their shrill cries call out a warning. "Turn back, turn back," the black devils seem to say.

And then, as I round a bend I see scattered evidence of what I have come to view: corroded machinery, rusted rails, wooden timbers framing a dank cliffside opening. Like a wonderstruck adventurer who stumbles across a secret laboratory in an ancient Bavarian castle, one thought keeps running through my mind: *This is where it happened. This is the Mi Vida mine.*

IN THE FIRST HALF of the twentieth century, southern Utah languished as the domain of a few hardy cowboys, ranchers, sheepherders, and hard rock miners. What little the general public knew of it came mainly from Hollywood, in movies like *Stagecoach, Fort Apache, She Wore A Yellow Ribbon*, and *Rio Grande*. In the minds of many, southern Utah was synonymous with Monument Valley. No matter that much of Monument Valley lies in Arizona, not Utah. The classic view of towering rock monoliths framing a lone rider atop a nearby ridge *was* Utah to them. That nearby ridge even had a name, John Ford Point, in honor of the famous director of those defining westerns.

In 1945, two blinding flashes half a world away changed everything. The Armageddon launched on Hiroshima and Nagasaki ushered in a new and terrible era: the atomic age. For the first time in history, the total destruction of earth by man was within the realm of possibility. Yet not all was despair. The new era also offered hope for the benefits nuclear energy could provide for such fields as medicine and power generation.

The atomic age was made possible by a single chemical element that most people of the time had never heard of—uranium, the heaviest of all elements found naturally on earth. Uranium is radioactive, meaning it is not stable. Over time, its atoms emit alpha particles to lose protons from their nuclei, causing it to decay into a series of other elements. The transition happens slowly, but given enough time, all uranium will eventually turn to lead.

Uranium exists in several different forms, called isotopes. The atoms of every isotope contain the same number of protons, 92, in their nuclei. The difference is in the number of neutrons. The nucleus of the most common uranium isotope contains 146 neutrons. It is known as uranium-238 because the total of its 146 neutrons and its 92 protons equals 238. Over 99 percent of all uranium is uranium-238. Scientists like to refer to it using the arcane nomenclature, ^{238}U, but I will save you that drudgery here. Fortunately, this isotope is not highly radioactive, or the entire world would have blown itself up long ago.

While all uranium isotopes are radioactive, only a tiny percentage is fissile, meaning it can sustain a nuclear chain reaction. The atomic bomb code-named Little Boy that was dropped on Hiroshima on August 6, 1945 was proof of the awesome power of fissile uranium.

Uranium can also be processed to create plutonium, another fissile element not found naturally on earth. The atomic bomb dropped on Nagasaki on August 9, 1945, code-named Fat Man, used a plutonium core bred from uranium in a reactor at Hanford, Washington.

The fissile uranium isotope used in bombs and power plants has only 143 neutrons and is known as uranium-235. Today, it comprises less than one percent of all uranium found in nature. Even though the Little Boy bomb used only about 140 pounds of uranium-235, this isotope is so rare that thousands of tons of uranium ore had to be processed to obtain it.

It wasn't always that way. When the earth first formed four-and-a-half billion years ago in the wake of a supernova explosion, uranium-235 was plentiful, accounting for perhaps as much as ten percent of all uranium. Even two billion years ago, uranium-235 was so common that it occasionally became concentrated enough to reach critical mass and form a natural nuclear reactor. Evidence of such ancient reactors can still be found near Oklo, Gabon, on the west coast of Africa.

Every radioactive isotope decays at its own rate. Scientists use the term *half-life* to describe how long it takes for half the isotope to decay into another element. The half-life of uranium-238 is over 4 billion years, but that of uranium-235 is only 700 million years. Over the eons uranium-235 decayed away much more rapidly and today accounts for only 0.7 percent of all uranium.

The uranium for the first atomic bombs came primarily from mines in the Belgian Congo and Canada. With the start of the Cold War, the US Government knew it was essential to build a stable supply from domestic sources. The Atomic Energy Act of 1946 established the Atomic Energy Commission (AEC) and made it illegal for anyone other than the government to purchase uranium.

The Four Corners Region of the American Southwest was known to be a promising source. During World War II, the government had contracted with several mines in the area to obtain vanadium, an element that, when added to steel in small amounts, dramatically increased its strength. Vanadium was extracted from a reddish-yellow ore called carnotite, and uranium was a waste byproduct of that process. Government contracts for vanadium had ended in 1944, and by 1947 the one plant still operating, the Vanadium Corporation of America out of Naturita, Colorado, ran at a much-reduced capacity. There is so little uranium in carnotite that production was virtually nil. What the AEC needed were sources of a high-grade uranium ore known as uraninite or pitchblende, like those found in Africa and Canada.

In April 1948, the AEC announced a 10-year incentive program that encouraged private industry to help the government find more uranium. It guaranteed a minimum price for high-grade ore and a $10,000 bonus to anyone who delivered 20 tons of ore from any single new mining claim. The AEC set up ore buying stations throughout the region, deployed government geologists to help in the search for ores, and bulldozed over 1,200 miles of dirt roads to give prospectors access to promising locales.

Almost overnight, the area swarmed with get-rich-quick hopefuls in a great uranium boom. Those with enough of a stake bought Geiger counters and waved them across the land, hoping to hear the rapid series of clicks indicating a strike. But the Colorado Plateau is a vast landscape, and uranium lodes are scarce. Most prospectors were amateurs with no idea of what they were doing. Even the professionals had limited success, in part because nobody had a good idea for where to look. It didn't help that the guidelines proffered by the AEC were mostly wrong. Before long, the region was littered with disillusioned prospectors now out of cash.

Into this fray came Charles A. Steen, an unemployed geologist from Texas out to make his fortune. Charlie was born in 1919 to a prospector who made and lost fortunes in oil booms. Charlie always claimed the only things he got from his father were his name and a Dalmatian dog, but later events would show he also picked up his father's penchant for wildcat mining speculation.

His mother and father soon divorced, and Charlie was raised in near poverty by a series of stepfathers. He never let his financial situation deter him; instead, he saw it as a challenge. He worked his way through college, first at the John Tarleton Agricultural College and then on to the Texas College of Mines and Metallurgy, where he graduated with a degree in geology in 1943. Poor eyesight kept him out of the military, so he worked the war years as a petroleum geologist in South America.

While at college he met the woman with whom he would share his life. Minnie Lee Holland—who preferred to go by her initials, M.L.—came from a strongly religious home where "about the only thing that wasn't a sin was going to church." An accomplished painter, she once signed on to a cruise ship as an art teacher. She was dedicated to supporting Charlie in his adventures, and Charlie was quick to admit that without her support his success would never have happened.

When Charlie returned to Texas after three years in Bolivia and Peru, he and M.L. got married. He joined Stanolind Oil and Gas as a field geologist, but the job didn't last long. Rebellious by nature, he had little tolerance for incompetent managers. After one too many arguments with his bosses he was fired for insubordination and blackballed throughout the tightly controlled industry.

Now on his own and locked out of the oil industry, Charlie looked for other opportunities. At one point he planned to prospect for gold in Alaska, but after reading a magazine article about the uranium boom in the Four Corners region, he decided that was the place to be.

The uranium frenzy had already been going on for over a year without a single strike of high-grade uraninite. A few of the luckier prospectors were making meager livings from carnotite strikes, but most were reminiscent of a grizzled Humphrey Bogart in *The Treasure of the Sierra Madre*. Poor but ever optimistic, they wandered the land in search of riches, accompanied by a forlorn burro or its army surplus mechanical equivalent.

Charlie scraped up enough money to buy an old jeep, and his mother mortgaged her home so he could buy a used drill rig. He packed up and moved to Dove Creek, Colorado, which was already overrun with pros-pectors. By now, in addition to M.L. his family included three boys. The brood joined him once his fourth son was born, squeezing into the close quarters of a 20-foot travel trailer. Ever short of money, the family lived on beans, rabbit stew, and the wild venison Charlie hunted regardless of whether it was in season.

Charlie's funding didn't include money for a Geiger counter, but he didn't feel it was necessary. The "experts" were sure uranium deposits would be found on the surface in a geologic layer called the Morrison Formation—the same layer rich in radioactive *Allosaurus* and *Diplodocus* fossils at Dinosaur National Monument. Charlie was convinced the best layers were deeper down, out of range of a Geiger counter. Uranium is heavy. It should naturally seep through more porous layers to accumulate over a hard bedrock layer below.

Eventually, to save money the family moved to Yellow Cat Wash north of Moab. The nearest town, if you could call it that, was Cisco, Utah, a tiny whistle stop on the Denver and Rio Grande Railroad. Today it is little more than a ghost town, and it wasn't much more than that back then. Its dubious claim to fame is having served as a filming location for the movies *Vanishing Point* and *Thelma and Louise*. At least the frugal Steens found Yellow Cat to offer rent-free accommodations.

Charlie staked out claims in the Big Indian District south of Moab. AEC geologists had discounted the region because there were no

Morrison Formation exposures anywhere in the area. Charlie thought it had potential, but he ran out of money before he could prove it. Reluctantly, he packed up the family and towed their trailer to Tucson, where for the next year he took work as a carpenter to replenish his stake.

In April of 1952 Charlie and M.L. decided to give uranium mining one more try. They sold the trailer and moved back to Cisco, where they rented a dilapidated tarpaper shack. His mother, recently recovered from a severe heart attack, sold her house and brought the proceeds with her to help her son.

Experienced miners laughed when they learned the "crazy geologist" had begun drilling on a claim in the Big Indian District. Charlie called it *Mi Vida*—Spanish for "My Life." The naysayers called it "Steen's Folly." With not a speck of Morrison Formation anywhere around, the experts knew it was bound to be a fruitless endeavor. Their feelings were confirmed when, on July 27th, the drill bit broke 200 feet down with no yellow carnotite in any of three weeks' worth of core samples, only an unidentifiable dingy black sludge.

The next morning while filling his jeep with gas (on credit, as usual), Charlie joked with the proprietor, Buddy Cowger, about how the black cores sitting in the back of his truck were rich with uranium. Buddy pulled out a Geiger counter to call Charlie's bluff. They were both astounded when the needle pegged and the counter sounded off like a machine gun. Charlie knew at once the black cores were high grade uraninite, not carnotite. The Steen family's future was now secure.

Not everyone agreed. When a private assay came back reporting the unheard-of average of 0.34 percent uranium—with some samples running better than 2 percent—the AEC accused him of salting the mine with pitchblende from Canada. When Charlie went to Salt Lake City, Houston, and Denver to solicit funding, he met with no success. Potential backers contacted the AEC to verify his claim and were told there was no way there could be any uranium in the Big Indian District.

Charlie finally talked the *Denver Post* into running a story about his find. Although the reporter was skeptical, the article did the trick. Charlie secured backers and by the end of 1952, the Mi Vida mine was in production. The mine where no uranium could exist started a new uranium boom. It eventually shipped over a billion dollars in ore and earned Charlie and M.L. $150 million. But their rags-to-riches story wasn't finished. Before it was, they would be back to rags.

༄

STORIES IN THE MAINSTREAM MEDIA frequently claim as many as a third of all lottery winners go broke within five years. That number may not be based in reality, but the fact is, people who suddenly come into money are faced with numerous challenges mere mortals don't have to worry about. Long-lost Uncle Billy shows up asking for a loan he never pays back. Neighbors pitch shaky business ideas that just need a bit of funding to get started. Salesmen hype fancy houses, cars, yachts, and airplanes that seem well within the newly-rich's budget. Strangers appear at the door with hard-luck stories only money can fix. And lurking in the background, federal and state tax collectors stand ready to swoop in to extract their dues. Winners with little financial expertise never seem to seek professional investment advice, figuring they have enough money to cover any expense. To paraphrase the late Senator Everett M. Dirksen, a million here, a million there, pretty soon you're talking bankruptcy.

Charlie Steen conducted himself like a typical lottery winner. When M.L. asked for a washing machine so she wouldn't have to keep washing clothes by hand, he wouldn't hear of it. He started flying their clothes to a laundry in Grand Junction for cleaning. When he decided the family needed something better to live in, he bought hillside property on the northeast side of Moab and built a $250,000 mansion complete with swimming pool, servant's quarters, and a grand view overlooking the valley. He held parties frequently, hosting such notable guests as Henry Fonda, Dorothy Malone, and Utah's Governor J. Bracken Lee. Generous to a fault, he gave away money to acquaintances on the slightest whim with little regard for the consequences. He bought an aircraft and hired a pilot as a business expense, then flew M.L. to weekly rhumba lessons in Salt Lake City. When poor reception at home prevented the family from watching a favorite TV program, he loaded the TV and everyone into the plane and circled high in the sky where the reception was better. He donated $50,000 for the construction of a new hospital in Moab. He threw annual parties for the entire town, attended by thousands of people. He and M.L. traveled the world in style. As M.L. said, "we were jet setters before there were any jets."

In 1958, Charlie was elected to the Utah State Senate. He soon discovered politics in a Mormon dominated state were not for him. He liked an occasional alcoholic drink, which is forbidden by their religion. But he claimed Mormon legislators never seemed to be shy about dropping by his hotel suite where they could have a taste of his booze without being seen. The hypocrisy grated on him, so he resigned before his term was over.

In 1962, he sold his mine and other business interests to the Atlas Minerals Corporation and moved his family to Reno, Nevada. Some say it was because he was frustrated the legislature had refused to pass his bill to permit the sale of liquor by the glass. Others say it was because he was uncomfortable being the only millionaire in Moab, where threats of kidnap forced him to install a chain link fence and hire armed guards to patrol his property. In Reno, he would be just one of many millionaires in the crowd.

His luck didn't follow him to the new state. He made disastrous investments in Arabian horses, silver mines, a pickle factory, and the rapidly declining business of propeller-driven aircraft manufacturing. Then the federal government came after him for $4 million in back taxes. By 1968 he was wiped clean and had to declare bankruptcy.

To rebuild his finances, Charlie returned to the only career he ever really knew, prospecting. While drilling for copper in California, he was severely injured when he was struck in the head by a piece of drilling equipment. After three surgeries and several weeks in intensive care he slowly recovered, but he was never the same. It took many more months of therapy to learn to talk normally. His life never returned to his former level of luxury, although income from his remaining properties allowed him to eke out a stable living.

M.L. died in 1997 and Charlie, after suffering for years with Alzheimer's Disease, died in 2006. In a fitting tribute, their ashes were mingled together and scattered near the entrance to the mine that had once been their life. Their sons, used to living lives of luxury, quickly began squabbling over their meager inheritances. Most of what they would have received was soon lost in legal fees.

~

As I EXPLORE the remains of the Mi Vida mine, I am struck by its size. Or more accurately, its lack of size. I'm used to open pit mines covering thousands of acres, where a 100-ton dump truck is but a tiny speck lost in the vast expanse of a quarry. Compared to this, Mi Vida is a mere backyard picnic area—bring in a few wooden tables and invite the neighbors over for a barbecue dinner. It even has a little cave for the children to play in. As long as no one brings a Geiger counter, you won't have to dwell on the level of radiation being emitted from the ground surrounding you.

Much of what once was here is now gone. Derricks, service buildings, miners' quarters, and most of the heavy machinery evident in historical photos have long since disappeared. The mine's entrance—what miners call an adit—is sealed with tons of rock. But not everything has vanished. Extending from the adit is a line of rusting ore cars complete with an engine on a low frame. Faded lettering on its side shows it to be the property of the Utex Exploration Company. Utex—an amalgam of Utah and Texas—was the first company Charlie formed after his big strike. The ore cars sit on rusting rails that still extend to what remains of a metal tower headframe at the edge of the cliff. It was there the ore was lowered to trucks far below to be hauled to mills for processing.

Initially the ore went to mills owned and operated by the AEC in Monticello and Blanding. In 1955, the AEC gave Charlie permission to open his own mill, the Uranium Reduction Corporation, on the northwest side of Moab. It began operation in October 1956 as the first independently owned uranium processing mill in the country. Charlie ran the mill until 1962. He sold it to Atlas Minerals Corporation when he moved to Nevada.

The Moab mill performed initial processing of the raw ore by first grinding it into a powder, then immersing it in acidic or alkaline solutions to draw out the uranium. The solutions were dried, leaving behind a yellow or brown powder of concentrated uranium called *yellowcake*. The Moab mill's work stopped there; the yellowcake was shipped to other facilities for further enrichment. The waste sludge left behind, containing little uranium but still hazardous from residual radium, radon gas, and other radioactive elements, was dumped in a tailings pile at the mill.

By 1970 the government declared it had all the uranium it needed for nuclear weapons. Atlas then turned its attention to supplying the nuclear power industry, but the partial meltdown of a reactor at Three Mile Island in 1979 turned popular sentiment against the industry and curtailed demand.

The Moab mill closed in 1984, but its legacy remains. Over the years, the tailings pile accumulated a total of sixteen million tons of mildly radioactive waste in a pile 80 feet high spread out across 130 acres on the north side of town. In 1977 the government prohibited Atlas Minerals from discharging any polluted wastewater directly into the Colorado River, so the company diverted it to the tailings pile, where it grew into an enormous radioactive pond. Without any protective lining under the pond, water seeped into the ground, potentially contaminating Moab's water supply. Atlas Minerals was ordered to clean up the mess, but the company declared bankruptcy in 1999.

Cleanup then became the responsibility of the US Government. In 2009, the Department of Energy began a multi-year, $400 million project to relocate the tailings, transporting them by train to a more secure site 30 miles to the north near Crescent Junction. The DOE estimates the project will not be complete until sometime in the 2030s. Meanwhile they assure the public the remaining level of radioactivity is nothing to be worried about.

MOST PROSPECTORS LEFT the uranium boom poorer than when they started, but Charlie Steen wasn't the only one to strike it rich. Forty-eight-year-old Vernon Pick (a good surname for a prospector) was one. In a classic self-portrait photo that accompanies virtually every story about him, he has apparently just come back from an extended trip to the outback. With a grizzled beard, deep-set eyes, bushy eyebrows, crumpled prospector's hat tilted rakishly to one side, and the serious look of someone who has seen it all, it is the kind of publicity shot that would do a Hollywood actor proud.

Vernon had no intention of becoming a mining baron. Together with his wife, Ruth, he was happily ensconced as the owner of an electrical repair business at Two Rivers, Minnesota. He had dropped out of high school after his freshman year, but he had an insatiable curiosity for learning. He taught himself electronics and read everything he could find, from technology magazines to the classics of literature. Similar to Charlie Steen, he was rebellious of authority and more comfortable living a life of solitude.

On May 9, 1951, his business burned to the ground, and insurance covered only about a third of his losses. Discouraged, he and Ruth decided not to rebuild. Instead, they took their insurance money, bought a panel truck and a travel trailer, and headed west. Vernon thought he could land a job at one of the aircraft factories in California, and they could have a little vacation along the way.

They got only as far as Colorado Springs. There, Vernon learned for the first time about the great uranium boom currently underway in the Four Corners region. Although he knew nothing about geology, he figured he could pick up what he needed to know by reading books and talking with experts. He imagined he could hit a strike worth at least $50,000— enough to set Ruth and him up with a nice standard of living.

Like Charlie's wife M.L., Ruth supported Vernon's vision. As she later told *Life Magazine*, "I could have said no, but that would have made him unhappy. Then I'd have been unhappy." Vernon launched into the venture enthusiastically. He sought out advice from the geology department of the University of Colorado at Boulder, bought a Geiger counter and some camping equipment, and headed over to the AEC office in Grand Junction, Colorado for more advice.

At the AEC office, he met with Dr. Charles Rasor, who recommended Vernon start looking near the tiny town of Hanksville, Utah. Even today, Hanksville is well off the beaten path. The land around it is so otherworldly that the Mars Desert Research Station, established in 2001 to explore the human factors challenges of sending humans to Mars, sits only seven miles away. In 1951 the Hanksville area was even more like a visit to the Red Planet.

Vernon set up Ruth in a trailer park at Grand Junction, then headed out. He spent the next nine months exploring the canyons and mesas around Hanksville with little success. He made a point of searching far from civilization, where he was unlikely to come across other prospectors. He mapped out a couple of claims, but they weren't productive. He battled sweltering summer heat, flash floods, rattlesnakes, scorpions, and cougars. Every few weeks he would return to Ruth to rest and have some good meals, then head out again.

By June of 1952 they were down to their last three hundred dollars. Vernon promised Ruth he would make only one more trip and if that didn't pan out, they would pack up and move on to California. One area he hadn't yet explored was a watercourse known as the Muddy River. It was a long walk from where he could park his truck—about 15 miles—but by now he was in good shape, so it wouldn't be impossible.

Over the next few days, he scoured the land around the river. As he did, he realized something was wrong. For some unknown reason he was becoming sicker by the hour. He needed to recover, so he set up camp. For the first time, he had doubts not only about whether he would find uranium, but even whether he would make it out alive. A dead cow lying near his camp only reinforced his concerns.

To get away from the cow, he moved his camp upstream. He was too weak to carry everything at once, so he moved it in stages. The last thing he moved was his scintillometer, an expensive but far more sensitive replacement for his original Geiger counter. When he picked it up, he absent-mindedly switched it on. The meter immediately pegged to the top of the scale. At first, he couldn't figure out why. Then he realized he was standing on an entire lode of uranium-bearing ore. He looked up to see the best exposures on the cliffs above him. The rocks on which he was standing had tumbled to the floor of the canyon from there.

With a new enthusiasm, Vernon made his way back to his truck. His first stop was to a doctor who diagnosed him as having contracted arsenic poisoning from drinking contaminated river water, which should clear with time. He then staggered to the county seat to record his claim, which he called the Delta mine. Vernon initially worked the mine himself, extracting about a million dollars' worth of ore before selling out in 1954 to Floyd Odlum of Atlas Corporation for $9 million plus a PBY amphibious aircraft (Vernon had learned to fly back in Minnesota). Atlas renamed it the Hidden Splendor Mine and worked it for three more years, recovering only about $2 million in ore before abandoning it in 1957. A series of other owners took control in later years, but the site is now abandoned.

Vernon Pick didn't make the same mistake as Charlie Steen. He avoided the thousands of people who hounded him for grubstakes, get-rich-quick schemes, and outright handouts. Instead, he set up the Vernon J. Pick Foundation, a charitable organization focused on providing college scholarships to deserving high school graduates.

Don't imagine that Vernon lived a normal life from then on. He moved to an 800-acre property outside of Saratoga, California, where he built a scientific laboratory that employed up to 20 researchers to investigate peaceful uses of atomic energy. He named it Walden West, after the book by Henry David Thoreau that was one of his favorites. Like Charlie Steen, he hosted annual barbecue parties for crowds of people and entertained celebrities such as Olivia de Havilland and the Duke and Duchess of Bedford.

The threat of nuclear war and his contributions to its possibility apparently weighed heavily on him. California would undoubtedly be in the crosshairs of any battle, so in 1965 he decided to get away. After considerable analysis of weather patterns and potential paths of radioactive fallout, he moved to Lillooet, British Columbia, where he established a new home he called Walden North. It was built sturdily enough to withstand any anticipated fallout. Shrouded in secrecy, little is known about what he did there. Vernon was a heavy smoker and died of cancer in 1986, but his foundation continues to provide scholarships to this day.

I'M HIGH ON A HILL overlooking Moab, having dinner at a restaurant called the Sunset Grill. Before me is an enormous steak that covers the entire plate, with grilled vegetables and country fried potatoes squeezed around the side. The food is good, but I've come here more for the experience than the meal. I've asked for a window seat where I can look out over the whole valley—the town to the south, Arches National Park to the north, and the radioactive tailings of the old Moab mill to the west. It's a view not unlike the one Charlie Steen would have seen over half a century ago, and for good reason. The Sunset Grill is the reincarnation of Charlie's old Moab mansion, and the room I'm sitting in was once Charlie's office.

When I explain my interest, the waiter encourages me to explore. The walls of the restaurant are covered with relics of the time—prospector's tools, pages from a Walt Disney comic book showing Goofy on a uranium hunt, a fanciful *Life Magazine* story that includes a cutaway diagram of an atomic-powered railroad locomotive. Charlie's faded red jeep is affixed to a ledge outside the restaurant, permanently poised as if ready to head out on one more expedition.

In the corner of one room stands a large ceramic jar called a Revigator, complete with spout for dispensing drinking water. The inside of the jar is lined with carnotite that leaches radioactive radon gas out of the ore into the water. The jar was marketed in the early 20th century as a product to improve your health. Fill it with water every night before you go to bed, and in the morning, drink the radioactive water to cure such ailments as arthritis, flatulence, or senility. Despite not a speck of evidence that it worked, the company sold several hundred thousand jars to an unsuspecting public. Somewhat surprisingly, when a team from Mount Saint Mary's University and the National Institute of Standards studied a vintage Revigator in 2009, they found the greatest risk to a person's health came from the toxic arsenic, lead, vanadium, and uranium that dissolved into the water from the carnotite, rather than from the water's high level of radioactivity. Sensibly, the Revigator at the Sunset Grill is no longer in use.

Moab has changed immeasurably in the decades since Charlie lived here. Mining no longer dominates the economy, replaced long ago by a steady stream of tourists who come to explore the land by four-wheel-drive vehicle, mountain bike, ATV, motorhome, or simply on foot. Few of these latter-day adventurers know the story of how the dirt roads they now travel came to be. Fewer still know the stories of Charlie Steen, Vernon Pick, and the many anonymous prospectors who once scoured these canyons and mesas in search of riches. Of those who do, some say the uranium boom was a scourge on the land, an era to forget rather than to memorialize. Besides leaving permanent scars on the landscape, it left permanent scars on the miners. Lung cancer and other illnesses from exposure to radioactive ores were common, especially among the many Navajo mine workers who were never told of the risks. In 1990 the government finally passed legislation to compensate those who suffered from the effects of radiation exposure. Although the law initially excluded Navajo workers, it was eventually changed to include them. As of 2020, over two billion dollars has been paid to survivors.

With my meal finished, I gaze across the valley to watch the sun descend behind Poison Spider Mesa. As it sets, billowing white clouds in a cerulean sky become bathed in a fluorescent red glow. The highway below swarms with jeeps, ATVs, campers, and family cars whose occupants are oblivious to the spectacle. These less adventurous souls are more interested in returning to prepared meals and warm hotel rooms for the evening. But out there somewhere, well beyond my view, lie a select few who avoid the bustle of civilization. As the gloom of night settles over the land, they pull into isolated clearings far from city lights, eat quick dinners of freeze-dried chicken à la King, spread out their bedrolls, and drift off to peaceful slumber while watching the inexorable flow of a thousand shimmering points of light glide across an indigo sky.

Sleep well my anonymous friends. I will join you soon. Tomorrow, as you drive down that rough dirt track wondering whether to turn left or right at the next fork in the road, remember it doesn't matter. Either direction will lead to adventure.

Mi Vida Mine, San Juan County, Utah

Mosquito Arch, Valley of Fire State Park, Nevada

15

CHANGE: NATURAL
AND OTHERWISE

OSQUITO ARCH is gone. Mosquito Arch, where I once stood at dawn, camera in hand, watching the sun cast its first rays of light on a cold winter morning. Where I trod carefully to avoid a six-foot rattlesnake lying motionless at its base, too cold to move, offering only a weak flicker of its tongue. Nothing there now but a pile of rock and fading memories. It was well off the beaten path and unlikely to have been vandalized. When I asked at the Valley of Fire Visitor Center, they confirmed it apparently fell in the middle of the night just a couple of months earlier. One evening it was there and the next morning it wasn't, which brings a new twist to an age-old question: if a sandstone arch falls in the middle of the night and there is no one around, does it make a sound? Perhaps not, but the snake sleeping at its base sure would.

Of course, it's not unheard of for arches to fall. In Arches National Park, a named arch crumbles every few years. In 1940, a large boulder tumbled from Skyline Arch and doubled the size of its opening. In 1991, an enormous slab from Landscape Arch fell onto the trail below. A Swiss tourist, alerted by cracking sounds, captured the event on video. In 2008, Wall Arch, a popular tourist destination, completely collapsed. And in

2018, Rainbow Arch, a small arch just above the park's visitor center, crumpled away. Miraculously, no one was injured in any of these incidents. I can't speak for the wildlife.

Someday, the park's most famous arch, Delicate Arch, will succumb to a similar fate, although if certain factions have their way, it won't be too soon. As far back as the 1950s, plans were concocted to preserve it with a coating of silicone-based epoxy. John M. Davis, the regional superintendent at the time wrote, "To allow this unique formation to fall without making some effort to prolong its existence would be to lose forever an integral part of the story justifying the existence of Arches National Monument."

The project went nowhere, primarily because local park staff led by Superintendent Bates Wilson realized it was a dumb idea and ignored instructions to apply the sealant. But that excuse would never fly with Washington bureaucrats, so the official explanation was that the epoxy was found to deteriorate quickly in the sun.

Every so often the topic comes up again. It wouldn't do for Utah's most recognized feature, one prominently displayed on state license plates and tourism brochures, to suddenly collapse into a pile of rubble. But no one has yet come up with a viable way to preserve it. Perhaps after it falls, it can be replaced with a steel-reinforced concrete replica, or in true Disney fashion, with a laser-light simulation in three-dimensional, full color virtual reality.

IT WOULDN'T BE the first time mankind has tinkered with nature in slickrock country. Even early Native Americans cleared space for agriculture by burning fields, but their meager attempts pale in comparison with what newcomers have done. That thought crosses my mind as I slog down Harris Wash toward the Escalante River. When I last came here ten years ago, the hike was long but manageable. Today I need a machete—an implement I thoughtlessly failed to pack—to forge my way through. Since my last visit, the canyon has become a nearly impenetrable mass of noxious brush, an obstacle neither the Ancestral Puebloans nor the early

Europeans ever had to face—an imported species that goes by several names: tamarisk, tamarix, saltcedar, or salt cedar. The crews tasked with removing its dense thickets use decidedly less charitable names.

The story of tamarisk is a classic example of the perils of tinkering with nature. Native to Mediterranean Europe and the Middle East, it was brought to America in the 1820s by nurserymen in Philadelphia and sold as an ornamental plant, a windbreak, and a way to stabilize riverbanks. It did a wonderful job, and by the early twentieth century US Army engineers thought it would be a good solution to an emerging problem out West. Historically, western rivers were protected from erosion by cottonwoods and willows that grew along their banks. These native species depended on spring floods to cleanse the riverbanks so they could sprout. Construction of dams along many rivers had so altered their natural flows that these spring floods no longer occurred. The barren banks were eroding away, and something needed to be done.

Tamarisk seemed to be the ideal solution. It had already proven its worth in eastern states, so army engineers brought it west. Initially, everyone loved it. In 1914 a proponent proclaimed in *Science* magazine how well it was suited to the dry soil of the west.

Over time, people began to realize it wasn't the savior they had imagined. It was pushing out native species and altering the environment. Tamarisk has a deep root system that makes it difficult to control. Chop it down and it grows right back. Burn it down and it erupts in even more vigorous blooms. Even herbicides don't always work. It is harder to kill than a *Jurassic Park* velociraptor.

Detractors also pointed out other problems. It absorbs salt and secretes it through its leaves, causing the salinity in its immediate vicinity to increase above levels native species can tolerate. Moreover, mature plants can consume over 200 gallons of water per day, lowering the water table in an already dry land. But there was a more sinister backdrop to some of the claims. Mining companies in western states needed water, but water rights were already oversubscribed to farmers. An enterprising mining engineer whose name is lost to history came up with a clever idea. He proposed that by eradicating the water-hungry tamarisk, it would free up more water that could be allocated to the miners. With the outbreak of

World War II, the US government, anxious to obtain metals for the war effort, stepped in to support the miners. The war on tamarisk had begun.

Over the ensuing decades all sorts of efforts were undertaken to eradicate the invasive pest. After trying bulldozers, flamethrowers, and aerial herbicides with little success, the U.S. Department of Agriculture looked for other solutions. In its native lands, tamarisk doesn't grow out of control because of natural insect predators. So, early in the twenty-first century the USDA imported a tamarisk-eating beetle, *Diorhabda elongata*, and dispersed it in controlled releases. The results were encouraging, with tamarisk thickets decreasing in areas where the beetles were released.

It's no surprise that in the intervening years the beetles have spread far beyond their initial release areas. But never fear. Researchers say the beetles feast exclusively on tamarisk, and when the tamarisk is gone, the beetles die. Why is it when I hear that I am reminded of the classic line from *Jurassic Park*, "Life will find a way"?

And there are other problems. Over the decades, a native bird on the endangered species list, the southwestern willow flycatcher, decided tamarisk was the perfect nesting place. Remove the plant and you threaten the bird. Suddenly tamarisk isn't quite the villain it was made out to be. To protect the flycatcher, tamarisk-eating beetles are now prohibited from further release.

Tamarisk, Grand Gulch, Utah

Tamarisk proponents also point out that while it may consume a lot of water, the amount isn't much different from amounts consumed by native willows and cottonwoods. That may be true, but if Harris Wash is any indication, tamarisk is so much more prolific than any native species that the total amount of water consumed is undoubtedly far more. As I trudge through the never-ending thickets, I am sorely tempted to side with the tamarisk detractors. Let the flycatcher go back to its traditional nesting methods.

༂

THE STORY OF TAMARISK is only a footnote in the story of the political battles for western water rights. One of the single most profound events to impact canyon country took place on January 21, 1963, when the steel gates of the Glen Canyon Dam were closed to begin filling Lake Powell. By the time it reached full capacity seventeen years later, Lake Powell had inundated over 250 square miles of land—a kill zone as large as fifty nuclear explosions the size of the Hiroshima detonation.

The loss of Glen Canyon was a stinging blow to environmentalists. David Brower, executive director of the Sierra Club, wrote in his foreword to Eliot Porter's book, *The Place No One Knew: Glen Canyon on the Colorado*:

> The best of the canyon is going or gone. Some second-best beauty remains along the Colorado of course, but much of its meaning vanished when Glen Canyon died. The rest will go the way Glen Canyon did unless enough people... are willing to ask if progress has really served good purposes or if it wipes out so many of the things that make life worthwhile.

Alas, a few paragraphs later Brower offered ideas that would send chills down the spines of today's environmentalists:

> The alternatives that could have saved Glen Canyon are still unused. Fossil fuels, for one. The states of the Upper Basin of the Colorado contain a major part of the earth's coal reserves ... and they are a much longer-

lived source of energy than the short-lived reservoirs planned for the silty Colorado.

Brower also suggested atomic energy as a superior solution. He must have later regretted those words, as only a few years later he became one of the most outspoken opponents of nuclear power plants.

The Glen Canyon Dam and Lake Powell were the culmination of a century of battles over water rights in the Southwest. The Colorado River and its tributaries provide much of the available water in an otherwise parched and barren land. When measured by water flow, it is not a large river. The Mississippi River is thirty times larger, the Columbia River ten times larger. But when measured by its importance to an arid land, the Colorado is a giant. Whoever controls the river controls the development potential of the region.

As usual in stories of the Southwest, California looms large. Although it lies at the ragged end of the river after it has already flowed through Colorado, Utah, Arizona, and Nevada, California needed water long before the other states. In the early 1850s, pioneers who had been disillusioned in the Gold Rush of 1849 began exploring other parts of the newly admitted state. Dr. Oliver Wozencroft and his colleague, the engineer Ebenezer Hadley, were the first to realize the potential of the lower Colorado River Delta. They set out southeast from San Francisco with several men and mules to explore what was then an unknown land. Upon reaching the Colorado Desert they found a sweltering, forbidding wasteland with impressive possibilities. Over the eons, the Colorado River had deposited countless acres of nutrient-laden silt across the land. Simply divert water from the river and you would have a fertile agricultural landscape to rival the Valley of the Nile.

Dr. Wozencroft had a bill presented to Congress in 1859. Its official description read:

> This bill proposes, in consideration of the introduction of a wholesome supply of fresh water into the Colorado desert tract as prescribed in the bill, to grant a tract of land. The tract embraces about 1600 square miles in the basin of what now is, and must remain, until an energetic and extensive

system of reclamation is inaugurated and brought to successful comple-
tion, a valueless and horrible desert.

Unfortunately for Wozencroft, the Civil War and its Reconstruction-
era aftermath made it impossible to get Congress's attention. He labored
unsuccessfully until his death trying to launch the project. The "valueless
and horrible desert" remained untouched.

In 1883, the Southern Pacific Railroad completed construction of a
major route between Los Angeles and New Orleans that travelled directly
across the Colorado Desert. With reliable transportation now in place,
interest in the desert blossomed. In 1896 Charles Rockwood and Anthony
Heber formed the California Development Company to establish irrigation canals and sell land to settlers. But an advertising campaign touting
lots in the "Colorado Desert" would never fly, so in 1900 the associated
Imperial Land Company came up with the name "Imperial Valley." Settlers soon flocked to the "valley" under the dream of easy wealth.

With the canals built, crops were planted and harvested. The Colorado
River, though, proved to be a formidable obstacle. Each spring, turbulent floods threatened to overflow the dikes. By fall, flows were reduced
to a trickle. In 1905 a raging flood burst through a poorly constructed
irrigation channel and for two years flowed unchecked into the Salton
Sink, inundating over two hundred thousand acres of farmland. It was
the genesis of the Salton Sea, the modern equivalent of an extinct, much
larger Ice Age lake known as Lake Cahuilla. The challenge of repairing
the break bankrupted the California Development Company. It fell to the
Southern Pacific Railroad, whose busy transcontinental line was threatened, to spend an estimated $5 million to complete the repairs.

Imperial Valley farmers knew they needed a reliable source of water
free from the risk of disastrous floods. At the same time, the growing city
of Los Angeles needed water for its residents. Californians began pushing
for a flood control and water storage dam upstream to serve these joint
needs. The U.S. Reclamation Service began studying possibilities.

The fact the Reclamation Service was involved at all was due to an
obscure legal precedent of interstate commerce. According to a doc-
trine in constitutional law known as "navigable servitude," the federal

government has the right to regulate all commerce on navigable waterways. Anyone who has read John Wesley Powell's reports of his harrowing journeys down the Colorado River would hardly consider it to be a "navigable waterway," but for a very brief period of time in the middle of the nineteenth century, steamboats traveled the lower reaches of the river from its mouth as far north as Callville, Nevada (remember Joseph Christmas Ives' trip up the river in 1857?). That history was enough for the federal government to lay claim to the entire river. Numerous court cases and further agreements since then have all reaffirmed it, together being known as "The Law of the River."

While the Reclamation Service (renamed the Bureau of Reclamation in 1923) was studying alternatives, the various state governments realized there was a serious potential problem. According to another well-established law known as the law of prior appropriation, whoever was first to divert a river's water for "beneficial use" had superior rights over those who came later, even if those latecomers were upstream. Because of the Imperial Valley canals, California had already established precedence and could potentially monopolize the entire water supply.

California knew if it were ever to get a dam approved, it would need the support of the other states. In 1922, representatives from the seven states of the Colorado River Basin met to deal with the issue. The outcome was the Colorado River Compact that divided the river into an Upper Basin, consisting of Colorado, Utah, Wyoming, and New Mexico, and a Lower Basin, consisting of Arizona, Nevada, and California. Half of the available water was allocated to each basin.

Authorization for the construction of Boulder Dam (renamed Hoover Dam in 1947) near Las Vegas was one outcome of the Compact. The federal government would recover the costs of construction through the sale of hydroelectric power and water rights to various Southern California agencies. It took more years of legal wrangling, but the project was approved in 1928 and the dam was completed in 1936. The reservoir it created was named Lake Mead.

With the immediate needs of the Lower Basin met, the Bureau of Reclamation turned attention to the rest of the river basin. In 1946 they published a report titled, *The Colorado River: A Natural Menace Becomes a National Resource.* In this report, a wild river was the enemy, something to be subdued to serve man. It presented a list of no fewer than 134 projects to do so. But even its authors realized it would be impossible to do them all: "There is not enough water in the Colorado River system for ... full development of all potential projects outlined in the report." Two of its highest priority recommendations were a dam along the Green River at Echo Park near the Colorado-Utah border and another along the Colorado River in Glen Canyon. These would assure reliable year-round water delivery to the Lower Basin and produce enough hydroelectric power to pay for their construction and operating costs.

Echo Park became a flashpoint for environmentalists because the dam would flood the wild and scenic Green River through Dinosaur National Monument. They remembered the battle lost over Hetch Hechy Dam in Yosemite National Park at the beginning of the century, in which the beautiful Hetch Hechy Valley was inundated to provide water for San Francisco. They were determined to prevent any future such desecration of national parklands.

Famed author Bernard DeVoto raised public awareness of the threat in a scathing piece in the *Saturday Evening Post* titled, "Shall We Let Them Ruin our National Parks?" The Sierra Club published a book edited by Wallace Stegner titled, *This is Dinosaur: Echo Park Country and Its Magic Rivers.* It told the story of the monument in compelling words and photographs. A companion foldout, "What Is Your Stake in Dinosaur?" showed photos of Hetch Hechy before and after the dam, not so subtly insinuating this would be the fate of Echo Park if a dam were built. Copies of the book were sent to every member of Congress. But Secretary of the Interior Douglas McKay pressed forward, publishing a report showing the benefits the project would accrue.

A major part of his analysis was a claim that there would be only minimal losses of water due to evaporation. That analysis was flawed, and David Brower, the Sierra Club's executive director, provided testimony before Congress telling them so. Conservationists played up the premise that if the Bureau of Reclamation couldn't even do the math right, why should you believe anything else they said? Aided by a growing public sentiment in support of national parks, the dam at Echo Park was killed, in large part due to Brower's efforts.

But the victory was not complete. The second dam at Glen Canyon was always a major component of the Bureau's strategy, and if they couldn't have Echo Park, there was no way they would lose Glen Canyon. No matter how beautiful the canyon, there were no parks or monuments nearby. It was a region few people had ever seen. Resistance was slight, and on April 11, 1956, authorization to construct the dam became law.

Some people blame Brower for not fighting more strenuously to protect Glen Canyon, and even Brower himself wrote in his foreword to *The Place No One Knew: Glen Canyon on the Colorado*, "Glen Canyon died in 1963 and I was partly responsible for its needless death. So were you. Neither you nor I, nor anyone else, knew it well enough to insist that at all costs it should endure."

But as every military general knows, dividing your forces is a recipe for disaster. In trying to prevent two dams from being built, the risk was great that both battles would be lost. By concentrating on one battle the odds were much better, and Echo Park had the largest potential impact. Winning there would establish a precedent that national parks and monuments must always be protected. Glen Canyon, no matter how beautiful a landscape, would not establish any precedent. To win at Echo Park, Glen Canyon was sacrificed.

I never got to see Glen Canyon in its pristine state before the dam. Those who did tell of towering monuments, carved walls, royal arches, tranquil glens, and wondrous grottoes. John Wesley Powell, the man who named it Glen Canyon, wrote in *The Exploration of the Colorado River and its Canyons*, of his discovery of Music Temple:

> The chamber is more than 200 feet high, 500 feet long, and 200 feet wide. Through the ceiling, and on through the rocks for a thousand feet above, there is a narrow, winding skylight; and this is all carved out by a little stream which runs only during the few showers that fall now and then in this arid country. ... When "Old Shady" sings us a song at night, we are pleased to find that this hollow in the rock is filled with sweet sounds. It

was doubtless made for an academy of music by its storm-born architect; so we name it Music Temple.

Music Temple, like the rest of Glen Canyon, is now drowned hundreds of feet under the waters of Lake Powell. Even if climate change someday reduces the lake to a puddle, a century's worth of accumulated sediment, sunken beer cans, corroded batteries, pop bottles, deck chairs, kayaks, water toys, and houseboat garbage will have changed it forever.

～

FORTUNATELY, THERE ARE THOSE who are committed to protecting this land. I am talking with one of them, Martin Stamat, an energetic millennial who serves as Executive Director of the Glen Canyon Conservancy. I want to understand more about the Conservancy and their mission. Because of a worldwide pandemic we are forced to talk by phone rather than in person.

I'm curious about Martin's background and ask him to enlighten me. It is a story I've heard often: an outsider comes to canyon country, falls in love with it, and decides to stay. In Martin's case, he was born and raised in North Carolina. His first exposure to canyon country came when his family took a road trip to San Francisco, stopping at places like the Grand Canyon and Hoover Dam along the way. With that as inspiration, he ultimately discovered Utah while working as a teacher's assistant for an anthropology professor and pursuing his bachelor's degree at Appalachian State University. The curriculum included visits to numerous Ancestral Pueblo sites, which piqued his interest in the area. In 2013 he moved to Page, Arizona to take a seasonal job as a river guide. He loved the area so much he stayed on, bought a house, and became a vested stakeholder in the community. In 2017 he joined Glen Canyon Conservancy as its Executive Director.

Martin explains the Conservancy's mission is "to preserve the magic and beauty of Powell country for generations of future explorers." This is encouraging. I had naively assumed they were only there for the boating community, which stereotypically is more interested in drunken parties than inquisitive explorations.

Martin gives me a quick overview of the organization. It was formed in 1986 as Glen Canyon Natural History Association, a philanthropic partner with Glen Canyon National Recreation Area. Money earned through donations and retail sales was funneled back to the park to support a variety of programs. Their track record of success opened opportunities for additional partnerships with Rainbow Bridge, Grand Staircase Escalante, and Vermillion Cliffs National Monuments. They now operate 10 stores over a 5,000 square mile area, conduct tours of Glen Canyon Dam, support educational, safety, outreach, and research programs, and run the John Wesley Powell Memorial Museum and Archaeological Society.

The National Park Service and the Bureau of Land Management are the primary beneficiaries of the Conservancy's funding programs. These agencies can request funds to do things that either don't fit within their budgets or that federal regulations don't allow to be done using public funds. I ask Martin to give me a quick overview of the kinds of projects they have funded, and he cites a litany of activities: engagement programs for underrepresented youth, Christmas bird counts for kids, after school dinosaur camps, photo contests, water safety education, upgrades to personal flotation devices for boaters' children, campsite cleanup, trail maintenance, improvements at leave no trace hot spots, public service safety announcements, and funds to help the five Native American tribes in the area interact with the public about appropriate visitation at sacred sites. Martin apologizes, "It's hard to have an elevator pitch for an organization that is so diversified."

One recent grant provided air conditioners for checkpoints staffed by conservation officers who inspect boats for invasive quagga mussels, a threat to lakes throughout the country. Originally from Eastern Europe, the mussels showed up in the Great Lakes in the 1980s, probably imported in water from a ship's ballast. Transported from there in recreational boats that weren't thoroughly cleaned, they have now entered Lake Powell, where they clog underwater fixtures and displace native species. It's too late to keep them out of Lake Powell, but the inspections can help prevent them from spreading to other lakes not yet contaminated. It's an important job, and I'm happy to hear the inspectors can now get relief from sweltering summer temperatures between inspections.

I'm particularly enthusiastic about another project Martin mentions—the removal of tamarisk and the even more invasive Russian olive from the Escalante River watershed. It is a collaboration between several organizations led by Grand Staircase-Escalante Partners. Martin tells me teams have already removed both species from much of Harris Wash, with more work planned. I make a mental note to plan a return to Harris Wash so I can check out the results of their work.

I ask Martin about the motivation behind the organization's name change from Glen Canyon Natural History Association to Glen Canyon Conservancy. I've noticed other cooperating associations have gone through similar name changes and wonder why. It turns out to have a very practical twenty-first century answer. "Our URL and email addresses were ridiculously long," he says. "It's a bit of an industry trend. There are two different patterns in naming cooperative associations. One is to add the word, 'Forever' to the organization's name, like Zion Forever or Yellowstone Forever, and the other is to add the word, 'Conservancy.' We quickly realized calling it 'Glen Canyon Forever' would be contentious because of the fact the controversial Lake Powell exists inside of Glen Canyon. And 'conservancy' more accurately communicates how we act as stewards of the landscape."

As a federal philanthropic partner, Glen Canyon Conservancy stays out of any sort of political activism or litigation. They have no official position on such controversial issues as whether or not Glen Canyon Dam should be torn down. It's a controversy that has lingered ever since the dam was built, and there are vocal contingents who advocate for its removal. In 1983, they came perilously close to getting their wish.

THE FALL OF 1982 was a severe El Niño year, inundating Utah with extraordinary amounts of rainfall. As fall turned to winter, reservoirs reached capacity, forcing managers of dams across the state to begin releasing water. Heavy snowfall continued into May, building a deep snowpack in the Rocky Mountains far above normal. Most dam managers knew they needed to make room for the melting snow, so they increased their releases in preparation for the inevitable summer melt.

In May, Mother Nature signaled she was not yet finished. Almost overnight, the weather turned unseasonably hot. Snowpacks that would normally melt gradually over several months turned into raging torrents, flooding towns, washing away highways and railroads, and damaging power, gas, and water lines. Governor Scott M. Matheson declared a state of emergency across 11 counties. At Glen Canyon Dam, water was rising a foot a day.

And what had Glen Canyon Dam's managers been doing to prepare for this onslaught? Not much. While managers at other dams had opened their gates enough to lower water levels in anticipation of the incoming floods, at Glen Canyon Dam they released only a trickle—not even enough to offset the water that was coming in. By keeping the dam close to full they could get the most out of its power generators, placing profit over safety. At the end of May, Lake Powell held more water than it had on New Year's Day. The reservoir was nearly full, and water was rushing in at twice the volume the dam could release through all normal means.

The dam's designers had anticipated such a possibility. On either side of the main concrete arch and set back several hundred feet, they had drilled tunnels through the sandstone for two emergency spillways, lined with concrete and controlled by steel gates. When opened, the spillways could send a total of 2 million gallons per second downstream, 70 percent more than the highest flow that had ever been recorded on the river at the time of the dam's construction. In theory this would relieve any concern, but in reality, this option had never been tested.

By early June, Lake Powell sat mere inches below the top of the spill-way gates. It was time to put the emergency plan into action. On June 2, engineers opened the left (east) gate slightly to test the spillway by releasing only a fraction of maximum flow. Over the next several days, they gradually increased the opening, still maintaining only a fraction of full flow—not enough to lower the level of the reservoir, but a start.

And then things took a turn for the worse. In the early morning hours of June 6, ominous rumblings came from deep within the dam. Some workers reported feeling the entire dam shake. As the sun rose it illuminated a terrifying sight. The water rushing from the spillway tunnel, previously pristine white, was flowing a dingy red. Enormous chunks of concrete and sandstone were shooting out from the opening. The torrent had obviously blasted through the spillway's concrete liner into the soft Navajo sandstone below.

If the erosion continued it would cut through the sandstone all the way back to the reservoir. At that point the concrete dam might ironically remain standing while all the water from Lake Powell rushed around it, sending a towering wall of water down the river through the Grand Canyon. At Lake Mead, it would overflow the top of the dam, probably causing it to fail. In turn, every dam downstream would be washed away. Thirty million people throughout the Southwest would suddenly be without water.

In a report issued several years after the event, the BLM estimated the wall of water through Grand Canyon would have been over 500 feet high. Even that is probably an underestimate. Due to software limitations in the industry-standard computer program the BLM used to model the dam's collapse (yes, such software programs actually exist), it assumed it would take a minimum of 1.9 hours after the dam breached for the full wall of water to build up and roar downstream. Based on historical

BUREAU OF RECLAMATION PHOTO ID #C557-400-900

Glen Canyon Dam with Emergency Spillways Active, 1983
Courtesy of Glen Canyon Conservancy – John Wesley Powell Museum

observations of other dam failures, a more realistic estimate would have been on the order of 10 minutes.

Engineers were faced with a stark reality. The spillway was obviously failing. There was nothing to do but close the gate and inspect the damage, even though the level of the reservoir was still rising and would soon top the spillway gates. If water flowed over the tops of the gates it would cause uncontrolled erosion of the spillways and a possible total failure of the dam. Opening the right spillway could buy some time, but not much. And neither spillway could be opened to anything near full capacity. Disaster was only hours away.

Once the gate was closed, an intrepid team of inspectors ventured into the tunnel. As long as the gate above them held and water didn't flow over its top, they were safe. What they found was a series of enormous gouges in the concrete, the result of a process called cavitation. As the rushing water bounced along the spillway, it hammered away at the concrete, breaking it into chunks swept along with the flow. After piercing the three feet of concrete it began eroding the sandstone underneath. This was not a new problem. Other dams had been victims of cavitation in the past, and a fix had already been developed. But to save money, the fix had never been installed at Glen Canyon.

Continuing to use the spillways would be risky, but there was no choice. They would have to let out enough water to keep the reservoir level below the top of the gates but not so much that the spillways failed and breached the dam.

In an emergency, good engineers rise to the occasion, and while their managers may have been inept, these engineers were clever. They realized if they could raise the height of the spillway gates only a few feet, it could buy enough time to get past the worst of the flood. But how do you raise the level of a 186-mile-long reservoir by four feet? Simple. Go to a local hardware store and buy a stack of four-by-eight-foot sheets of marine-grade plywood. Then weld together all the angle iron you can find and use it to hold the plywood to the top of each spillway gate. So that's what they did. It may seem ludicrous to think that 4x8 sheets of plywood could hold back a reservoir nearly 200 miles long, but according to the law of hydrostatic pressure, it doesn't matter how long the reservoir is.

It could be 2 feet or 200 miles long, the pressure the water applies to the plywood will be the same.

The patch job was hastily constructed and leaked everywhere it could, but it did the job. Once in place, the spillway gates on both the left and right sides were partially opened, and millions of gallons of water soon rushed downstream. Although warnings had been broadcast throughout Grand Canyon, hundreds of hikers, rafters and kayakers were caught in the deluge. Thanks to the heroic efforts of helicopter pilots, over 150 people were rescued. Many were injured, but only one is known to have drowned.

Over the coming weeks the plywood held (it was eventually replaced by steel plates), the spillway erosion slowed, and by mid-July the water level began to drop. The crisis was finally over. Tom Gamble, Glen Canyon Dam's Power Operation Manager, later claimed the dam was never in any danger. Reclamation Commissioner Robert Broadbent said the crisis was an act of God and couldn't have been predicted. He blamed the problem on a faulty computer model and a bad forecast from the National Weather Service. But it's interesting to note that every other dam along the greater Colorado River drainage, working from the same data, was sufficiently prepared to avoid the problem. And when you realize the only things saving the dam from disaster were a few sheets of plywood—a solution never even imagined in the dam's formal disaster management plan—you have to wonder about the sincerity of the apologists.

❧

CLIMATE CHANGE virtually assures that a such catastrophe a will never occur again. The water level in Lake Powell has never returned to that of 1983, and water flow into the lake has been below its historical average every year since 2003. As the lake's level drops, critics are once again asking whether we need Lake Powell at all.

One of the most prominent of those critics is the Glen Canyon Institute, founded in 1996 by Dr. Richard Ingebretsen. The Institute's mission states they are "Dedicated to the restoration of Glen Canyon and a free flowing Colorado River." The Institute doesn't advocate that the dam itself be torn down (which would be prohibitively expensive), only that it be opened up so that Lake Powell can drain. They call this the "Fill Mead First" plan. Lake Powell and Lake Mead are each only about half full. At the current rate of water consumption and with the predicted effects of climate change, they will never reach full capacity again. This plan would allow Lake Mead to get to a level closer to its capacity.

The Institute says Lake Mead is a better place to store water because it is deeper and narrower than Lake Powell, so less water is lost to evaporation. This is important because Lake Mead, not Lake Powell, is the reservoir that supplies water to millions of people in Arizona, California, and Nevada. Except for a few thousand people living in Page, Arizona, Lake Powell doesn't directly supply water to any of the surrounding areas. Its primary purpose is to regulate downstream flow to assure Lake Mead always has sufficient water.

The Fill Mead First plan could have other benefits. The Colorado River carries a tremendous load of sediment, estimated to be about 100 million tons annually. (Colorado means "red" in Spanish, reflecting the impact these sediments have on the river's color.) Today, the sediments get trapped at the base of the dam. Most estimates predict Lake Powell will fill with sediment sometime over the next 100 to 500 years. By opening the dam to natural river flow, the sediments could eventually be washed downstream to the Grand Canyon, where they would replace sediments that have been depleted in the years since the dam was built. This could help the recovery of native aquatic species and improve the river experience for rafters. And exposing again the many side canyons that were drowned by the reservoir would encourage a new wave of visitation by those who have read about but never seen the canyon before the dam. (And yes, these newly flowing sediments would hasten the silting of Lake Mead, but that is an issue for another day.)

By not tearing down the dam, it could still be used to temporarily store excess water in very wet years that will undoubtedly occur occasionally in the future. The Institute proposes maintaining the reservoir at what is called a "dead pool" level—the lowest 237 feet of water that is unusable because it is below the level of the outlets at the dam.

Such a drastic change would have a major impact on the region. Recreational boaters would have to look elsewhere—to Lake Mead or other reservoirs in the Southwest—to enjoy their pastime. Local businesses would lose revenue from those visitors, although it could be offset by revenue from new classes of visitors: hikers, backpackers, and campers on the land, rafters and kayakers on the 180 miles of newly opened river.

Not everyone agrees with the rosy predictions made by the Glen Canyon Institute. An analysis by John C. Schmidt of Utah State University predicts the loss to evaporation across the two lakes would be essentially unchanged if the plan were implemented. And he contends the other major loss of water at Lake Powell, that due to seepage into the sandstone, is not really lost, it just seeps around the dam and back into the river below it. This itself is certainly a controversial theory, but I will leave it to the experts to thrash it out.

Would Glen Canyon ever recover from being underwater for nearly a century? It is hard to say. Glen Canyon Institute is encouraged by their observations of side canyons that have already been exposed as the water level has dropped. In only a few years, normal rainfall and flash floods have scoured sediments and removed much of the white "bathtub ring" left by the lake on canyon walls.

The Fill Mead First plan hasn't gotten much traction from the agencies who would be chartered with carrying it out, so it may never come to pass. Regardless of the immediate circumstances, the silting of Lake Powell will eventually need to be addressed. In the not-too-distant future, Glen Canyon Dam will transition from being a useful source of water and power to an abandoned relic much like the pyramids of Egypt or the cliff dwellings of Mesa Verde. At that point the late David Brower may finally get his wish. Glen Canyon might someday become a national park, but its main attraction could well be the ancient concrete structure he so despised, not the incomparable canyon itself.

Harris Wash, Grand Staircase-Escalante National Monument, Utah

16

GROUND ZERO: GRAND STAIRCASE-ESCALANTE

D ESERTS PRESERVE their relics passionately. This first became apparent to me as a youth in the early 1960s. My family had been driving from Southern California to Arizona along US Route 66 on one of our many trips into the Mojave Desert. West of the town of Needles we pulled well off the road to enjoy a leisurely lunch. While my mother prepared sandwiches, I set out to explore. As I scuttled across the desert lost in the thoughts typical of a preteen boy—baseball, fast cars, girls, not necessarily in that order—a gradual sense of unease came over me. I looked up to survey my surroundings and was startled to discover I was walking across a broad series of bulldozer tracks, and fresh ones at that—possibly made only earlier that day. It was evident from their sharp angles and crazily contorted paths these were aggressive bulldozers that had run rampant over the land. I suddenly felt completely exposed. Standing in the open desert, I would have little protection from their onslaught should they return.

I paused to listen and scan the countryside. Nothing but the faint ripple of a breeze as I stood under the noonday sun. I tried to process the evidence before me. Why would bulldozers be running roughshod over the land? They hadn't been doing anything productive. There was no evidence they were trying to build a road or clear land for a building. Had drunken bulldozer drivers been doing nothing more than spinning donuts in the desert?

Slowly, the glimmer of an idea crept into my mind. Perhaps these weren't bulldozers, and perhaps it wasn't today they had been here. I scoured the ground for the evidence I thought I might find. And there it was. I picked up and examined a dull metal cylinder, its head cryptically stamped "U 4 2." Then another, and another, and another. And scattered about, the steel links that had once held these brass cartridges together in an ammunition belt for a .50-caliber machine gun.

Despite the freshness of their appearance, these tracks had not been made today, or yesterday, or at any time during my lifetime. They had been made in 1942. And not by bulldozers but by Sherman tanks whose crews were training in the Mojave Desert before being shipped to Tunisia to fight the German Afrika Korps. This was hallowed ground. I stared in wonder across the landscape. Did the crews who fired these rounds ever come home? Did General George Patton himself once stand on this very site, castigating tank crews he thought were not performing up to par? Nearly a quarter of a century later, the tracks from those tanks still looked as if they had been made only that morning.

THE SUBJECT OF BULLDOZERS in the desert comes up again as I talk with Kya Marienfeld, Wildlands Attorney for the Southern Utah Wilderness Alliance. SUWA is one of the primary non-profit organizations dedicated to protecting the wilderness of the Colorado Plateau. Since it was founded in 1983, it has had enormous success doing so.

Kya has the kind of background you might imagine for an attorney who specializes in environmental law. She was born in Minnesota, the offspring of two free-spirited naturalists. While in college at the University of Minnesota, she spent summers as a guide in Yellowstone, the Missouri Breaks, and the Boundary Waters Wilderness. She earned her law degree at Lewis and Clark Law School, "the Harvard of environmental law." After spending a year as a law clerk for a judge in Alaska she joined SUWA and moved to Moab. For someone accustomed to the cold climates of Minnesota and Alaska, moving to southern Utah in the heat of July was almost overwhelming. But after five years she's used to it now.

Kya and I are having a leisurely cup of coffee at Moab Coffee Roasters. I had contacted her some weeks earlier after learning she had just testified before Congress regarding the BLM's involvement in a controversial Watershed Restoration Initiative led by the State of Utah. I wanted to learn more about the controversy and what SUWA was doing about it. She was happy to oblige, so we arranged to meet while I was passing through Moab.

"Utah's Watershed Restoration Initiative is a coalition of public and private entities created to fund vegetation and habitat projects across federal, state, and private lands in the state," she says. "The coalition includes the BLM, the Forest Service, the Utah Division of Wildlife Resources, and various hunting advocacy organizations, all coordinated by the Utah Department of Natural Resources. Many of their projects, such as the removal of invasive species like Russian olive and tamarisk or the restoration of river systems, are beneficial. But they have also funded many large-scale, mechanical vegetation removal projects that are causing irreparable damage to native pinyon pine, juniper, and sagebrush ecosystems."

I have heard about these projects. They are usually given innocuous names like "vegetation treatments" or "habitat restoration," but the names seem intentionally deceptive. One particularly savage method is known as "chaining," although it is never called that in official materials. It uses a giant ship anchor chain of the type found on naval destroyers or cruisers, often weighing more than 10 tons, stretched between two bulldozers spaced dozens of yards apart. The bulldozers pull the chain back and forth across the land, uprooting trees, shrubs, flowers, squirrels, chipmunks, rabbits, mice, gophers, bird nests, insects, spiders, beetles, butterflies, and every last ounce of biological soil crust in their path. The chained earth can stretch for thousands of acres. Chaining is not something performed only on designated multiple-use public lands. It has already been done in Grand Staircase-Escalante National Monument, with more areas in the planning stages.

How this serves as "habitat restoration," I've never figured out. Clear cutting acres of native pinyon-juniper landscapes only to have them replaced with non-native cheatgrass and other invasive species would hardly seem to qualify. So, I question Kya. "I don't understand. The only justification I can come up with for such projects is 'we have bulldozers and we want to use them.' What am I missing?"

"You're not too far wrong," she says. "Proponents claim they are necessary for restoring a natural ecosystem to benefit wildlife like deer and elk, and to help prevent wildfires. But the best available science shows that, more often than not, large scale vegetation removal doesn't help. It either has non-significant or detrimental effects."

I'm astounded. "Don't they have any evidence to justify what they are doing?"

"Proponents say they see more wildlife after an area has been chained, but what do you expect? Without the pinyon-juniper forests, of course you can see more. That doesn't mean there is more, only that you've removed what was blocking you from seeing it. There may even be less, but you didn't make counts before and after, so you don't know for sure. And

Results of mechanical mastication on BLM Land in Southern Utah –
Photo courtesy of Ray Bloxham / Southern Utah Wilderness Alliance

replacing pinyon-juniper forests with highly flammable cheatgrass isn't a way to reduce fire risk. The real reason for these projects is to clear away native species so the land is more suitable for cattle grazing."

Kya tells me that chaining, because it is so obviously destructive, has gotten enough bad press to have fallen mostly out of favor, at least for now. In its place have come other methods of similar destructiveness. One popular approach is called mechanical mastication (often referred to by the trademarked name, "Bull Hog" mastication). It uses an enormous mulcher attached to the arm of an excavator. If you've ever watched a tree trimming company cut down a tree and turn it into sawdust by shoving it into a shredder one branch at a time, you get the idea. With a mechanical masticator, you don't even need to cut the tree down. The mulcher simply shreds the living tree from the top down to turn it into a pile of wood chips left scattered across the ground.

Kya says she explained all this to the House Committee on Appropriations, most of whose members had no idea what was going on. When the BLM says they are working on habitat or watershed restoration it sounds innocuous enough, and legislators have so much more on their plates they don't have time to dig deeper. Kya's objective was to educate them on the real story behind the projects.

Kya points out that much of this work isn't scientifically defensible. She refers me to a comprehensive report with the impressive title, *Do Mechanical Vegetation Treatments of Pinyon-Juniper and Sagebrush Communities Work? – A Review of the Literature.* It is a 73-page document that analyzes over 300 published technical papers to answer the question posed in its title. Edited by Allison Jones of Wild Utah Project, it was peer reviewed by 11 experts from such diverse agencies as the US Forest Service, US Geological Survey, US Department of Agriculture, Bureau of Land Management, Utah Geological Survey, Colorado State University, and non-profits like the Grand Canyon Trust and Bird Conservancy of the Rockies.

Later, I pore over it in detail. I'm not intimidated by its technical depth, which is extensive. I've written plenty of technical papers myself, even a whole 500-page textbook for engineers working in the arcane world of electronic printed circuit technology. I'm confident I can tell whether what I am reading is scientifically sound or merely a mouthpiece for a preconceived point of view. This one is valid. Its conclusions are much too detailed to more than summarize, but it makes several key points. One example:

> Managing habitat for wildlife is complex. Species often specialize for spe-
> cific habitat conditions, and what benefits one species may be a detriment
> to another. The best strategy is to maintain heterogeneous, patchy mosaics
> across the landscape of vegetation types in all stages of succession. This
> argues against large expanses being treated with one method that creates
> a single homogenized vegetation community.

The report's overall conclusions are unmistakable. Well over half the time, large scale treatments produce no significant benefits. Of the remainder, the results are about equally divided between those showing positive effects and those showing negative effects. Even in baseball, an average under .250 is nothing to get excited about. I think back to the decades-old tank tracks I stumbled across as a teenager and realize that for the other seventy-five percent of these lands, it will be many more decades, if ever, before they recover.

Kya's testimony appears to have been effective. The BLM has withdrawn their proposed projects in Grand Staircase-Escalante, at least for the moment. Whether they will be resurrected later remains to be seen. Organizations like SUWA are committed to remaining vigilant.

❧

THE IDEA OF DESTROYING natural habitat in Grand Staircase-Escalante National Monument to make it more suitable for cattle grazing flies in the face of the monument's very reason for existence. Established in 1996 by President Bill Clinton as an outdoor science laboratory, the original proclamation is unambiguous in its intent:

> This high, rugged, and remote region, where bold plateaus and multihued
> cliffs run for distances that defy human perspective, was the last place in

the continental United States to be mapped. Even today, this unspoiled natural area remains a frontier, a quality that greatly enhances the monument's value for scientific study...The monument presents exemplary opportunities for geologists, paleontologists, archeologists, historians, and biologists.

During the first decade of the monument's existence, scientific research was extensive. Of its 140 full-time and seasonal employees, over half conducted research in such areas as archaeology, botany, hydrology, paleontology, ecology, and geology. In addition, the BLM dispensed money from a $1 million annual fund to support university research. Accomplishments spanned a wide range of disciplines, some of which include discovery of over 25 new species of dinosaurs, cataloguing of over 600 species of bees, and uncovering new insights into the relationship between the modern Hopi Tribe and the Ancestral Pueblo culture.

Over the years, the Monument has sponsored several science symposia. In the 2006 symposium, researchers presented over 60 technical papers with such titles as, "Aquatic Invertebrates of the Grand Staircase-Escalante National Monument," "Late Cretaceous Ornithopod Dinosaurs from the Kaiparowits Plateau," "Using Biological Soil Crusts as an Indicator of Rangeland Health," and, "Architecture and Cultural Identity Along the Fremont-Anasazi Interface." In an introductory paper, Matthew Zweifel of the BLM set the tone for the symposium:

Archaeologists and cultural resource specialists at Grand Staircase-Escalante National Monument are fortunate that the Monument emphasizes its science programs and research to a greater extent than most other federal land management agencies. As a consequence, the Monument has a notable list of scientific accomplishments that BLM can be proud of, and that we should bring to public awareness whenever possible.

Alas, even as those words were written, fundamental changes were underway that would completely gut the monument's scientific charter. But before we go there, we need first understand the tortuous history behind the monument's creation.

❧

THE GENESIS OF THE IDEA for a national monument in the Escalante area predated Clinton's proclamation by decades. The first proposal for an Escalante National Monument was put forth by Secretary of the Interior Harold Ickes in 1936. At 4.5 million acres it would have dwarfed the 1996 monument. Looking something like a mirrored image of the State of Texas, its western border was set just east of the town of Escalante and its eastern border roughly along the eastern edge of today's Canyonlands National Park. The San Juan River formed its southern border and the junction of Wayne and Garfield Counties much of its northern border. A narrow panhandle around the Green River extended almost as far north as today's Interstate 70. While it would have been an impressive monument, the proposal never made it out of congressional committee.

In 1963, flush with the success of Glen Canyon Dam, Floyd Dominy, the director of the Bureau of Reclamation, pushed forward with plans for two more dams along the Colorado River. One would be at Marble Canyon above the Grand Canyon and the other would be at Bridge Canyon below it. While neither dam was within Grand Canyon National Park's boundaries at the time, the dam at Bridge Canyon would have flooded the lower portion of the park.

Environmental groups led by David Brower and the Sierra Club were quick to oppose the plans. Strengthened by an emerging environmental sentiment within the general public, both projects were eventually killed. But once again, the win came with a tradeoff. In stopping the dams, environmental groups agreed not to oppose construction of a nearby coal-fired power plant.

In 1974 the 2.25-gigawatt Navajo Generating Station at Page, Arizona, just six miles from Glen Canyon Dam, began operation. To get coal to the plant, the Black Mesa and Lake Powell Railroad was constructed. It was a 78-mile, 50,000-volt electric railway that ran on power provided by the station. It carried up to 24,000 tons of coal per day from a mine on Navajo land at Black Mesa, near Kayenta, Arizona. The plant and railway remained operational until late 2019, when competition from less expensive natural gas and renewable energy plants drove both to close permanently. Across the nation, other coal-fired plants are suffering similar fates. While coal accounted for 48 percent of all electricity production in 2008, by 2020 it had fallen to less than 20 percent.

Today, it seems incredulous that environmental groups would support construction of a coal-fired power plant, but in the 1960s, saving rivers from dams was their highest priority. They were still stung by the loss of Yosemite's Hetch Hetchy Valley half a century earlier, and the battles of the 1950s—winning at Echo Park and losing at Glen Canyon—were fresh on their minds. Giving up a couple thousand acres for a power plant and not opposing a coal mine on Navajo land few had ever seen seemed a small price to pay. It was the continuation of a legacy spanning more than a hundred years: ignoring the interests of Native Americans whose lands were in the crosshairs.

Navajo sentiment is stated succinctly by John Redhouse, an Indian rights activist who was a member of the Navajo Committee to Save Black Mesa at the time the events unfolded. In an article titled, "Red Truth, White Cover-Up at Black Mesa" published in *Censored News*, a newsletter for Indigenous peoples, he pulled no punches. He first railed against "anti-Navajo, anti-Indian environmentalists like Edward Abbey and David Foreman," then blasted the entire mainstream environmental movement because "the major foundations and rich environmental philanthropists like Harvey Mudd were already funding the white groups," leaving little for the Navajo and other Indian groups. He wrapped up by saying "in terms of resource allocation and equity, it was the same old shit then as it is now."

Ouch! Having earned both my bachelor's and master's degrees in engineering from Harvey Mudd's namesake college, I can only cringe at the reference. Although I do need to point out that Harvey S. Mudd, the mining engineer for whom the college was named, died in 1955, over a decade before the Navajo Power Station controversy. I decided to contact the college to learn what I could and was put in touch with Victoria Mudd, Harvey Mudd's granddaughter. Tory was very familiar with the story of the Black Mesa controversy. Her film of that story, *Broken Rainbow*, won the Academy Award for best documentary feature in 1986. She told me it was her brother, also named Harvey Mudd, who was the target of Redhouse's ire for funding only the white groups.

જ

THE POWER PLANT'S most obvious impact on the Escalante area was a noticeable deterioration of air quality, as was seen throughout the Southwest. This was not unexpected. Even before the plant opened, a government analysis predicted that burning so much coal every day would degrade air quality by orders of magnitude.

Even more concerning to environmentalists was the dangerous precedent that had been set. If coal could be extracted from Navajo lands, it could just as easily be extracted from the coal beds around Escalante and Big Water. Their fears were confirmed when the Interior Department began issuing coal leases on federal lands throughout southern Utah. For the next twenty years, environmental groups agonized over the threat of mining in the area. Fortunately, the steep, rugged country in this region was so far from any major highway or railroad that the cost of extracting its coal was prohibitive.

When President Clinton established Grand Staircase-Escalante National Monument in 1996, he bypassed Congress and used the Antiquities Act of 1906 to create it by executive order. The Antiquities Act, signed into law by President Theodore Roosevelt, came about as a result of widespread looting of prehistoric Native American ruins throughout the Southwest in the late nineteenth century. Scientists and educators across the nation pressed Congress to protect public land from further desecration. The legislators who passed the Act may never have envisioned it being applied on such a broad scale.

The Antiquities Act gives the president the power "to declare by public proclamation historic landmarks, historic and prehistoric structures, and other objects of historic or scientific interest that are situated upon the lands owned or controlled by the Government of the United States to be national monuments...the limits of which in all cases shall be confined to the smallest area compatible with proper care and management of the objects to be protected."

The wording of the Act was the result of numerous negotiations among legislators. Although originally envisioned only to protect archeological sites, certain factions wouldn't support such a narrow definition. The words, "or scientific interest" were inserted to appease those factions. It was those three words on which Clinton based his proclamation.

It is tempting to imagine Clinton's declaration being the result of his love of the area, similar to how Theodore Roosevelt's love of the Grand Canyon inspired him to declare it a national monument in 1908. The reality was much different. In a series of interviews starting in 2014, Bruce Babbitt, Clinton's Secretary of the Interior, John Leshy, the Department's General Counsel in charge of the effort, and Charles Wilkinson, the attorney who wrote much of the proclamation, shared the story with Marsha Holland as part of the Southern Utah Oral History Project initiated by the BLM soon after the monument was created.

The year 1996 was an election year. One of Clinton's pollsters, Dick Morris, whom Babbitt calls a "weird character," told Clinton that polling showed soccer moms were going to be very influential in the election, and they were all interested in the environment. He encouraged Clinton to do something "big and spectacular" to show he cared about the environment.

Clinton's staff knew Congress wouldn't pass anything controversial in an election year, so they would have to figure out a way for him to do it using executive power. The Antiquities Act was an obvious tool, and Grand Staircase, being a darling of environmentalists, was an obvious opportunity. But the Antiquities Act would need to be applied differently from how it had been used before. According to Babbitt, in the past, it had primarily served as sort of a "conveyor belt" into the National Park System. Sites would start as national monuments and eventually be transformed by Congress into national parks. Grand Canyon, Arches, Grand Teton, and Death Valley are just a few examples of national monuments that followed this pathway to becoming national parks.

That was not the vision for Grand Staircase. It was a large landscape, not all of which was wilderness. The idea was to protect it from new mineral leasing and road networks while avoiding unnecessary conflict. Babbitt explains they didn't want to remove grazing rights or people's ability to hunt and fish, nor did they want to invoke all the other restrictions that would come with making it a national park.

That led to another important decision. With very few exceptions, previous national monuments had been managed by the National Park Service. None had ever been managed by the Bureau of Land Management. They wanted that to change. Leshy explains:

> Babbitt and I argued that the BLM should manage it, because the rap on BLM was that it was the "Bureau of Livestock and Mining," and that becomes a self-fulfilling prophecy if all it has to manage is rangeland and mining lands. We thought it was very important from a long-term legacy standpoint that BLM should be given some good recreational and habitat lands to manage.

Fifteen people worked in closely guarded secret during the spring of 1996 to craft the proclamation, putting it on the President's desk that August.

And there it sat. The monument may never have happened if not for the President's daughter, Chelsea Clinton. Later that month, the Clintons were in Wyoming for another event. Chelsea was with them. In an interview for the Oral History Project, Wilkinson described the scene:

> She is down at the breakfast table; there are a lot of papers lying around. Clinton comes down for breakfast and Chelsea grabs the Monument Proclamation and supporting documents and says, "Dad, what's this?" He says, "That is some National Park out in Nevada or some damn thing, I don't know." She said, "Dad! This is where I went backpacking last quarter and I told you how wonderful it was and you gotta do this!"

President Clinton made the proclamation on September 18, 1996, in a ceremony held at the South Rim of Grand Canyon National Park, with Vice President Al Gore and numerous dignitaries in attendance. In an interesting coincidence, Harold Ickes, Jr., son of the man who promoted the original Escalante National Monument in 1936, attended as White House Deputy Chief of Staff.

Critics note that by holding the ceremony at the Grand Canyon in Arizona, Clinton didn't even enter Utah. They imagine he did this to thumb his nose at the state, but the reality was much more practical. Leshy explains: "The truth was, the logistics of doing it in Utah were too complicated. It was too difficult to get to any place close to the monument in Utah. I mean, could you imagine Air Force One flying into Escalante? They couldn't figure out the logistics ... it was not going to happen." Not only did Clinton avoid the monument at the time of the proclamation, he has never been there in all the intervening years.

The proclamation got the ball rolling, but there was still much to be worked out. One issue was how to deal with all the state-owned lands inside the monument. When Utah was admitted into the Union it, like other states at the time, received four sections of every 36-section township. So, the proposed monument was riddled with state inholdings. In an ingenious solution driven by Babbitt, the Federal Government and the State of Utah agreed to an enormous land swap. The state-owned parcels inside the monument were exchanged for federal lands elsewhere in Utah—most of these on mineral-rich lands the state was happy to acquire.

Similarly, agreements were negotiated to buy out the mineral leases from holders in the monument. Since the cost of extracting coal and other minerals from such a remote location was prohibitively expensive, most holders were more than happy to sell these essentially worthless leases and acquire new ones on the lands received by the state.

All these secondary negotiations had to be approved by both Congress and the State of Utah before they could be completed. This gives Grand Staircase-Escalante National Monument an important distinction. It is much more than a simple Presidential proclamation. It has also been ratified by both federal and state legislative bodies.

In his statement upon signing the Act approving the land exchanges in 1998, Clinton felt the trade agreement had resolved longstanding issues:

> This Act brings to an end six decades of controversy surrounding State lands within Utah's national parks, forests, monuments, and reservations, and ushers in a new era of cooperation and progressive land management.

We have shown that good faith, hard work, bipartisanship, and a commitment to protect both the environment and the taxpayer can result in a tremendous victory for all.

Such was not to be.

❧

IN MY QUEST to learn the history of Grand Staircase-Escalante, I sought out insights from numerous people. In almost all of my conversations, one name kept coming up: Carolyn Shelton, former assistant manager at the monument. "Carolyn will tell it like it is," I was assured on multiple occasions, "unlike many others who even in retirement are afraid to talk about their former employer."

It wasn't hard to reach her. An unsolicited email arrived in my inbox as soon as she heard I was working on a book about the area. Before long, we were talking and exchanging emails regularly. I gained a perspective on the monument's history from someone who had been there almost from the beginning.

Carolyn arrived in 2001 to design the monument's visitor centers and set up the visitor services program. Within a few years, she was promoted to Assistant Monument Manager for Science and Visitor Services. It was a position she held until she retired in 2016.

As we talked, it was clear how much Carolyn loved the monument. "I think the experiment that was Grand Staircase-Escalante National Monument was absolutely successful," she said. "I can go on about the value of the knowledge we are gleaning from this area—the last mapped in the continental United States. You're probably aware of the paleontological discoveries, but did you also know we are the darkest and quietest place in the continental US? I think that's pretty significant, considering you can't make new wild places anymore. You can only wreck them."

Carolyn brought up another important point. "I assume that you realize Utah's connections with the LDS faith form a very unique dynamic, a very powerful and influential one at all levels of society." Yes, I assured her, I knew the importance of this connection.

In Utah, sentiment against the federal government runs rampant. It has been that way since the Mormons first came to Utah in 1847 to escape persecution for their beliefs and their practice of polygamy. The so-called Utah War ten years later, in which the Army attempted to introduce federal authority over the renegade territory, cemented this resentment.

It's no surprise, then, that outrage at Clinton's proclamation was immediate and vocal. In the town of Escalante, Babbitt and Clinton were hung in effigy. Utah counties sued Clinton in a case that eventually reached the Supreme Court. Although sympathetic to the plaintiffs, the court ruled it had no authority to second-guess the president.

Carolyn recited an experience she encountered when she first arrived in Kanab. She had been warned not to get her hair done in town because "they will know you work at the monument." She decided to go to the hairdresser there anyway and was greeted with a warm welcome. When they learned she had just moved to the area, she was asked, "What brought your husband here?"

"I brought my husband here," was her reply.

"Oh, what do you do?"

"I work in the monument."

The entire shop went deathly quiet, and she spent the rest of the appointment in silence. But when she returned every month afterward, they were all anxious to hear everything about her job.

In the monument's early years, the BLM had the budget to do significant scientific research, and they collaborated with numerous universities from around the world to do even more. Much of the anti-monument sentiment died down as it became evident it was a boon to the economy. The BLM staff was another matter. "Half of them did everything they could to subvert it and half of them loved it," says Carolyn. It was a challenging time.

The funding decline began when George W. Bush became president and the Republicans took over both houses of Congress in 2001. The Republican-controlled legislature soon began making cuts. Rather than occurring in one lump, the cuts came in smaller doses stretched out over the years. Science budgets grew smaller. Whenever someone left the organization they were not replaced regardless of the importance of their role.

There was a conscious decision not to do any strategic planning. Initial optimism when Barack Obama was elected in 2008 was soon quelled when it became obvious there would be no significant improvements. In 2001, the monument had a $16 million budget. By 2016, it had shrunk to $4 million.

Politicians in Utah across all levels of government—county, state, and federal—rather than being incensed at the loss of funding, cheered the reductions. Even in the face of data from the US Bureau of Economic Analysis showing that economic growth in the region had surpassed Utah's average throughout the 2000s because of the monument, they were unmoved. A group of business owners from the Escalante and Boulder Chambers of Commerce met with several Utah Representatives and Utah Senator Mike Lee to explain the boom, only to find no one was interested. Regardless of the facts, the position of Utah legislators was that the area had been blighted by the monument.

Carolyn Shelton went through similar experiences whenever she met with local county commissioners. "The attacks were unrelenting," she says. At public meetings, they laid into her with an onslaught of preposterous claims: "You have closed all the roads; grazing has been completely curtailed." In reality, the ground rules laid down by Babbitt assured that little had changed. When Carolyn privately asked one county commissioner, "Why do you say these lies?" his answer was, "Because that is what people want to hear."

As a former elected public official myself, I have encountered this kind of hubris too often before. Like so many politicians of every faith who cloak themselves in religion until it becomes inconvenient, some Mormon legislators apparently feel the ninth commandment doesn't apply to them. To paraphrase John Redhouse, "it's the same old shit now as it was then."

In spite of the budget reductions, scientific research continued, although most researchers had to seek other sources of funding. Carolyn says that over her 40-year career, she had never seen an organization's mission change so radically and so quickly. Anyone who didn't "toe the line" was accused of being disloyal. She explains:

I worked mostly through Republican administrations. We had to be creative, seek funding from offices that couldn't spend theirs, and seek lots of grants in coordination with scientists. We also worked with our Friends group, Grand Staircase-Escalante Partners. In a sense, they hired the staff I couldn't get to do the work in archaeology, paleontology, Escalante River Restoration, and education, as well as a Science Program Administrator, a vacant position I struggled for over four years to fill thru BLM. They helped me fulfill my need for "capacity." We basically "pieced it together" with a LOT of dedication to mission.

I think we had actually "healed the wounds," working patiently with locals to shift the dial. I believed that since the Monument is here "forever," why shove it down people's throats. Let's take our time, live in these communities, listen to people through things like the oral history program, share the science we learned through educational 'Walks & Talks" from scientists in the communities and schools.

By 2016, an equilibrium had been achieved. A few locals were still vehemently opposed, a few others vehemently in support, but the vast majority had no strong opinion. But nothing lasts forever. A newly elected President of the United States decided he had unilateral power to undo legislation passed by Congress without need for their approval. Things were about to heat up.

House on Fire Ruin, Mule Canyon, Utah

17

GROUND ZERO: THE BEARS EARS

Bluff, Utah, is one of the hardest towns in the lower 48 states to reach. If the roads are clear, it's at least a six-hour drive from any major airport like Albuquerque, Phoenix, Salt Lake City, or Las Vegas. Even from a small, regional airport like Moab or Cortez it's a two-hour trip, and then only after you've spent the day waiting for a connecting flight out of a major airline hub. You can only hope the rental car counter hasn't already closed by the time you finally arrive.

I contemplate these facts as I pore over maps trying to decide the best way to get there. Friends of Cedar Mesa, a non-profit organization dedicated to ensuring that public lands in Southern Utah are protected, is holding its 2020 annual Celebrate Cedar Mesa conference in Bluff, and I want to attend. After pricing out several airline itineraries I give up and decide to take two days each way to drive the two-thousand-mile round trip from California. I'm not deterred by the fact the conference is in early March. Climate change virtually assures that none of the mountain passes I cross along the way will be snowed in. I should be more concerned about the dark clouds of an incipient worldwide pandemic, but at this point, its impact is still uncertain. Although I don't know it at the time, had the conference been scheduled for two weeks later, it would have been cancelled.

The weather is good, so I decide to bypass the most direct route from Northern California. Instead, I head south to Barstow to join Interstate 40—the 1970s-era replacement for US Route 66—which roughly follows the heavily used BNSF (formerly Santa Fe) transcontinental rail line through Arizona. With the railroad industry's obsession on improving internal efficiency rather than customer satisfaction, trains now routinely stretch two or more miles in length. A never-ending series of double-stack container trains lumber past Needles, Kingman, Williams, Flagstaff, Winslow, and Holbrook, where I spend the night before taking a quick detour to visit Petrified Forest National Park the next morning.

Petrified Forest is a different kind of red rock country. The red here comes from the agatized remains of 200-million-year-old petrified wood scattered across the landscape, ranging from nearly intact 140-foot-long trees to the tiniest shards of rainbow-colored quartz. Scientists say much of the fossilized wood here came from conifers that fell into ancient rivers and were carried downstream to where they collected in logjams, similar to how the tyrannosaurs of Chapter 8 were washed into a jumbled pile at the edge of a lake. The logs were quickly covered with ash erupting from nearby volcanoes. Over the centuries, minerals from the ash seeped into the wood and replaced the organic material. Like victims of a prehistoric Medusa, the trees turned to stone. When the Colorado Plateau began rising millions of years later, its movement placed enormous stress on the buried stone trees, fracturing them into the innumerable pieces that cover the landscape today.

There is something about petrified wood that corrupts people's behavior. Individuals who would never bother to pick up a discarded can or paper bag lying right at their feet think nothing of going far out of their way to illegally cart off petrified wood. If it weren't for alert park rangers who aren't opposed to handing out stiff fines, the park's entire supply of petrified wood would have vanished long before now. Since the park protects only a tiny portion of the region's petrified wood, it's easy enough to buy legal samples from any of the nearby souvenir shops and avoid the risk of fines or jail time.

The multicolored hills of the park's Triassic-age Chinle formation clearly illustrate why this landscape is known as the Painted Desert. Muted pastels of red, yellow, gray, and alabaster are layered across the land like brush strokes from an artist's pallet. I stop to explore the remnants of three ancient logjams scattered across the illitic clays of its badlands: Rainbow Forest, Crystal Forest, and Long Logs. Some of the logs here are giants that have remained intact over the eons, but many have been fractured by geologic forces into multiple slabs as if they had been sliced by a logger's chainsaw. I would like to explore more of the park, but Petrified Forest is only a brief detour on my way to Bluff, and it is soon time to leave. I drive to Chambers, then turn north on US Highway 191 for the 170-mile drive to Bluff.

It is early evening when I pull into the parking lot at the Bluff Dwellings Resort and Spa, the town's newest hotel—so new that its festive grand opening celebration takes place the next day. It is an impressive resort designed with an Ancestral Pueblo influence. Like all of Bluff, it borders the original boundary of Bears Ears National Monument. I am not much of a spa person, so I pass on that opportunity, but I do enjoy relaxing around an outdoor fire pit chatting with other guests. Then I find dinner at a nearby restaurant and retire to prepare for the coming conference. My goal is to understand all I can about the controversy surrounding the monument's creation.

THE LANDS OF SOUTHERN UTAH are sacred to Native American cultures. From Paleoindians to Ancestral Puebloans to historic Utes, Paiutes, Navajos, and Puebloans, these lands served as homelands for thousands of years. Even after those who lived here in the middle of the nineteenth century were forcefully removed—culminating in the cavalry's forced march of 8,000 Navajos out of the region to New Mexico in 1864 on what is known as the Long Walk to Bosque Redondo—their bonds with this land remained strong. Today, Native Americans come to visit sacred sites, practice traditional methods of hunting and fishing, and collect medicinal and ceremonial plants and herbs. It is a place where they can connect with their ancestors, where they can learn about and understand their heritage.

For decades, these people agonized over what they saw as wanton destruction of that heritage through such practices as mining, oil drilling, irresponsible use of off-road vehicles, and deliberate vandalization of the relics of their past. They saw graves robbed, ruins looted, rock art destroyed. By 2010, they had had enough. Five nations—the Hopi, Navajo, Uintah & Ouray Ute, Ute Mountain Ute, and Zuni—formed the Bears Ears Inter-Tribal Coalition to do something about it. They spent the next five years creating a comprehensive proposal for a 1.9-million-acre national monument that would protect their heritage.

When the proposal was ready, they petitioned President Barack Obama, asking him to use the power of the Antiquities Act to create the monument. It would protect over 100,000 archaeological and sacred sites, more than the total number of similar sites across all five of Utah's national parks. They asked that the monument be named "Bears Ears" after the culturally significant twin buttes rising high above the surrounding landscape near the heart of the monument.

A key request was that the monument be managed by a Bears Ears Commission comprised of representatives of each of the five Tribes plus federal land management agencies. The commissioners would collaborate to develop a comprehensive management plan for the monument. Such a collaboration between the Tribes and government was an unprecedented idea.

Utah legislators knew that President Obama was being lobbied to create a national monument, so in 2013 they decided to craft an alternative. Congressmen Rob Bishop and Jason Chaffetz led an effort called "Public Lands Initiative" that they claimed would be a compromise that best met the needs of all stakeholders. But they did little to include inputs from all those stakeholders. During public hearings, only current residents of the area were allowed to make comments. Native Americans whose ancestors had lived on the land for countless generations until being forcibly evicted in the nineteenth century were treated as if they had no claim to the land. The final bill heavily favored commercial usage, and it included a provision that would prohibit future presidents from using the Antiquities Act to create monuments in Utah. The bill was so flawed it never even made it to the full House for a vote.

President Obama had expressed interest in working with the bill's authors on compromise legislation, but once it became apparent they weren't interested, he knew he had to act. On December 28, 2016, as one of the last acts of his administration, he issued Proclamation 9558— *Establishment of the Bears Ears National Monument.* It wasn't quite everything the Tribes had asked for, but it was close. Rather than the full 1.9 million acres of the original proposal, it came in at 1.35 million acres. In part, this reduction was the result of a compromise with the mining industry. Owners of an existing uranium mine in Red Canyon wanted to expand its operation. That would have been prohibited had the canyon been included in the monument, so Obama left it out. This resulted in two separate tracts: the main monument to the east and a smaller detached segment to the west.

In addition to protecting Native American heritage, the Proclamation cited numerous other reasons for creating the monument: its geology, paleontology, flora and fauna, historic legacy, and the wonders of its natural beauty. It also recognized the need for Tribal participation by creating the requested Bears Ears Commission of representatives from each of the five Tribes to "partner with the Federal agencies by making continuing contributions to inform decisions regarding the management of the monument."

Reaction to the proclamation was predictable. Utah legislators called it the unconstitutional act of a tyrant. They promised they would demand Trump undo it once he became president. Native Americans, the environmental community, and Democratic legislators praised it. State Senator Jim Dabakis of Salt Lake City spoke for the proponents when he was interviewed by the *Salt Lake Tribune* for an article summarizing public reaction to the Proclamation.

> Before the deafening outcry from Utah GOP spin, remember, Rob Bishop had every opportunity to make a great deal for Utah...sadly he chose the ugly political path. Obama was ready to deal, but the hostile GOP chose

defiance...Don't like Bears Ears? Blame Utah's GOP leadership. Like Bears Ears? Thank tone deaf Rep. Rob Bishop.

It didn't take long for the new president to act. In April 2017 Trump signed an executive order directing Secretary of the Interior Ryan Zinke to review not only the Bears Ears proclamation but also numerous others. Zinke was a former Navy SEAL and Montana state politician who admitted in his 2016 autobiography that he "viewed the conventional rules as guidance rather than the law." (By 2018, like so many other Trump appointees he was out of the administration, having resigned in disgrace after he was exposed for having private discussions with the leader of a company he regulated about a possible commercial development project he would benefit from.)

Zinke actually did something Trump has never done: he visited Bears Ears. Calling himself a "Teddy Roosevelt Republican," he met with San Juan County Commissioners, who told him Obama's Bears Ears Proclamation stood in the way of the county's oil, gas, and mining industries. Zinke pointedly refused to hold any public hearings to listen to other viewpoints. Even though during an online public comment period nearly 90 percent of the comments submitted by people who identified as Utahns opposed shrinking the borders, Zinke's recommendations to Trump heavily favored doing so.

In December, based both on Zinke's recommendations and on strong lobbying by Utah Senator Orrin Hatch, Trump issued executive orders reducing the size of Bears Ears by 85 percent and Grand Staircase-Escalante by nearly 50 percent. His justification was that the Antiquities Act "requires that only the smallest area compatible with the proper care and management of the objects of historic or scientific interest to be protected." He claimed the existing monuments far exceeded what was necessary to protect those objects. He claimed many were under no threat and others were "not of scientific or historic interest." But he also acknowledged he had never been to Bears Ears to make those assessments himself: "I've heard a lot about Bears Ears, and I hear it's beautiful, (but) the Antiquities Act does not give the federal government unlimited power to lock up millions of acres of land and water." Never mind that the Antiquities

Act includes no such limitation, and that the Supreme Court has already agreed. Such a claim played well with Utah Republicans.

A legitimate question is whether the full 1.35 million acres constitutes the "smallest area" necessary to protect the objects in question. From the perspective of a city-bred businessperson who has never spent a single night camping out alone in the wilderness and who views "objects" simply as trophies to be mounted on a wall, it is too large. But from the perspective of Native Americans whose ancestors from time immemorial called this region home, it is not enough. To them, an "object" is not limited to an individual relic displayed next to a lion's head or an elephant's tusk; it is the sacredness of the entire region that is important. More than a hundred thousand heritage sites are dotted across the land. Large prehistoric cities are not the only objects in need of protection. Even the smallest sites can have archaeological significance. Something as tiny as the Clovis point found on Lime Ridge can be monumentally important.

How can you say that Moon House in Cedar Mesa qualifies for protection, but that House on Fire or Fallen Roof Ruin, also in Cedar Mesa, do not? Archaeologists estimate that only ten percent of the region's sites have been surveyed. What about the many thousands that have not yet been examined? Writing them off as "unimportant" before you have even looked at them is the action of someone far more interested in commercial development than in preservation. And Native Americans consider the whole concept of "objects" to be irrelevant. To them, it is the whole of their ancestral homeland that is sacred.

The relics of the Ancestral Pueblo people are not the only objects that need protection. Bears Ears is home to remains of dinosaurs from the Jurassic Period and giant reptiles and plant-eating crocodiles from the Triassic Period. Other reptiles, amphibians, and fish from the Paleozoic Era and mammals from the Pleistocene Epoch are also found within its borders. The paleontology of the region is only imperfectly understood because until Obama's proclamation, the funds to study it had been limited.

Environmental groups, the Native American Tribes, and the outdoor retailer Patagonia immediately filed lawsuits challenging the legality of Trump's proclamations for both Bears Ears and Grand Staircase-

Escalante. Their claims were simple: the Antiquities Act gives the president the legal authority to create national monuments, but not to reduce or eliminate them. As of 2020, the suits were still moving slowly through the courts without any sign of a forthcoming decision. That was where things stood when I made my way to Bluff for the Celebrate Cedar Mesa conference.

⌘

THE CONFERENCE WAS HELD in the Bluff Community Center, built in 1978 with funds from a grant to the Navajo Nation and upgraded twenty years later. For a town the size of Bluff, it is an impressive facility. It can hold up to 300 people, and when I did a quick count during the meeting, I came up with a rough estimate of 250 attendees.

The conference covered a wide range of topics, including the history and geology of Cedar Mesa, perspectives from various Native Americans, and an update on the status of the litigation. In a sign of the coming times, Josh Ewing, then Friends of Cedar Mesa's Executive Director, launched the ceremony with instructions to everyone on what to do and not do to prevent the spread of COVID—use hand sanitizer, cough into your sleeves, and avoid shaking hands. At the time face masks were not thought to be necessary, so we avoided having to wear them.

At an awards ceremony the previous evening, Bill Lipe was given the Lifetime of Service award and the National Parks Conservation Association was recognized as the Conservation Partner of the year. Laura Lantz and Scott Edwards, well-respected BLM rangers in Cedar Mesa since 1991, were presented the Legends of Cedar Mesa award for their lifetime of service excellence.

Native American perspectives were introduced in several presentations. Joseph Naranjo of the Santa Clara Pueblo talked about the importance of prehistoric relics in a talk titled "Gifts from our Grandfathers." Shanna Diederichs of Woods Canyon Archaeological Consultants told about the World Monuments Fund's recent action to add Bears Ears to their "watch list" of the twenty-five most important and threatened archaeological sites throughout the world. Hopi Vice Chairman Clark

Tenakhongva and Gary Stroutsos offered a different perspective with "A Song for Bears Ears."

While I had read about how Native Americans view their relationship with the land differently from those of us of European descent, talking with and listening to those representatives of Native culture brought it home to me in a way I had never before understood. It is no more possible to divide a Native American from his land than it would be to divide a European's body from his soul. The result in both cases would be death, either literally or figuratively. I knew that just by attending, I had done more to understand the Native perspective than either Donald Trump or Ryan Zinke. I could only hope this understanding would somehow get to those who make the decisions. Even at the conference, it was obvious this could only happen under a new administration.

~

WHEN JOE BIDEN DEFEATED Donald Trump in the 2020 Presidential Election, it was an encouraging sign for both Bears Ears and Grand Staircase-Escalante. Yes, as expected, the transition of power did not occur smoothly. Sore losers have always been known to cry foul, but they don't usually storm the Capitol in an attempt to overturn legitimate results. The storming of the Capitol by Trump supporters on January 6, 2021, was perhaps the most perilous threat to our democracy the nation has ever seen, but at least for now, democracy has prevailed. President Biden did the right thing by moving quickly past this distraction and getting down to the business of running the government.

Even before he was sworn in, Biden announced he would nominate Deb Haaland as Secretary of the Interior. A member of the Laguna Pueblo in New Mexico, she would become the first Native American since the nation's founding to serve in a cabinet post. As a single mother, it had been a challenge for Haaland to put herself through college, but she eventually prevailed. She earned a bachelor's degree in English and a doctoral degree in law, both from University of New Mexico. In 2018 she became one of the first two Native American women elected to the U.S. House of Representatives. She became vice chair of the

House Committee on Natural Resources, she chaired the Subcommittee on National Parks, Forests, and Public Lands, and she served on the Subcommittee for Indigenous Peoples of the United States. She was confirmed as Secretary of the Interior on March 15, 2021, with bilateral support in the Senate.

On his first day in office, President Biden signed an executive order that instructed Secretary Haaland to conduct a review of Trump's actions to reduce the size of Bears Ears and Grand Staircase-Escalante. She was to submit a report to him with recommended actions within 60 days. Once she was confirmed by the Senate, Haaland quickly took action. In April, she traveled to Utah, where she toured both monuments and spent time with elected officials including Governor Spencer Cox and Senators Mike Lee and Mitt Romney. She also met with Tribal leaders, BLM and Forest Service employees, and Friends of Cedar Mesa. Dr. Alan Titus introduced her to scientifically significant fossils from Grand Staircase-Escalante. And unlike Zinke, she held forums to gather inputs from the general public, including local leaders, business owners, mining companies, ranchers, and representatives of the scientific community.

In June, Haaland recommended to President Biden that both monuments be restored to their original boundaries. But by September, Biden had still taken no action. The Tribes and the environmental community were in a state of panic—would he ever do anything? The answer was yes, but he was taking the time necessary to ensure his proclamations would survive legal scrutiny. Finally, in early October he made the announcement. In two executive orders, he restored both monuments to their original boundaries. The text of each order was explicit on why the protection was necessary and why the boundaries represented the smallest area compatible with the protection of the objects of scientific and historic interest.

In an ironic twist, the proclamation not only restored Bears Ears' original boundaries, it included another 11,200 acres that Trump had added as sort of a "consolation prize" when he made his cuts. There is a certain logic to this. If Trump can't legally make cuts to national monuments, then those components of his proclamations would be null and void. But the acreage he added would be legal, so the revised boundaries would need to combine both Trump's and Obama's acreage.

The one unanswered question is whether presidents can legally reduce or eliminate existing national monuments. The court has never resolved that question and until they do, the spectre of a future president taking a similar action will continue to hover in the background.

Yavapai Point, Grand Canyon, Arizona

18

TO THE EDGE
OF THE ABYSS

NOTHING WILL QUITE prepare you for your first view from the South Rim of the Grand Canyon. No matter how many photos or videos you have seen, they pale in comparison to standing at the edge of the abyss, taking in the enormity of a landscape whose scale is impossible to comprehend. In part, it is because of the bland prelude you went through to get there, a prelude never shown in videos: a sixty-mile drive from the town of Williams, Arizona, through nondescript grasslands and pinyon-juniper forests—a prelude that reveals nothing of the grandeur ahead. Even after entering the park, there is no hint of anything new. But as you approach the rim of the canyon still obscured by the forest, you sense a change. A brilliant yellow glow radiates from between the trees, as if the sun were rising in the north. When you reach the rim and gaze far down into its depths, you realize you are at the boundary of a different world, a world like nothing you have seen before: a world of brilliantly glowing, rainbow-colored rocks stretching back two billion years in time; a world of pillars and mesas, of cliffs and valleys. Look closely at the floor of the canyon and you will see a slender silver thread running the full length of the chasm: the hand of the canyon's creator, a ribbon of water known as the Colorado River. It is a view you will never forget.

President Theodore Roosevelt, on his first visit in 1903, set the tone for the canyon's preservation. He knew speculators were plotting to develop it and mine it for copper, lead, and asbestos, possibly destroying much of its grandeur forever. Some of the more enterprising "miners" had staked out dubious claims along the Bright Angel Trail, earning far more by charging fees to tourists than they ever did by extracting minerals. In a speech for the ages, Roosevelt laid down the challenge:

> I have come here to see the Grand Canyon of Arizona, because in that Canyon Arizona has a natural wonder which, as far as I know, is in kind absolutely unparalleled throughout the rest of the world. I shall not attempt to describe it because I cannot. I could not choose words that would convey or that could convey to any outsider what that Canyon is. I want to ask you to do one thing in connection with it in your own interest and in the interest of the country—to keep this great wonder of nature as it now is.... Leave it as it is. You cannot improve on it; not a bit. The ages have been at work on it and man can only mar it. What you can do is keep it for your children and your children's children and for all who come after you as one of the great sights which every American, if he can travel at all, should see....We have gotten past the stage, my fellow citizens, when we are to be pardoned if we simply treat any part of our country as something to be skinned for two or three years for the use of the present generation, whether it is the forest, the water, the scenery; whatever it is, handle it so that your children's children will get the benefit of it.

Roosevelt backed his words with deeds. In 1908 he used the power of the Antiquities Act to preserve the canyon as an 800,000-acre national monument. Local miners objected, but their lawsuit was quickly dismissed by the Supreme Court.

When I drafted the outline for this book my plan for this chapter was to build on President Roosevelt's vision. I would portray the grandeur of the canyon, share its history, and describe some of the colorful characters who have passed through it over the years.

That was the plan. It was a good plan, but sometimes life gets in the way of the best laid plans.

❧

My daughter Juliana and I have come to the South Rim on a brilliant April day in 2019. Clouds to the north shed rain like tears into the canyon, but from where we stand at Yavapai Point, sunlight bathes us in warmth. From here, the canyon's full range of geologic wonders are exposed. Directly across the chasm, the sharp defile of Bright Angel Canyon rises from the river all the way up to Grand Canyon Lodge on the North Rim. Layer upon layer of sediments in various shades of red, orange, and yellow rise from the canyon floor like sheets of an enormous multicolored layer cake. The most distinguished of these, two layers below the mesa top, is a broad white band known as the Coconino Sandstone, laid down in the Permian Period 250 million years ago. While fossils are common in many of the Grand Canyon's sediments, don't look for dinosaurs here. Even the youngest layer, the Kaibab Formation at the top of the North Rim, is far older than the first dinosaurs.

We are here on the kind of day every tourist hopes for: sunny and comfortably warm, with billowing white clouds floating leisurely across the sky. But we are not tourists today. In all my years of canyon country explorations, today is the only day I have ever wished I didn't have to be here. The fact we are here at all is only because of a phone call we received five days earlier.

Nicki's brother Mike was on vacation in the Southwest and had included a visit to the Grand Canyon on his itinerary. The trip was our gift to him, a thank-you for watching our home several months earlier while we visited our son Greg and his family in England. It was Mike's first visit to the canyon, and he had sent us a text when he arrived the day before: a photo and a single word, "Wow!" It was a sentiment remarkably similar to that of every other first-time visitor.

A day later we had heard nothing more from him. Then we got a call from one of Mike's business associates. He said a park ranger was trying to reach us, but he didn't know why. When we called the ranger's number, there was no answer; we had to leave a message.

The ranger, Hannah, called us a short time later. It was immediately evident this wasn't the first time she had made this kind of call. She confirmed we were related to Mike and that we were in a place where we could talk. Then, in solemn tones, she told us the story. The day before, Mike had slipped and fallen four hundred feet to his death from the South Rim. It had happened only a few minutes after he sent us the text.

Our immediate reaction was denial. It had to be impossible. Mike was a cautious person; he couldn't have been so careless. Someone must have stolen his wallet and cellphone, and it was that stranger who had fallen. But we were grasping at straws. Through dental records, his identity was confirmed a day later. As his only relatives, it was up to us to take care of his affairs.

Nicki didn't feel she could make the trip, and I couldn't blame her. The Grand Canyon has never been one of her favorite places, for this very reason. Call it a premonition, an apprehension she has had ever since our first visit four decades earlier. On that trip we were traveling with our two-year-old son Greg, and it was a legitimate concern. I had assured her not to worry, the locations we would visit were protected by sturdy railings. Since Congress designated the Grand Canyon a National Park in 1919, it has been visited by nearly a quarter of a billion people. As of 2016, fewer than 60 of those visitors had died in falls—most of those while doing something stupid. (The classic story tells of the father who decided to scare his daughter by pretending to fall, then lost his balance and really did fall four hundred feet to his death.) Using my best engineering judgment, I calculated the probability of falling to be about equivalent to that of winning the lottery, which we all know never happens.

But as any statistician will tell you, every once in a very long while it really does happen.

⇗

THE NEXT FEW DAYS passed in a blur. I flew to Phoenix and met Juliana at the airport. We rented a car, drove to Flagstaff, and got rooms for the night. The next morning we met with a representative of the town's mortuary to arrange for Mike's cremation. Then we headed out for the somber drive to the park.

We met Hannah near the Yavapai Museum of Geology. She took us the short walk to where it had happened. From the museum, the Rim Trail follows the edge of the cliff, guarded for several hundred feet by a low rock wall, then by a steel frame railing. When the railing ends, only a few feet of loose sandstone lies between the trail and the edge of the canyon.

I could picture the scene. Crowds had been swarming the railing to view the canyon in relative safety. Mike had never been one to be patient, so rather than waiting for a spot to clear he had walked ten feet to the right to gaze into the depths directly from the edge. It was an unnerving view. He had been overcome with vertigo, and his weak knee—a problem he had dealt with for years—may have buckled. It was over in less than ten seconds. He may not even have had time to fully realize what was happening.

I documented the site with a few pictures, and we watched in amazement as others ventured dangerously close to the edge. Finally, with little more to see we returned with Hannah to her office to begin the process of wrapping up a life ended too soon: fill out paperwork so we could retrieve his car and belongings, drive his nearly new Nissan Rogue back to California, organize a memorial service, clean out his apartment, close out his finances. Every family goes through a similar list when they lose a loved one, but that doesn't make it any easier.

Due to the nature of Mike's death, we had to deal with certain formalities most people never face. Mike had been the third person to die there in less than two weeks, making it national news. We politely declined requests for camera crews from NBC, ABC, and CBS to interview us and film what they undoubtedly hoped would be a tearful lament. We had no interest in providing the world with that kind of entertainment. Then, less than a week later a seventy-year-old woman fell to her death near Mather Point, and the reporters moved quickly on to the next story.

There is a level of shock associated with an accidental death that typically isn't there when a loved one succumbs after a lengthy illness.

Everyone deals with that shock in their own way. Friends and acquaintances offer what they hope will be words of comfort. I've heard it all: "It is such a beautiful place, that's where I'd want to go." "At least he died quickly; my grandmother was in pain for years." "He's at peace now." All well-intended sentiments, but only marginally comforting. And yet there is a certain truth to all of them. I too, would rather end my days in an inspiring place, not in a dim hospital room connected to a multitude of dripping tubes and humming electronic instruments, even knowing those instruments used technologies I helped invent. And lingering in such a state for months or years would not be my favorite way to go. But I have resolved to face what comes my way stoically, hopefully not for many years to come.

Whenever this kind of event happens there is an inevitable clamor for protective railings to be installed along the entire rim of the canyon. But in Grand Canyon National Park alone the combined length of the north and south rims is over 550 miles. The cost to taxpayers to install railings along even a significant portion of it would be enormous. And it might not make much difference. Most victims fall to their deaths after climbing over a railing and tempting fate.

Would additional railings have protected Mike? Possibly, but I don't know what was going through his mind. If he were just impatient, an additional length of railing might have given him space to view the canyon safely. But if he were like many other victims, it wouldn't have mattered. Michael Ghiglieri and Thomas Myers, in their macabre book, *Over the Edge: Death in Grand Canyon*, tell the story of one Richard Peña, who in 1985 ignored his son's warning and climbed over a railing to peer into the abyss, saying, "You gotta take some chances in life." It took only one errant step for Peña to plunge more than 300 feet to his death. Some people are driven by the excitement of taking risks, never contemplating the possibility of a fatal outcome or the trauma it would inflict on stunned survivors.

&

As a Vietnam-era Air Force veteran, Mike was eligible for certain recognition. A military honor guard carried the flag at his services, the

Department of Veterans Affairs provided a marker for his grave. He was an active member of his church, and well over a hundred people attended the event. Everyone we spoke with commented on how excited Mike had been about his upcoming vacation, which he had planned out in minute detail to be shared with anyone who would listen. It included not only the visit to Grand Canyon, but also stops in Las Vegas and Valley of Fire. The last item on his itinerary was to be a day of digging for fossil trilobites at a site I had pointed him to in eastern Nevada. It never came to pass.

It took a few weeks to wrap up the bulk of his affairs and several more months to close out the last details. Then our duties were over, and it was time to move forward with our lives. But some things will never be the same. Sunday dinners will always be one person short. Weekly cribbage games are now a thing of the past. And the Grand Canyon, that magnificent wonder of the natural world, that canyon of unsurpassed light and beauty, will never be quite as magical again.

Metate Arch, Grand Staircase-Escalante National Monument, Utah

19

SUNSET

A N OCTOBER AFTERNOON in canyon country. October is my favorite month in the desert. Summer crowds are long gone, spring crowds won't be here for months. The days are comfortably warm, and the snows of winter have not yet arrived. The landscape is flush with golden yellow cottonwoods. Most wildflowers are well past their peak blooms, but stragglers linger—rabbitbrush, nightshade, yucca, and more—especially when summer monsoons have been prolific.

I've driven to a remote location down a primitive dirt road to enjoy a last night of solitude before returning home to California. The sun is sinking low in the sky, half hidden by a line of clouds blowing in from the northwest. The clouds end abruptly overhead, leaving blue sky to the south. Red hillocks to the north cast a neon glow in the fading sunlight, while lengthening shadows to the west serve as precursors of the night to come. Rain is in the forecast, but as usual in the desert, if it comes at all, it should only come briefly.

I am sitting on a rock outcrop absorbing the view. A steady wind whips through the air. Beside me, a moth has pressed itself flat against the rock, trying to shield itself from the gusts. A hopeless task—its wings are regularly blown upright, as if being raised in surrender. Between gusts, it scrambles a few steps at a time toward better shelter. Eventually it scurries behind a small outcrop where it seems more protected. I turn away, and when I look again, it is gone. But where? Burrowed further into shelter or blown away by the wind? It's a question I can't answer. Fare thee well, my tiny friend.

I'm surprised that with the clouds and wind, it's not colder. I sit comfortably in shirt sleeves, while as usual, a never-ending progression of commercial airliners passes overhead, flying between Southern California and points east. I've been coming to Southwestern deserts for decades and never seem to be able to avoid the faint rumble of turbofans high above. Today, with the wind, they're not always discernible.

As afternoon drifts into evening, the line of clouds moves east and the wind eases. There will be no rain this evening. Whether it will come later tonight, only time will tell.

Although I am far from a developed campground, I am not the first to camp here. Near my car lies a ring of rocks some previous traveler arranged into a fire pit, a layer of ash still evident within it. The pit could be centuries old, marking a place of respite for travelers since the days of Paleoindians. In years past, I would have built my own campfire here and cooked dinner over the coals, but today, that is prohibited. Too many careless campers didn't maintain their fires, resulting in devastating conflagrations throughout the parched Southwest. In this time of drought, campfires are prohibited on BLM lands outside of developed campgrounds. Tonight's dinner will be prepared on a camp stove, leaving me only to dream of the days long ago when I could sit before a campfire cooking steaks over the flames and roasting marshmallows over the coals.

Alone with my thoughts, it is easy to lament all the changes in the desert since the years of my childhood. Campsites once far from the beaten track today sprawl with housing developments. Sand dunes I could explore in silence now bristle with off-road vehicles. Even the remaining remote spots are frequently littered with trash.

While I remember the campfires of my youth fondly, the adults seated around those same campfires groused about how much had already changed since the "good old days" of their own childhoods. A generation earlier, their cattle rancher fathers had complained about fences strung across previously open rangeland. Navajos and Utes no doubt lamented how much better life had been in the days before the first European settlers. And for all I know, mastodons and mammoths may well have reflected ruefully on the days before the first Paleoindians crossed the Bering Strait.

Change is inevitable, my own family being a prime example. Juliana earned her degree in anthropology, then decided to change careers and move into the medical profession. In what I thought was an astute observation, she pointed out, "Bones are bones, whether you're looking at 4,000-year-old mummy bones or modern bones. But there's more money to be made looking at modern bones." After deciding doctors' hours were not for her, she has gone on to a successful career in medical education administration.

My son Greg made the most dramatic change. He moved to England on a "temporary assignment" to help a friend launch a start-up company. There, he met and married Katie, bought a house in the English countryside, started a family, and settled in as a distinguished English gentleman. United Airlines and Marriott Hotels, among others, have been happy to help Nicki and me deal with that change.

CHANGE MAY BE INEVITABLE, but not all change is necessary or appropriate. The land I am now on, part of a diminishing enclave of wilderness, is the perfect example. Wilderness has been an integral part of the American identity since even before the first Europeans crossed the Atlantic—Native Americans have always understood the need to live in harmony with nature.

We need wilderness today more than ever before, as a way to escape the seduction of social media, of video games, and of a virtual reality designed to draw us ever farther from actual reality. If we someday wake to find all wilderness was destroyed while we were seduced, it will be too late. Never again would we be able to re-energize our minds and bodies amid the primeval vistas and the primordial silence of wilderness lands.

Artificial intelligence and virtual reality will never be a substitute for the freedom of the wild places. We need landscapes unchained from the scourge of cellphone service and Internet connectivity—places where it is possible to meditate in peace while breathing free air and listening to a robin sing in the forest or a coyote howl in the desert.

ॐ

EVERYONE NEEDS WILDERNESS, although as I learned from my corporate career, I may not be an unbiased observer. Being a senior executive in a multi-national company, I had access to my own executive coach, an outside consultant whose job was to help develop my leadership skills. My coach, Rose, was a no-nonsense expert with twenty years' experience working with executives from such companies as Microsoft, Apple, and Hewlett-Packard. When she gave me a test to assess my personality, she was astounded. I was the most introverted senior manager she had ever met.

That didn't mean I was a shy and retiring person—far from it. The image of an introvert as someone who hides in the corner in group settings is just a myth. Rose explained that the difference is in how you like to spend your time. As she framed it, "If your idea of a perfect vacation is to spend a week partying with a hundred other people on a cruise ship in the Caribbean, you're an extrovert. If your idea of a perfect vacation is to spend a week alone in the wilderness, you're an introvert." To which I replied, "You're kidding. A week alone in the wilderness? That wouldn't be nearly enough."

Yes, I'm an introvert. I need my time alone in the wilderness (a valuable trait during pandemics). But I'm not the only one. We may be a society that is today accustomed to living indoors, but the need for wilderness remains within us, lingering in our psyche a few layers beneath the stressors of everyday life, poised to emerge when the time is right. It is why so many of us love to get outdoors, why sales of outdoor recreation equipment are booming, and why visitation to national parks and monuments is at an all-time high.

Historically, the main argument environmental groups have used to promote the need for wilderness is as a place to get away from the bustle of city life. That argument by itself hasn't been compelling enough to sway public opinion, which is why the signature legislation for preservation of canyon country's wilderness—America's Red Rock Wilderness Act, or ARRWA—has never been passed by Congress. Developed after much scientific study by a coalition of environmental groups under the auspices of the Utah Wilderness Coalition and first introduced in the House of Representatives in 1989, ARRWA has been reintroduced in both the House and Senate in every session of Congress since 1997. It would designate nine million acres of lands in Utah as wilderness while including concessions to preserve existing rights and roads. Almost all the lands covered by the act are already owned by the Federal government and managed by the BLM or Forest Service, but for state-owned lands that lie within its boundaries, the act clearly states, "if State-owned land is included in an area designated by this Act as a wilderness area, the Secretary shall offer to exchange land owned by the United States (elsewhere) in the State of approximately equal value." Although this would assure the act was at least neutral or even positive to the state, opponents who presumably have never read its text branded it as a "Federal land grab." Polls have shown the majority of Utahns approve of the act, but Utah's congressional delegation has been adamantly opposed, evidently for no other reason than because it was drafted by environmentalists. They have blocked passage in every session.

The reality of climate change, and with it the prospect of mass extinctions, has changed the game. Since 1980, greenhouse gases have doubled, raising temperatures around the world by over a degree Fahrenheit. Droughts, floods, hurricanes, and wildfires are all more extreme than ever before. Glaciers are retreating and sea levels rising. The United Nations issued a report in 2019 showing that nature is declining globally at rates unprecedented in human history—as many as a million species are now at risk of extinction. Even climate change deniers have begun to accept that climate change is real, although their latest claim is that it won't be bad for humanity. To which I ask, having admitted you were wrong before, why should I believe you now?

Wilderness is no longer just a place to go to get away from the stress of everyday life, it is key to maintaining the future health of the planet.

Plants and soils help reduce greenhouse gases by removing carbon dioxide from the air, releasing its oxygen and storing its carbon within their structures, a process called *carbon sequestration*. The more plants—especially woody plants like trees and shrubs—that grow undisturbed in the landscape, the more greenhouse gases are sequestered, an important justification for retaining canyon country's pinyon-juniper forests rather than bulldozing them. Large tracts of contiguous wilderness also help maintain biodiversity in plant and animal species, reducing the threat of extinction—what could be called the "final sunset" for a species.

President Biden announced a national initiative in the war on climate change within his first week of taking office. Known as the 30 by 30 plan, its goal is to accelerate removal of greenhouse gases and improve biodiversity by protecting 30 percent of America's land and water from development by the year 2030. Although some scientists would prefer the amount of protected land be 50 percent, 30 by 30 is a powerful first step in the war on climate change.

America's Red Rock Wilderness Act would make a significant contribution to the 30 by 30 plan. Studies have shown it would contribute 1.5 percent of the additional acreage needed to reach the plan's goal and would remove enough greenhouse gases to contribute nearly six percent of the plan's carbon reduction budget. It would also conserve five key wildlife corridors necessary to maintain healthy biodiversity.

Despite the importance of wilderness to the future health of the planet it continues to be at risk, threatened by those who, as Theodore Roosevelt warned more than a century ago, see the land as nothing more than "something to be skinned for two or three years for the use of the present generation." If Roosevelt hadn't taken bold steps to preserve the Grand Canyon, it might already have been decimated. Large stretches would be off limits due to mining, and what little remained would be overrun with commercial development similar to that at Niagara Falls.

In the Slickrock Desert, two of the biggest threats are oil and gas development and unrestricted use of motorized vehicles. The BLM continues to promote the sale of new oil and gas leases throughout Utah even though thousands of existing leases have never been developed. According to statistics reported on the BLM's own oil and gas website, in 2020 the state of Utah had 2.9 million acres under lease, but only 1.1 million acres actually in production. That means *sixty-two percent* of the acreage under current lease has never been drilled. Over half of those leases are more than ten years old—plenty of time for lease owners to have developed them if they were ever going to. According to industry data, the average total yield of each well drilled in Utah is only 581 barrels. That's not per day or even per year. That is the average total lifetime yield from each well. Even at $100 per barrel that hardly covers the cost of drilling. Why would companies want to lease even more?

Evidently, like those "miners" at the Grand Canyon back in Theodore Roosevelt's day who earned more by charging fees to tourists than they ever did by extracting minerals, today's leaseholders seem more interested in removing land from possible wilderness designation than in extracting oil or gas. With annual lease rates of only $1.50 to $2.00 per acre, it's a small expense for most companies. About the only development likely to be seen on any new leased land is bulldozing of primitive dirt roads to nonexistent wells in an attempt to eliminate the land's potential for future designation as wilderness.

Unrestricted use of motorized vehicles, primarily recreational off-road vehicles known as ORVs, is another growing threat. BLM lands are mandated by law to be "multiple-use lands" managed for a variety of uses such as recreation, energy development, mineral extraction, livestock grazing, wildlife management, and timber harvesting. It is entirely appropriate that some of this land be accessible to ORVs. But not all of it. Multiple-use is not a license to run roughshod over delicate wildlife habitats or irreplaceable archaeological sites. And multiple-use must also meet the needs of outdoor lovers who want to get away from it all—away from the whine of gas engines, away from the threat of death or injury by speeding vehicles.

The BLM initially did little to regulate the use of ORVs in Utah, with predictable results. Previously pristine landscapes were scarred with innumerable vehicle tracks, destroying the very shrubs and soils necessary to help reduce climate change. Archaeological sites were ruined. In 2008, the BLM finally published an initial set of resource management and travel plans for the 2.1 million acres of BLM land in south-central Utah.

These plans heavily favored drilling and motorized vehicles to the detriment of wilderness preservation. Environmental groups immediately filed lawsuits (eventually merged into a single suit), led by Southern Utah Wilderness Alliance, Natural Resources Defense Council, The Wilderness Society, Grand Canyon Trust, Sierra Club, National Parks Conservation Association, National Trust for Historic Preservation, Rocky Mountain Wild, Utah Rivers Council, and the transpicuously named Great Old Broads for Wilderness. This coalition claimed that the BLM failed to follow numerous federal laws requiring that they protect wildlife and sensitive archaeological sites, minimize impact on soil erosion, and avoid opening new trails in officially designated wilderness areas or primitive areas. In 2013, the court agreed, ordering the BLM to spend the next eight years developing new plans. The State of Utah and various ORV groups filed lawsuits challenging that decision, but by 2018 the U.S. Court of Appeals for the Tenth Circuit had dismissed the challenges. The BLM has moved forward with new planning efforts, working in conjunction with both the environmental groups and the ORV groups. This being Utah, however, future lawsuits are probably inevitable. In rejecting Utah's suit, the court left the door open by saying it was too early for the state to file a claim because "at this point, no one knows how BLM will implement the Settlement Agreement." Whatever the BLM decides, things will probably end up in court again. Fortunately, the coalition of environmental groups will continue to serve as defenders of that wilderness.

It will certainly continue to need defending. When I attended the Friends of Cedar Mesa conference in March 2020, one of the hot topics was how to engage a younger set of advocates. Defense of wilderness can't be left only to aging Baby Boomers who cut their teeth on Vietnam war protests. Fortunately, advocates from that younger generation have already emerged—people like Kya Marienfeld of SUWA and Martin Stamat of Glen Canyon Conservancy, both of whose stories I shared in earlier chapters. More are on the way.

ॐ

SUNSETS SHOULD BE something to enjoy, not dread. It is time to turn away from the dispiriting thought of species-level final sunsets and take in the sunset unfolding before me now. It is going to be a good one. The wind has eased to a light breeze. Scattered clouds are drifting slowly in the west, streaked with a ruby red glow. A nearby grove of golden-leaved cottonwoods shimmers in the fading sunlight, its presence proof of water still underground even after a summer of drought. From some-where in a nameless canyon the faint song of a spotted towhee wafts through the air. Other birds occasionally streak across the sky, but in the dim light I can't tell what they are. And as always, commercial aircraft rumble overhead, fortunately at intervals sufficiently far apart to be tolerable.

Dinner tonight will be my last in the outback on this trip, so I have decided to make it a culinary delight—a can of beef stew warmed on the camp stove rather than my usual fare of freeze-dried backpacker meals. I eat it right out of the pot, saving both time and dishes. I also indulge in a small bottle of red wine the size of those served to economy class airline passengers. I've reached an age where I'm not sure how many more times I will be able to make these kinds of solo trips, so I have resolved to enjoy each one to the fullest.

As the sun retreats behind a distant line of mountains, I sense a flurry of frantic activity overhead. Fluttering wings dart randomly across the sky like balls in a pinball machine. Bats. The creatures emerge from caves, trees, or rock shelters soon after sunset to spend the evening feast-ing on flying insects. They stalk their prey by emitting sounds far higher than humans can hear and using their enormously oversized ears to track the reflections of those sounds. Known as *echolocation*, it is nature's original form of radar. It serves them well: bats can eat half their weight in mosquitos every night. I thank them for their efforts.

Apparently I'm not under their main flight line. The bats soon leave and do not return.

In the gathering darkness, the night's first glowing diamond appears in the western sky—the planet Venus. Other than the moon and occasion-ally the International Space Station, it is the brightest celestial object in the night sky. Countless more shimmering diamonds emerge as the veil of night deepens, mapping heavenly constellations onto an inky black background. Pegasus, Cygnus, Andromeda, and Cassiopeia all lie near the zenith, while a dozen others sit lower in the sky. Away from city lights the view is sublime.

I spot a faint smudge between Cassiopeia and Andromeda that I would never be able to see from the city: the Andromeda Galaxy. It is the spiral galaxy that lies closest to our own Milky Way. The light I am seeing was emitted from that galaxy nearly three million years ago. If there is life within it, the Earth those beings now see would be the one that existed at the beginning of the Ice Age, long before the emergence of the first modern humans.

What might those Andromedans see three million years from now, when light from today's Earth reaches that distant galaxy? Will it be a nurturing Earth with a hopeful future, or will it be one running headlong into a final sunset not only for innumerable plant and animal species, but also for humankind? It is a weighty question I will not be able to answer tonight. Decisions society is making today are ones that will plot our fate.

I turn again to the sky to bask in a last night of unblemished starlight. The air is turning cold, wrapping its frigid tendrils around my face, my neck, and every other exposed part of my body. I will need to envelop myself in the warmth of a down sleeping bag soon. Tomorrow's drive will be long, and I should try to get a full night's sleep. That won't be easy. The shimmering stars are calling to me. A coyote in the distance is howling at me. Night breezes are whispering to me. Come back, come back, come back, they are saying to me.

It would be easy to obey, but my other life is calling to me, too. People are depending on me. Tomorrow I will return to that other life, a life where I can make a difference—for my family, for my company, for at least a small segment of society at large. It is a responsibility I welcome.

But even before I depart, my mind is at work spinning plans for my next journey to the Slickrock Desert. I need those plans. It is good to have plans.

ACKNOWLEDGEMENTS

This is the fourth book I have written on outdoor-related subjects. Why would a senior executive in the high-technology industry write so many books on a subject not even peripherally related to his job? Simple: I needed an excuse to get out into the wilderness. While I loved my job, it meant spending my days sitting behind a desk at my office or in windowless meeting rooms at other offices in bustling cities around the world. Exploring the outdoors has always been a necessary part of my life, and I needed to come up with a way to do more of it. One day I told my wife, Nicki, that I was going to write a book about the state parks near my home in Northern California. To do that I would need to get out and hike every one of the trails in those parks. And so I did. When that book was finished, I turned my attention to a guidebook for hikers and backpackers showing them how to use map, compass, and GPS to navigate in the outdoors. That was an excuse to get out to remote locations to verify that what I wrote would actually work. After the third edition of that book, it was time for a completely new version of my state parks book. Once that was done, *The Slickrock Desert* became my next excuse for spending more time in the wilderness.

Nicki has been amazingly supportive of all of these follies, so I first thank her for letting me pursue them, and for coming along on some of those adventures herself. She has learned a lot. After watching me teach so many classes on GPS navigation and helping answer the many questions from perplexed students, I'm sure she could teach that class herself.

Getting out into the wild helps satisfy my need for adventure, but it doesn't help with the research that must be done to write a book like this. For that, I thank a number of people who have been generous with their time. I will start by singling out two of them. First is Carolyn Shelton, the now-retired Assistant Monument Manager for Grand Staircase-Escalante National Monument. In live discussions and email correspondence, Carolyn gave me extensive insight into the history and the issues of the monument and its surrounding areas. At least as important, she read an early version of my entire manuscript and offered welcome advice on how to improve it. I can't overstate how valuable her help has been.

Second is Kya Marienfeld, wildlands attorney for the Southern Utah Wilderness Alliance. Wedged between testimonies to Congress she found time to meet with me live in Moab near the beginning of the pandemic to share the major threats to the Slickrock Desert and what SUWA is doing to deal with them. She has always responded quickly to my follow-up questions and when necessary, put me in touch with others who could provide additional insight.

Sarah Bauman, Executive Director of Grand Staircase-Escalante Partners, was helpful in both a live conversation and in follow-up emails. She shared the work her non-profit is doing to honor the past and protect the future of the national monument, and she introduced me to two others who provided valuable insight. First is Christa Sadler, a paleontologist who is the author of several excellent books on the dinosaurs of the region. Christa gave me an overview of the paleontology of the Kaiparowits formation and the research currently underway there. Equally important, she was the one who introduced me to Carolyn Shelton. Second is Scott Berry, an attorney on the board for Grand Staircase-Escalante Partners. Scott described the legal challenges he has dealt with in supporting the monument—challenges that became especially difficult after the Trump administration gutted it. Like me, Scott is trying to be retired but is not being very successful at it.

I also thank several others who have provided me with valuable information. Alan Titus assured my story of the Rainbows and Unicorns Quarry was accurate. Martin Stamat and Deanna Smith shared the work of the Glen Canyon Conservancy, while Sam Wainer and Roxanne Bierman did the same for Canyonlands Natural History Association. Peekay Briggs, historian for the National Park Service, dug wholeheartedly into the research necessary to answer all my questions about the history of Wolfe Ranch. Marsha Holland showed me how to access to the remarkable archives of the Southern Utah Oral History Project, a "monumental" compilation of more than 300 interviews she and others have conducted over the last twenty years. Jocelyn Meyers, Communications and Development Director for Friends of Cedar Mesa, gave me helpful insight as I planned my attendance at the Celebrate Cedar Mesa event. Jedediah Rogers of Utah Historical Quarterly gave me access to their journals.

Another set of thanks go to those who have helped me in the field—not just while writing this book but across all the years I have been exploring this land. First is Bruce Barnbaum, the professional photographer extraordinaire who long ago introduced me to hidden treasures in the Slickrock Desert by way of two multi-day photography workshops spaced several years apart. The camping may have been primitive, but the landscape was great! Some of my photos from those trips appear in this book. Others who have joined me on photographic expeditions include Doug Campbell, Art Reitsch, and Mike Alltucker. I described some of my expeditions with them in this book, but as Sargeant Joe Friday always said, "the names have been changed to protect the innocent." (Or was it the guilty?) I also thank Gary Gianniny of Fort Lewis College, who led me on a geology hike near Comb Ridge and who was quick to answer my many email questions afterwards.

Two of my go-to sources for information about the Native American cultures of the prehistoric Southwest are Archaeology Southwest and Crow Canyon Archaeological Center. Archaeology Southwest publishes a quarterly magazine full of insightful research, and Crow Canyon sponsors regular webinars that are always extraordinary. I also thank William Doelle and Paul Reed of Archaeology Southwest for answering questions I posed during my research.

In my quest to learn more about the history of the Navajo Generating Station at Page, Arizona, I turned to Stephanie Graham, Senior Director of Communications at Harvey Mudd College. She put me in touch with Victoria Mudd, granddaughter of the college's namesake. Tory, as she is known, shared with me the story of the plight of the Navajo at the time the power plant was built, a subject she knows well. It was the topic of her Academy Award-winning documentary, *Broken Rainbow*.

Finally, I thank all those who reviewed early versions of my text and provided helpful guidance to make it a better book: Charlie and Beth Horton, Larry Yujiri, Wayne Raymond, Wilson Hom, and John Rosebaugh. My advice to them is not to get too complacent. Now that this book is done I need to come up with my next excuse for getting out into the wilderness. When I do, I will undoubtedly ask them to review whatever manuscript emerges from that folly.

Chukar, Alectoris chukar, *Utah*

SELECTED REFERENCES

CHAPTER 1

Boothby, Thomas C., et al. "Tardigrades Use Intrinsically Disordered Proteins to Survive Desiccation." *Molecular Cell* (2017) 65:975-984.

Chan, Marjorie A., et. al. "Desert Potholes: Ephemeral Aquatic Microsystems." *Aquatic Geochemistry* (2005) 11:279-302.

Davis, Jim. "What are "Potholes" and How are Organisms able to Live in Them?" *Utah Geological Survey – Survey Notes* (2007) v.39 no.3.

Oberhaus, Daniel. "A Crashed Israeli Lunar Lander Spilled Tardigrades on the Moon." *Wired* (August 5, 2019).

Zwinger, Ann. *Wind in the Rock: The Canyonlands of Southeastern Utah*. 3d ed. University of Arizona Press, 1986.

CHAPTER 2

Larsen, Randy T., et al. "Conservation risks of exotic chukars (Alectoris chukar) and their associated management: implications for a widely introduced phasianid." *Wildlife Research* v.34 no.4 Pp. 262-270 (2007).

Larson, Lane, and Peggy Larson. *The Deserts of the Southwest: A Sierra Club Naturalist's Guide*. Sierra Club Books (2000).

Schaafsma, Polly. *The Rock Art of Utah*. University of Utah Press (1994).

Slifer, Dennis. *Signs of Life: Rock Art of the Upper Rio Grande*. Ancient City Press (1998).

Wright, Aaron M., ed. "New Horizons for Southwestern Rock Art." *Archaeology Southwest Magazine* (Spring 2016) v.30 no.2.

CHAPTER 3

Davis, George H. and Alex P. Bump. "Structural geologic evolution of the Colorado Plateau." *Backbone of the Americas: Shallow Subduction, Plateau Uplift, and Ridge and Terrane Collision Memoir 204*. Geological Society of America (2009).

Fillmore, Robert. *Geological Evolution of the Colorado Plateau of Eastern Utah and Western Colorado*. The University of Utah Press (2011).

Flowers, R.M. and K.A. Farley. "Apatite ^{4}He/^{3}He and (U-Th)/He Evidence for an Ancient Grand Canyon." *Science* (December 21, 2012) v. 338.

Ranney, Wayne. *Carving Grand Canyon*. Grand Canyon Association (2012).

Swaby, Andrielle N., Mark E. Lucas, and Robert M. Ross, *The Teacher-Friendly Guide to the Earth Science of the Southwestern US. PRI Special Publication no. 50*. Paleontological Research Institution (2016).

CHAPTER 4

Burnett, Jim. "Did the First Europeans to See the Grand Canyon Leave This Mysterious Inscription?" *National Parks Traveler* (November 21, 2010).

Huseman, Ben W. *Wild River, Timeless Canyon. Balduin Mollhausen's Watercolors of the Colorado*. University of Arizona Press (1995).

Kenny, Ray. "A 16th-century Spanish inscription in Grand Canyon? A hypothesis." *U.S Department of the Interior: Park Science* (Fall 2010) v.27 no.2.

———. "Why the 16th Century Spanish Conquistadors likely did not Descend into Grand Canyon (USA) near Desert View: A New Perspective." *Journal of Arts and Humanities* (2015) v.04, no. 08:40-4.

Miller, David H. "The Ives Expedition Revisited: Overland into the Grand Canyon." *Journal of Arizona History* (Autumn 1972) pp. 177-196.

Pierson, Lloyd M. and Bruce Louthan. "Julian, Denis, Inscription 42 GR 0111." *National Register of Historic Places* (1990).

Roberts, David. *Escalante's Dream: On the Trail of the Spanish Discovery of the Southwest*. W.W. Norton & Company (2019).

Bolton, Herbert E. "Pagent in the Wilderness: The Story of the Escalante Expedition to the Interior Basin, 1776." *Utah Historical Quarterly* Vol. XVIII (1950).

CHAPTER 5

Canby, Wm. M. and J. N. Rose. "George Vasey: A Biographical Sketch." *Botanical Gazette* (May 1893) v. 18 n. 5 pp. 170-183

Lissandrello, Stephen. "Expedition Island." *National Register of Historic Places* (1976).

Marston, O. Dock. "The Lost Journal of John Colton Sumner." *Utah Historical Quarterly* (1969) v.37, no. 2.

Morgan, Dale L., et al. "The Exploration of the Colorado River in 1869." *Utah Historical Quarterly* (1947) v. XV.

Powell, J. W. *The Exploration of the Colorado River and its Canyons*. Dover Publications, Inc. (1961).

Stegner, Wallace. *Beyond the Hundredth Meridian: John Wesley Powell and the Second Opening of the West.* Houghton Mifflin Company (1953).

CHAPTER 6

Chapin, Nicholas PhD. *Oshara Revisited: The Archaic Period in Northern New Mexico. Anthropological Papers No. 10.* University of New Mexico, Maxwell Museum of Anthropology (2017).

Gladwin, Harold Sterling. *The Chaco Branch: Excavations at White Mound and in the Red Mesa Valley.* Gila Pueblo, Globe Arizona (April 1945).

Havnes, Mark. "Artifact is tiny, but ancient find is big." *The Salt Lake Tribune* (September 6, 2005).

Irwin-Williams, Cynthia. "The Oshara Tradition: Origins of Anasazi Culture." *Eastern New Mexico University Contributions in Anthropology* (September 1973) v.5 n.1.

Madsen, David B. and Steven R. Simms. "The Fremont Complex: A Behavioral Perspective." *Journal of World Prehistory* (Sept 1998) v.12 n.3 pp 255-336.

Mann, Charles C. "The Clovis Point and the Discovery of America's First Culture." *Smithsonian Magazine* (November 2013).

Reed, Paul, ed. "Social Identity in the Northern San Juan." *Archaeology Southwest Magazine* (Summer 2010) v.24 n.3.

Repanshek, Kurt. "Traces of a Lost People." *Smithsonian Magazine* (March 2005).

Scheffer, Marten, Egbert H. van Nes, Darcy Bird, R. Kyle Bocinsky, and Timothy A. Kohler. "Loss of resilience preceded transformation of pre-Hispanic Pueblo societies." *Proceedings of the National Academy of Sciences of the United States of America* (May 4, 2021).

U.S. Department of the Interior. Bureau of Land Management, Utah. *Analysis of the Management Situation: Grand Staircase-Escalante National Monument and Kanab-Escalante Planning Area.* U.S. Department of the Interior (June 2018).

Woodbury, Richard B. Looking Back at the Pecos Conference. *The Kiva* (1983) v.48 n.4.

CHAPTER 7

Clark, Jeffery J. and Barbara J. Mills, eds. "Chacoan Archaeology at the 21st

Century." *Archaeology Southwest Magazine* (Spring and Summer 2018) v.32 nos. 2 & 3.

Crown, Patricia L. and W.H. Wills. "The complex history of Pueblo Bonito and its interpretation." *Antiquity Publications Ltd.* (2018) v.92 issue364.

Heitman, Carrie C. "Houses Great and Small: Reevaluating the 'House' in Chaco Canyon, New Mexico." *University of Nebraska – Lincoln, Anthropology Faculty Publications* (2007) pp. 248-272.

Reed, Paul F. ed. "Chaco's Legacy." *Archaeology Southwest Magazine* (Winter 2014) v.28 n.1

CHAPTER 8

Cook, Terri. "Down to Earth With: Martin Lockley." *Earth Magazine* (June 16, 2014).

"Leader Religious Colony Awaits Life Restoration." *Cumberland, MD Evening Times* (February 26, 1937).

Lockley, Martin G., et al. "Limping Dinosaurs? Trackway evidence for abnormal gaits." *Ichnos* (1994) v.3 pp.193-202.

McCaslin, Bob. "Mrs. Marie Ogden celebrates 80th birthday on May 31." *San Juan Record* (May 30, 1963).

Murtaugh, Taysha. "The 14-Room House Inside This Rock Has Been Frozen In Time Since the '70s." *CountryLiving.com*.

Pinkowski, Jennifer. "Utah's 'Grand Staircase' Leads Back in Time to Dinosaur Shangri-La." *New York Times* (July 21, 2015).

Titus, Alan L., et al. "Geology and taphonomy of a unique tyrannosaurid bone-bed from the upper Campanian Kaiparowits Formation of southern Utah: implications for tyrannosaurid gregariousness." *PeerJ* (April 19, 2021).

CHAPTER 9

Bloomer, William W. *Moon House: A Pueblo III Period Cliff Dwelling Complex in Southeastern Utah*. Master's thesis, Department of Anthropology, Washington State University, Pullman (1989).

Lipe, William D. ed. "Tortuous and Fantastic: Cultural and Natural Wonders of Greater Cedar Mesa." *Archaeology Southwest Magazine* (Summer and Fall 2014) v.28 nos. 3 & 4.

Roberts, David. *In Search of the Old Ones*. Touchstone (1997).

———. *The Lost World of the Old Ones*. W.W. Norton & Co. (2015).

CHAPTER 10

Decker, Elizabeth Morris. "Letter from the Trail." Hole in the Rock Foundation, Bluff Fort Visitor Center (2015).

Miller, David E. *Hole-in-the-Rock: An Epic in the Colonization of the Great American West*. Literary Licensing, LLC (October 15, 2011).

Yardley, William, Matt Pierce, and Nigel Duara. "Seven hikers' descent into doom at Zion National Park." *Los Angeles Times* (Sept. 20, 2015).

Sahagun, Louis, "Hikers Feared Dead After Canyon Flood Wall Of Water Washes Away 11 Tourists." *The Spokesman-Review* (August 14, 1997).

CHAPTER 11

Sundeen, Mark. "Utah Wanted All the Tourists. Then It Got Them." *Outside Online* (January 29, 2020).

Carlton, Jim. "Tourists Heeding Utah's 'Mighty 5" Campaign Overpower Moab." *The Wall Street Journal* (September 16, 2019).

CHAPTER 12

Drugova, Tatiana, Man-Keun Kim, and Paul M Jakus. "Marketing, congestion, and demarketing in Utah's National Parks." *Tourism Economics* (July 23, 2020).

Red Emerald Strategic Plan, 2020-2023. Utah Office of Tourism (2020).

CHAPTER 13

Fillmore, Robert. *Geological Evolution of the Colorado Plateau of Eastern Utah and Western Colorado*. The University of Utah Press (2011).

James R. McDonald Architects. *Wolfe Ranch Historic Structures Report, Arches National Park*. National Park Service (October 1999).

Newell, Maxine. *A Story of Life at Wolfe Ranch*. Canyonlands Nat. Hist. Assoc.

CHAPTER 14

Coughlan, Robert. "Vernon Pick's $10 Million Ordeal." *Life Magazine* (November 1, 1954).

Epstein, M., D.G. Miles, Jr., and L.L. Yu. "What were they drinking? A critical study of the radium ore revigator." *Applied Spectroscopy* (December 2009) v.63 no. 12.

Hayes, Peter J. "Uranium King Wishes People to Forget Him." *The Desert Sun* (November 6, 1961).

Glionna, John M. "Utah uranium mine is more of a bad memory than a historic site for many." *Los Angeles Times* (December 27, 2014).

Steen, Charles A. et al. *Uranium-Mining Operations of the Utex Exploration Co. in the Big Indian District, San Juan County, Utah.* United States Department of the Interior (October 1953).

Zoellner, Tom. *Uranium: War, Energy, and the Rock That Shaped the World.* Viking (2009).

CHAPTER 15

Bishara, Yara. "Invasive tamarisk tough to eradicate." *The Durango Herald* (August 26, 2015)

Latham, Stephen. *Glen Canyon Dam Arizona: Dam Failure Inundation Study.* U.S. Department of the Interior, Bureau of Reclamation Technical Service Center, Denver, Colorado (July 1998).

Mast, Katherine. "The Battle Over the Tamarisk Tree." *DiscoverMagazine.com* (January 3, 2019).

Powell, James Lawrence. *Dead Pool: Lake Powell, Global Warming, and the Future of Water in the West.* University of California Press (2008).

Schmidt, J. C., Kraft, M., Tuzlak, D., and Walker, A. *Fill Mead First: a technical assessment.* Utah State University Quinney College of Natural Resources, Center for Colorado River Studies, white paper no. 1. (2016)

Stiles, Jim. "The Stabilization of Delicate Arch." *Canyon Country Zephyr* (December 2015).

CHAPTER 16

Holland, Marsha, interviewer. *Interview with Bruce Babbitt.* Southern Utah Oral History Project-Monument History Segment (November 13, 2015).

———. *Interview with Charles Wilkinson.* Southern Utah Oral History Project (December 1, 2011).

Jones, Allison, ed. *Do Mechanical Vegetation Treatments of Pinyon-Juniper and Sagebrush Communities Work? A Review of the Literature.* Wild Utah Project (February 2019).

Prose, Douglas V. and Howard G. Wilshire. *The Lasting Effects of Tank Maneuvers on Desert Soils and Intershrub Flora.* Open-File Report OF 00-512. U.S. Department of the Interior, U.S. Geological Survey (2000).

Redhouse, John. "John Redhouse 'Red Truth, White Coverup' at Black Mesa." *Censored News* (April 2, 2012).

The White House. "Remarks by the President in Making Environment Announcement Outside El Tovar Lodge, Grand Canyon National Park, Arizona." Office of the Press Secretary, Grand Canyon National Park, Arizona (September 18, 1996).

U.S. National Park Service. "Proposed Escalante National Monument, April 1936." *Utah Government Publications Online*, digitallibrary.utah.gov.

CHAPTER 17

"Tribal Concerns Ignored by Bishop's Public Lands Bill." *Bears Ears Inter-Tribal Coalition* (July 14, 2016).

Griffin, Steve. "Reactions to Utah's new Bears Ears National Monument, from scathing to celebratory." *The Salt Lake Tribune* (December 29, 2016).

Yachnin, Jennifer. "Antiquities fight could land Utah monuments in Supreme Court." *E&E News* (October 12, 2021).

CHAPTER 18

Ghiglieri, Michael P. and Thomas M. Myers. *Over the Edge: Death in Grand Canyon.* 2d ed. Puma Press (2012).

Squillace, Mark. *The Monumental Legacy of the Antiquities Act of 1906.* Colorado Law Scholarly Commons, University of Colorado Law School (2003).

CHAPTER 19

America's Red Rock Wilderness Act, 117th Cong., 1st Session. H.R. 3780.

Crumbo, Kim. *America's Red Rock Wilderness Act: Moving America Closer to 30x30 and Enhancing Wildlife Connectivity.* Southern Utah Wilderness Alliance (January 2021).

Pictographs, Barrier Canyon style, Sego Canyon, Utah

INDEX

ABOUT THE AUTHOR

Stephen W. Hinch has explored the lands of the American Southwest for over forty years, either on solo hikes into remote areas or with like-minded photographers on multi-day expeditions. A recognized expert on the use of GPS in the outdoors, his book, *Outdoor Navigation with GPS*, now in its third edition, is a bestselling guide to the subject. He is the author of four books and a contributing author to three more. Trained as an electrical engineer, he holds Bachelor

Nicki Hinch

of Science and Master of Engineering degrees from Harvey Mudd College. He has received three patents in telecommunications technologies. Steve claims his expeditions into the Slickrock Desert have been a necessary counterpoint to his life as a senior executive in the high-technology industry.

CPSIA information can be obtained
at www.ICGtesting.com
Printed in the USA
LVHW050448030322
712339LV00003B/63